LIFE
AFTER
DOOM

ALSO BY BRIAN D. McLAREN

Do I Stay Christian?

Faith After Doubt

Cory and the Seventh Story

The Great Spiritual Migration

We Make the Road by Walking

Why Did Jesus, Moses, the Buddha, and Mohammed Cross the Road?

Naked Spirituality

Everything Must Change

The Secret Message of Jesus

A Generous Orthodoxy

A New Kind of Christian

The Story We Find Ourselves In

The Last Word and the Word After That

A New Kind of Christianity

LIFE
AFTER
DOOM

Wisdom and Courage for
a World Falling Apart

BRIAN D. MCLAREN

ST. MARTIN'S
ESSENTIALS
NEW YORK

First published in the United States by St. Martin's Essentials, an imprint of
St. Martin's Publishing Group

www.stmartins.com

The Library of Congress Cataloging-in-Publication Data is available upon request.

ISBN 978-1-250-89327-7 (hardcover)
ISBN 978-1-250-89328-4 (ebook)

First Edition: 2024

10   9   8   7   6   5   4   3   2

CONTENTS

LIFE
AFTER
DOOM

Introduction

That Unpeaceful, Uneasy, Unwanted Feeling

> So at the moment the situation appears grim. And yet there are plenty of reasons to feel hopeful about the future. To name just a few: (NOTE TO EDITOR—Please insert some reasons to feel hopeful about the future, if you can think of any).
>
> —Comedian Dave Barry[1]

> More than any other time in history, mankind faces a crossroads. One path leads to despair and utter hopelessness. The other, to total extinction. Let us pray we have the wisdom to choose correctly.
>
> —Woody Allen[2]

> "Do you know what the opposite of love is?" "Hate," I said. "Despair," Sister said. "Despair is the opposite of love."
>
> —Poet Lisa Wells[3]

You woke up again this morning with that familiar unpeaceful, uneasy, unwanted feeling. You wonder what to do about it. You suspect that if you pay attention to it, it will unleash some inner turmoil. You could keep trying to ignore or suppress it—but that can't be good either.

You see a book with this title and you wonder, "Am I ready for this? My unpeaceful, uneasy, unwanted feeling could be ignored for another day, right? After all, it's only an intensifying and persistent sense

---

1 "Dave Barry's 2022 Year in Review," *The Washington Post Magazine,* December 2022.
2 "My Speech to the Graduates," *The New York Times,* August 1979.
3 From *Believers: Making a Life at the End of the World* (Farrar, Straus and Giroux, 2021). See Paul Swanson's interview with Lisa Wells on one of my favorite podcasts, *Contemplify* (August 2, 2023).

of anxiety growing from the realization that we humans have made a mess of our civilization and our planet, and not enough of us seem to care enough to change deeply enough and quickly enough to save it."

Or maybe it's even worse than that: yes, enough of us care, but it's already too late for us to change fast enough to make a significant difference. It's the feeling that catastrophe of some sort is inevitable, that we're on the moving sidewalk to the end of the world. We can ignore that for a while longer, right?

Many of our friends and family don't seem very concerned. They think there's something seriously wrong with anyone who would pick up (or write!) a book called *Life After Doom*. They see our shared sense of dread as a character flaw or maybe a mood disorder. "What's your problem? Cheer up!" they say, which teaches us to keep our real feelings to ourselves.

You can't blame folks who don't smell what we smell—something burning, something decomposing. For them, just making it to Friday takes all the energy they can muster. They don't have the time or energy to think twice about the well-being of our civilization or of the thin, fragile layer of air, water, and soil in which the web of life trembles. They certainly don't have the bandwidth to read a book about anything so depressing or grandiose as *doom*. When they see you carrying a book like this, you can't blame them for giving you a side glance that says, "Give me a break. Talk about champagne problems! I'm worried about running out of paycheck before I run out of month, and you're worried about the collapse of civilization? What's wrong with you?"

Sometimes we ask that question of ourselves. But here we are.

Sometimes the feeling is crushing, as if the Wall Street bull were standing on our chest.

Sometimes it's as vague and quiet as a plague, ready to suck the life out of our whole beautiful blue, fragile planet.

It's anxiety that we feel, yes, and a tender, sweet, piercing sadness, not just for ourselves, but also for everyone and everything everywhere, all at once. First, we feel it like a lump in our throats. We worry that it's cancer. Then we see it tightening like a noose around the throats of our children and unknown descendants who will be born into a future much uglier than our own. It's that feeling we had when the United States Capitol was breached in 2021, or when the towers fell in 2001, or (if we're old enough to remember it) when the Space Shuttle Challenger blew up in 1986. Sometimes it leaves us so angry we scare ourselves. Sometimes it leaves us feeling like we're mourning a dying friend or lover . . . or mother.

We feel this doom because we are awake, at least partially awake. The more we wake up, the worse we feel. It's so tempting to fall back to sleep.

No wonder certain politicians hate the idea of being "woke."

It's because of our common sense and uncommon sensitivity that we feel this way. It's our moral seriousness, our commitment to keep our eyes open, even through tears.

Sure, like most folks, we smile, tell jokes, do our jobs, cook, tend our gardens, fight traffic, create traffic, enjoy our hobbies, sip a cup of coffee in the morning, and maybe have a beer or something stronger at night. But even as we go about our normal routines as normal people, we can't shake this sense that we're in trouble—all of us, really serious, tangled-up trouble. It's the feeling that our civilization's Jenga tower is about to crumble, our inner sanctum of normalcy is about to be breached, our global status quo is about to blow, our scariest worst-case scenarios are about to stop being imaginary.

If we felt doom about the global climate crisis alone, that would be bad enough. But we have also come to see that global overheating is the toxic cherry on top of a hot, festering mess of other global problems, problems that go untreated because they remain unacknowledged.

We're like a selfish partner in a long dysfunctional marriage: one afternoon we find a note on our pillow, an empty bedroom closet, and a half-emptied bank account, and we suddenly realize that things have been worse than we thought, and this moment has been decades in the making.

We're passengers on a brakeless economic runaway train engineered by and for a feckless global elite who amass more economic, media, and political power every second. No, it's even worse than that:

we aren't passengers on the train; we—along with the whole Earth—are the fuel.

We simmer in a social stew of overheating human emotions that spawn intensifying storms of extremist resentment, racism, and bigotry. We are barraged by breaking news bulletins from global social and mass media conglomerates obsessed with profits and page views and largely oblivious to truth and harm. We vote as conflicted citizens in divided electorates trying to salvage corrupted democracies in which craven politicians again and again prove themselves too ignorant to understand our current situation and too impotent to do anything about it.[4] If we're religious, we can't help but notice how many of our religious leaders look less like their founding prophets and more like those craven politicians on whose laps they dance for swelling profits.

We observe this writhing knot of intensifying trouble, and the whole mess feels not only too big to solve, but too big and snarly to fully understand.

So the open secret of doom finds us everywhere. Trees tremble as they tell us about it, weeping. Water whispers it to us. Birds and insects testify about it through the heartbreaking silence that speaks of their absence. Forgotten forests, bulldozed into shiny new housing developments, haunt us like ghosts. Even though politicians try to distract us with their daily gush of hot air, the scorching winds of a destabilized climate breathe the chilling truth down our necks.

Those of us who are younger wonder if we should bring children into this unstable world. We wonder if they'll curse us for giving them life in a house-of-cards society that their parents and grandparents perfectly designed to collapse on their heads.

Those of us who already have young children are fully occupied changing their diapers, helping them with homework, driving them to soccer and basketball games, and paying the bills, all while saving too little for their college funds. As we fall exhausted into bed at night, we whisper a prayer that somebody somewhere is, please God, addressing

---

4 These paragraphs serve as a workable description of "our current situation," a phrase that will come up again and again in the pages to come.

these global problems that we don't have the energy to even think about or talk about, much less solve.

Those of us who are older want to write our grandchildren apology letters, lamenting we didn't do more sooner.[5] But we hesitate because we don't want to traumatize them with information they're not ready to handle. We wonder what difference we can make for future generations with the precious time we have left.

I began writing these words a few days after an unexpected visit by Hurricane Ian to Southwest Florida where I currently live. (I love the Florida weather for about nine months of the year. I love what's left of Florida's natural environment, a priceless treasure which is sold piece by piece to the highest bidder, day after day after day. I don't know how much longer I'll last here. But I stay—for now—inspired by this maxim: "Live so that if your life were a book, Florida would ban it.")

The weather was eerily calm in Ian's aftermath, but I felt a sense of doom rumbling like a bass note in my chest, because we humans are making increasing numbers of increasingly violent storms increasingly inevitable. *You think this is bad? You haven't seen bad yet,* a little voice inside me whispered. I haven't been able to shake this feeling: the world we consider safe and normal is just one disruption away from upheaval.

Normal is so easy to take for granted. Our climate and environment, our political and economic systems, our social norms and institutions, our hospitals and schools, our can-do spirit and our shared spirituality—they seem as dependable as electricity, running water, and the availability of Google and Amazon. But one hurricane or wildfire; one terrorist attack or coup; one election result, or one voice making one declaration of war; one middle finger pressing one fateful button; one bacterium or virus against which we have neither immunity nor vaccines, and everything normal is pounded to wreckage and washed away in a surging storm of change.

---

5 Larry Rasmussen wrote a book of such letters: *The Planet You Inherit* (Broadleaf, 2023), and I include one in appendix 5.

We can't believe we ever took for granted something as precious as "normal."

Doom is a kind of *pre-traumatic stress disorder* that arises when our old normal is deteriorating and no new normal has come into view. For our purposes, it isn't a single catastrophic event at some point in the future. Instead, it is *the emotional and intellectual experience shared by all who realize the dangerous future into which we are presently plunging ourselves, our descendants, and our fellow creatures.*

Many of us have experienced a sense of doom on an individual level. Yesterday we were living a normal, healthy life. Today we get a scary biopsy result or blood test or heart scan, and suddenly we are counting our remaining days and updating our will. We grieve the arrival of this devastating new reality with cycles of shock and denial, anger, bargaining, and depression. Eventually, we may resolve our inner turmoil with a degree of acceptance. With the help of our family, friends, and faith communities, we may even find or make some meaning in this madness, as the biopic starring us moves toward its final scenes.

These days, more and more of us are experiencing the stages of grief as a shared social experience. Our whole society seems to be ping-ponging back and forth between shock and denial and anger and bargaining and depression.[6]

Those are the kinds of unpeaceful, uneasy, unwanted feelings that might lead you to pick up a book like this one.

Before you read on, I need to be clear about who this book is and isn't for.

First, if you are already on the edge of a narrow ledge of anxiety and depression because of personal challenges, grief, or illness, this book is not for you, at least not right now. You have enough on your plate; this book will still be here when you are in a less stressed place.

Second, *Life After Doom* is not for you if you think that problems like climate change, ecological overshoot, economic inequality, racial injustice, and religious corruption are nothing but a hoax. Nor is it for you if you are looking for statistics and charts to convince you

---

6 These are the stages of grief as proposed by psychologist Elisabeth Kübler-Ross in *On Death and Dying* (Scribner, 1997, originally published 1969).

how bad things are. There are others who specialize in that important work.[7] Nor is it for you if you're looking for a book that is primarily religious or theological. As you'll learn in chapter 2, I was for many years a pastor and have written books that focus on spirituality. But this book is written by a human being for you as a human being, whether you consider yourself religious or spiritual or secular or skeptical, because we're all in this mess together. I promise to do my best to make my spiritual background an asset rather than an obstacle for you.

Life After Doom is for everyone who has reached a point where *not* facing their unpeaceful, uneasy, unwanted feelings about the future has become more draining than facing them. It's for anyone who understands that we've entered a dangerous time and we need to prepare ourselves to face that danger with wisdom, courage, character, and compassion.

You should know something about the way this book has taken shape. As I'll explain in chapter 1, I began waking up to our current situation nearly thirty years ago. Then, nearly twenty years ago, I researched and published a book on global crises. About two years ago, I felt I should return to the subject and immersed myself in the latest data. During my research, there have been moments when I felt like the ground was falling out from under my feet. I have thought about things I've never thought about before and felt things I've never felt before. I wondered why I took on this project, then reminded myself that I felt this project, in some ways, chose me.

Many days, I've gotten up from my desk and walked for miles, mindfully putting one foot in front of the other, contemplating the realities to which these words can only gesture, hoping St. Augustine was right when he said, "*Solvitur ambulando*" ("It is solved by walking"). As I walked, waves of fury, despondency, dread, grief, and wordless groaning would wash over me. I was not only processing my own emotions: I was also wondering how I could best help you, because I don't want to traumatize you, but I don't want to sugarcoat anything for

---

7 Jane Goodall often says, "So many people thank me for not putting statistics in my lectures," (Jane Goodall and Douglas Abrams, *The Book of Hope* [Celadon, 2021], p. 29). Following her lead, I'll keep statistics scarce in this book. For trustworthy resources that detail the evidence about our current situation, see appendix 1.

you either. I want to provide you the same kind of honest and humane guidance I need in these crazy times.

As I wrote, I found myself distilling what seemed most important into short, simple statements, what you might call "moral guidelines" or "resilience mantras." Eventually, I threw out my original outline for the book and chose those mantras as the book's chapter titles. I realized that these chapters took a familiar U-shaped journey, from *letting go* (a path of descent) to *letting be* (a place of insight) to *letting come* (a path of resilience) to *setting free* (a path of agile engagement). Those four movements became the four parts of this book.[8]

It's very difficult to dance with doom alone. That's why, at the end of each chapter, I have included a "Dear Reader" section, a kind of author's aside. I'll offer some journaling questions, conversation prompts, and dialogue guides. Hopefully you can find a trusted friend or two with whom you can share the thoughts and feelings that arise as you read. Perhaps they'll want to read through the book with you. If you recommend this book for a class or reading group, be sure to make it easy to opt out, because, as I said, this book isn't for everybody. Then again, those who need it really need it, and those who aren't ready for it now may be ready for it surprisingly soon.

Here's one thing I've learned already: when you dance with doom, doom changes you.

Yes, it can change you for the worse. It can scare you and exhaust you and leave you paralyzed in despondency, cynicism, and bitterness. Doom can win and life can lose.

But the dance can also change you for the better, leaving you more humble and honest, more thoughtful and creative, more compassionate and courageous . . . wiser, kinder, deeper, stronger . . . more connected, more resilient, more free, more human, more alive.

So here we are, you and I, about to spend several hours together in each other's heads and hearts, learning to dance with reality with all its doom and delight. We're in this together. That's our starting point.

Welcome to reality.

---

8 For more on this *U*-shaped journey, see Otto Scharmer's *Theory U* (Berrett-Koehler, 2009).

Dear Reader,

Thanks for reading this introduction. I encourage you to open a new document on your computer, or get a journal to handwrite your responses to the questions below. You can also use these questions to prompt needed conversation with friends who read this book with you.

I explain in this chapter that I don't think this book is for everyone, but that those who need it really need it. Do you think this book is for you? Why or why not?

Have you been dancing with doom alone? Or have you had conversation partners to share the dance with you? How has it been?

Share your experiences with the stages of grief relating to our current situation: shock and denial, bargaining, anger, depression, acceptance, meaning.

How might you benefit by reading this book? Have you ever practiced journaling before? What benefit might you receive from journaling? Have you ever been part of a reading group before? What benefits might you experience by forming or joining one?

One more thing. If at any point as you read, you feel emotionally overwhelmed, I invite you to either take a break for a week or two, or to skip ahead to parts 3 and 4, chapters 13 through 21. Yes, chapters 2 through 12 are really important, but for some readers, going to the end and then coming back to the middle may make more sense.

PART 1

LETTING GO

A Path of Descent

I Am Waking Up

There's no rug in the world
that's big enough
to sweep this under.

—Author Britt Wray, PhD[1]

The seven stages of climate denial: 1. It's not real, 2. It's not us, 3. It's not that bad, 4. We have time, 5. It's too expensive to fix, 6. Here's a fake solution, 7. It's too late: you should have warned us earlier.

—Professor Mark Maslin[2]

I wish you could have known my beloved Grandpa Smith. He was funny. He told jokes and did tricks, anything to make us laugh. He sometimes took out his false teeth, which truly amazed my cousins and me. Grandma would hear us giggling and see him fooling around with his dentures and she would say, "Oh, Steve," shaking her head as she turned away to hide her smile.

Grandpa Smith had lots of tools and could fix anything. He could play ragtime songs on the piano, his hands pouncing on those black-and-white keys like two cats on ten mice. We would dance around the room in childish ecstasy, the only time dancing was acceptable in our conservative religious family.

Grandpa told amazing stories that always began with "Back in . . ." It might have been "Back in 1908 . . . ," or "Back in 1929 . . . ," or maybe "Back during the war . . . ," which meant World War II.

---

1 Adapted from her TED Talk, available here: https://www.youtube.com/watch?v=-IlDkCEvsYw.
2 From a post available here: https://twitter.com/ProfMarkMaslin/status/1677228464670212097/.

However the story began, it would almost always end with "I'll never forget it."

He always carried a handkerchief. And a pocketknife.

He radiated goodwill and the simplest, purest love.

I remember opening my eyes while he said a prayer before a meal during one of our visits. I was seated to his right. I saw his right hand at rest on the table beside me, his fingers gently tapping the tablecloth for emphasis as he prayed. The skin on his forehand looked like cellophane, full of age marks and bruises and wrinkles, with raised purple veins meandering like rivers, so different from my skin back then, so like my skin now.

Almost every winter, he and Grandma joined my parents, brother, and me for a long drive from upstate New York to Florida for a late winter vacation. One year when I was ten or eleven years old, we were passing through a part of Central Florida where the fields were dotted with strange contraptions that looked like giant steel sandpipers bobbing up and down. "What are those?" I asked. Grandpa explained that they were pumpjacks. They pumped oil out from the ground, and from that oil we made gasoline, the same gasoline that fueled my parents' 1957 Pontiac Star Chief.

"What happens when they pump out all the oil?" I asked. You know how kids ask questions.

My grandfather was born in 1894, and he left school to start working after the eighth grade. He was smart and wise, but not highly educated. Over the course of his life, he had a variety of jobs. First, he was a vegetable huckster in a horse-drawn cart, then a house painter, a piano maker, a maker of plywood aircraft in World War II, and a factory worker for the auto industry. He was a simple, practical man and a devout Christian, and his answer to my question about running out of oil was as immediate and innocent as was everything else he said: "That will never happen, Brian. The Lord put enough of what we need in the Earth to last us until the Second Coming of Christ."

It was a sweet answer, a sincerely pious answer. But I couldn't buy it.

My grandfather shaped me in so many ways, and the years since he died have only made me love him more. But I realized even as a boy that Grandpa had grown up in a different time, a different world. To my grandfather, the Earth still felt unimaginably huge, and our loving God designed it especially for us as a giant store of free resources, so there was nothing to worry about.

My ten-year-old psyche was being shaped by different influences, including the first photographs of Earth from space. To me, informed by those photographs, our planet was a small clouded blue-and-white sphere floating in the vast darkness of space. It was obvious to me that in that small sphere, there was only a finite amount of oil—or anything else.

Fast-forward thirty-three years from ten-year-old me sitting beside my Grandpa Smith in our 1957 Star Chief. I had left my first career as a college English teacher to become a pastor, serving an innovative Christian congregation just outside Washington, DC.

One Sunday, I preached a sermon on our moral and spiritual responsibility to care for the Earth. For me, faith in God didn't absolve us from ecological responsibility or guarantee that we could take all we wanted since the world would end soon. Instead, the beauty and belovedness of creation issued a moral summons to humanity to care for every sparrow, every wildflower, every river and mountain and meadow.

After the service, a student from a nearby university came up to thank me.

"I'm an environmental science major. That was such an important sermon. I've never heard any minister say what you said. But I noticed you didn't mention global climate change. You know about it, right?" she asked.

"You mean nuclear winter, the global cooling that would follow a nuclear war?" I replied.

"Wow. *You don't know about global warming*," she replied, obviously shocked. She told me to go home and search "global warming" on my computer, which I did that very afternoon. Soon I came upon a graphic that showed the reduction of the Arctic ice sheet over the previous forty years. I saw the patch of polar white shrink before my eyes, and my life has never been the same.

Seven years later, my concern about global warming and related environmental problems led me to write a book on the subject. I wanted to explore the question, "What are the biggest problems, challenges, and threats we face as a human species?"

That research project might sound depressing to you. But the question had seized my curiosity for three reasons.

First, to put it bluntly, as a pastor, I had gotten sick of religious problems. I was sick of people complaining about the style of music in our services, or the way I interpreted a Bible passage in my last sermon, or that I wasn't as dynamic as that handsome young preacher on cable TV. I felt that I was constantly being drawn into big arguments about tiny religious matters. Religious triviality was not only boring to me; it felt dangerous. While we were arguing about gnat-sized religious problems, I suspected that a giant camel of trouble was sneaking into the tent in the form of global overheating, to be sure, but also resurgent racism and white supremacy, accumulated power among the super-rich, the dissemination of more and more weapons with greater and greater kill power, a growing susceptibility to authoritarianism among frightened and easily misled religious people, and more.

Second, for well over a decade, I had been going through a deep theological re-thinking, what many people now call "faith deconstruction." I had been taught that the purpose and focus of Christianity was to help people end up in a good place after they die. But as a preacher who had to engage with the Bible week after week, I had become convinced that this assumption was faulty. Every week when we prayed, "Your kingdom come, your will be done on Earth as it is in heaven," I realized that we weren't praying for our souls to go up to heaven after death. We were praying for a better way of life to come to fruition down here on Earth, while we were still alive. That theological revolution made me ask questions I had never asked before: If God cares about what is going on here in this life, shouldn't we care too? If so, what are the biggest problems here on Earth, anyway? I had been so focused on heavenly problems for so long, I felt like I needed to take a crash course in earthly problems.

Third, something was happening to me that often happens to people at midlife. I was becoming less obsessed with my own success and well-being, and more concerned about the success and well-being of my four children and future generations beyond them. What kind of world would my kids face as they grew up and perhaps had children of their own?

So in 2006, at the age of fifty, I embarked on a research project that turned into a book.

The title, *Everything Must Change*, tells you something about what I learned. (That title was tame compared to the title I originally proposed to my editors: *Jesus and the Suicide Machine*.)

In that year of research and writing, I became convinced that human civilization as we knew it was destroying itself. It was on a suicidal, eco-cidal trajectory arcing toward the collapse of the global ecosystems upon which we depend. We were already on course to plunge billions of people into great danger and suffering, and tragically, the most vulnerable would suffer most. I wish the intervening years proved that I had overestimated those dangers. I wish.

As I finished the book, one huge new question had arisen and remained unanswered. Some of the experts I encountered were confident that a great turning or turnaround could happen before a civilizational collapse. Others were convinced it was already too late for that, and we should put all our efforts into preparing survivors of the collapse to create resilient local communities in the aftermath. Still others believed that the collapse would be so total that there would be no economies at all, global or local, because there would be no humans, and perhaps little in the way of complex life left on the planet. Which experts were right?

I felt that question was too dire to include in the book, so I held it in my pocket like a stone, like a bullet that had been removed from my body. I have held it as my deep secret ever since, seldom mentioning it to anyone.

As a writer and speaker over the years since I left the pastorate, I've come to realize that precious few of the clergy, church folk, and other spiritually oriented people who come to hear me want me to talk about civilizational collapse. (Why did that surprise me?) They're too busy trying to help individuals, local communities, and humanity in general survive in this pre-collapse civilization. Survival is a tough enough assignment in these fractious and anxious times. So religious organizations pay for my travel, lodging, and honorarium because they want me to give them hope and some practical guidance for the current "normal" world and its challenges. I've done my best to do so.

But in the last several years, it's been harder and harder to keep doing that. Part of me wants to grab every pope, bishop, denominational executive, pastor, and seminary professor by the lapels and start yelling, "What the frack are you doing? Arguing about theological trivialities while the world burns? Worrying about preserving organ music and quaint architecture as the sixth mass extinction is unfolding? Why aren't you reorganizing everything, rewriting every liturgy, restructuring every hierarchy, and revolutionizing all your priorities so that you can re-mobilize all your resources to help save our precious, fragile planet? Aren't you supposed to be in the saving business? Don't you see? Without a healthy planet, there will be no healthy people, and certainly no healthy congregations, denominations, religions . . . or organ music!"

But I haven't assaulted anyone, physically or verbally, at least not yet, and I don't plan to. I realize that, whether in the world of religion or in the worlds of politics, business, education, and science, until things get bad enough, most people don't change. They don't even notice. They just go on, doing the best they can, and feeling that the future of humanity and the health of the Earth are way above their pay grade. They hope somebody else is worrying about it.

Maybe a few of them feel like my Grandpa Smith, that God has the past, present, and future fully scripted already, so we humans don't need to worry about such things. Whatever happens will be God's will.

But I suspect that most folks have their secret worries just as I've had.

So I began planning this book for all those people who have been hiding how worried they are, who know we're in trouble and aren't sure what to do or how to be, who realize that pretending to have hope is more exhausting than waking up to reality.

I remember what it felt like when I clicked on that website with the shrinking ice cap graphic. I remember what it felt like when I wrote *Everything Must Change*, or read William Catton's *Overshoot*, or Bill McKibben's *The End of Nature* and *Falter*, or, more recently, Dahr

Jamail's *The End of Ice,* or listened to lectures by Michael Dowd or Sid Smith. I remember the alarm, even panic, that arose within me.

At points in my ongoing awakening, when I felt that I couldn't bear any more grim statistics or dire predictions, I learned to say to myself, "It's OK. *I'm waking up.* It's a process. It takes time." My learning process has zigzagged back and forth, taking a bipolar path between optimism and despondency. I expect yours will too. So I'll do my best to guide you through this gently, knowing that we humans need to be awakened gradually, or we get really grumpy.

So here we are. We share this *emotional and intellectual experience of doom, of waking up to our precarious predicament.*

We'll explore questions like these:

What are the best-case and the worst-case scenarios that we face—environmentally and socially?

If some degree of civilizational collapse is coming, how shall we live on the bumpy ride toward the bottom? And how bad will the bottom be?

How do we manage a recurring temptation to retreat into a bubble of denial?

How can we manage encroaching feelings of doom without becoming despondent, overwhelmed, buried in gloom?

How can we avoid turning our worst-case scenarios into self-fulfilling prophecies?

Because facing current available data forces us to think about our own deaths and the possible demise of our civilization or even the whole human species, how can we predispose ourselves to live well while we're still alive?

Where can we find spiritual support when our religions seem to be living in another world?

How can we organize for meaningful action when our political systems are failing so pathetically?

How do we, who have lived in a time of extraordinary progress and plenty, prepare for a future of decline and collapse?

How can we help our children and grandchildren grow up in a world that often feels like it's falling apart, where their lives will almost certainly be less prosperous, less secure, and less comfortable than our lives have been?

When we were driving past the pumpjacks in Central Florida, Grandpa Smith was about the age I am now. He had lived through two world wars, a global pandemic, and the Great Depression, in the middle of which he fell from a ladder and broke his spine, forcing him to spend many months in a Stryker frame in a hospital. When we were sitting there in the back seat of the Sky Chief, he was about to begin the long journey of walking with his beloved wife through her long decline from cancer.

He didn't know anything about climate change, ecological overshoot, or the dynamics of civilizational collapse. But he did know how to survive in a scary century, how to endure great hardship, and how to sustain a kind and resilient spirit through it all. That's why I can't stop thinking about him now, as I begin this book. And that's why I wish you knew him.

Dear Reader,

I introduce myself in this chapter by sharing my story about waking up to our current situation. Here are some questions you can use as journal prompts alone, and as conversation starters with a reading group.

What did you learn about me in this chapter that interested you, or maybe concerned you?

Did you have a wise grandparent or other inspiring example like Grandpa Smith, and if so, what did that relationship mean to you?

Tell your story of waking up to our current situation.

Review the list of questions we'll address in this book. Which three or four questions do you resonate with most strongly, and why?

Before we move on, before you read chapter 2, I need to prepare you for some rough sledding. This is the one chapter in the book where I'm going to try to guide you as deeply as I can into the current state of understanding shared by scientists and other experts about the realities that are giving so many of us an intensifying feeling of doom.

If you're not already familiar with it, this kind of information might stir up strong emotional and intellectual reactions within you. You may not feel ready for those reactions at this moment. If that's the case, you may want to skip ahead to chapter 3, which describes how our brains typically respond to disturbing information; then you can return to chapter 2 . . . or not. Do what you need to do. And if what you read pushes you into a place of excessive stress or anxiety, please stop reading and process your feelings with a trusted family member, friend, spiritual leader, or mental health professional.

If you feel prepared to do so, if you want to do so, then please read on. I can assure you that I have tried to take the posture of a doctor with both bad news and a good, sensitive bedside manner. Even so, I can't promise you that reading chapter 2 will be easy. I can only promise you to do my best to be clear, concise, and honest. Your strongest response may simply be relief—relief that we're getting things out on the table, because on some deep level, I think we all know that we don't live in our grandparents' world anymore.

With that in mind, let me encourage you to take a few deep breaths and center yourself. Find a comfortable place to sit, maybe with a cup of tea or coffee in hand and with a pen or pencil nearby to underline passages or jot down notes. Rather than preparing yourself to agree or disagree, like or dislike, accept or reject what you'll read, let me suggest you read with double curiosity: first, with curiosity about what I have to say based on my research, and second, with curiosity about how you are responding and why you are responding that way.

Welcome to Reality

Until the late twentieth century, every generation throughout history lived with the tacit certainty that there would be generations to follow. Each assumed, without questioning, that its children and children's children would walk the same Earth, under the same sky. . . . That certainty is now lost to us, whatever our politics. That loss, unmeasured and immeasurable, is the pivotal psychological reality of our time.

—Buddhist author Joanna Macy

Our suicidal way of life is accelerating civilizational collapse.

—British environmentalist Sir Jonathon Porritt

Within each one of us there is some piece of humanness that knows we are not being served by the machine which orchestrates crisis after crisis and is grinding all our futures into dust.

—Womanist author Audre Lorde

Not everything that is faced can be changed, but nothing can be changed until it is faced.

—American writer / civil rights leader James Baldwin[1]

There is life after doom, but to get there, first you have to face the doom.

None of the likely scenarios ahead of us are pleasant, and that explains why a lot of people make a lot of money helping others avoid waking up to the dimensions of reality we will consider in this chapter. If you would like to opt out of doing so, now is the time. As I've said, you can come back to it later. (You may find it helpful to go to the

---

1 From a 1962 editorial in *The New York Times*. For more on Baldwin and this quotation, see https://www.npr.org/transcripts/912769283.

Dear Reader section at the end of this chapter and use the first four prompts as you read.)

Among people whose profession or conscience requires them to pay broad and deep attention to our current situation, everybody agrees that we are in a heap of trouble. The fact that you're reading this book suggests you are already part of this reality-based community.

In this chapter, I will summarize the best current thinking on "our current situation," a term I'll use often in the coming pages to refer to the complex reality we find ourselves in. I'll assume that you feel as I do when I go to the doctor: "Give it to me straight, Doc. Don't hold back or sugarcoat anything."

So, first, the diagnosis: Our global civilization as currently structured is unstable and unsustainable.[2] Ecologically, our civilization sucks out too many of the Earth's resources for the Earth to replenish, and it pumps out too much waste for the Earth to detoxify. Economically, our civilization's financial systems are complex, interconnected, fragile, and deeply dependent on continual economic growth. Without continual economic growth, financial systems will stumble toward collapse.[3] But with economic growth, we intensify and hasten ecological collapse. In addition, our global economic systems distribute more and more money and power to those who already have it, creating a

---

2 I'll use the term "civilization" as a synonym for any large complex society. When I refer to "our civilization," I mean our current global civilization, which consists of regional and national complex societies bound together by the global economy, global media and culture, world religions, science and education, and other global institutions and movements. When I refer to "our current situation," I mean the current instability of our current civilization.

3 Growth is essential in contemporary capitalism for a variety of reasons. Shareholders expect returns. Poor people seek better-paying jobs. Rich people seek more wealth and bigger profits. Without growth, especially in the presence of automation, unemployment grows, and with it, the risk of social unrest grows. Meanwhile, the banking system depends on loans that generate interest. Without economic growth, loans will not be repaid, debtors will default, banks will fail, and the system will crumble. Economists are trying to imagine a post-growth economy, but resistance to the idea remains strong because economic growth has been widely adopted as an absolute norm and necessity. Alternatives to growth are, to many economic fundamentalists, not simply unacceptable, but utterly unimaginable. See https://www.newyorker.com /magazine/2020/02/10/can-we-have-prosperity-without-growth. See also https://en .wikipedia.org/wiki/Economic_collapse. Appendix 1 lists other recommended resources.

small network of elites who live in luxury and share great political power, while billions live in or near poverty with little political power.[4] Speaking of politics, as we face increasing ecological and economic instability, social unrest and conflict will also increase. As a result, our democratic political systems will be strained to or past the breaking point. Like a person of my age who transitions from stability and health to sickness and decline, our civilization will become weaker and more expensive to maintain.

The process of civilizational collapse has been studied in depth by historians, leading among them, Joseph Tainter. In simplest terms, Tainter says, complex societies collapse when their key institutions can no longer solve the civilization's problems. He gives over a dozen historic examples, and focuses in depth on three: the Western Roman Empire in Europe, the Mayan society in Central America, and the Chaco society in the American Southwest desert. Each civilization faced problems. When it overcame those problems, it grew. Its growth created new problems that it would overcome, leading to more growth. However, each solution required new levels of complexity, infrastructure, and bureaucracy, which were increasingly expensive to maintain. Eventually, the cost of maintaining existing complexity, infrastructure, and bureaucracy would be so great that the civilization could not afford to solve new problems. The growth curve would peak and a time of decline would follow.

The Roman Empire, Tainter explains, was especially effective at solving problems. Rome's growing agricultural output led to population growth, and eventually the rising population needed even more food. The solution? Rome invaded neighboring nations, colonizing them and exploiting their land, labor (in the form of slaves and vassals), agricultural output, and other resources (such as precious metals, art, and knowledge).

Maintaining these colonial holdings, however, proved expensive for Rome, requiring ever-growing numbers of soldiers, garrisons, and

---

4 For more on inequality in the United States, see https://inequality.org/facts/income -inequality/. For more on global inequality, see https://www.imf.org/en/Publications /fandd/issues/2022/03/Global-inequalities-Stanley.

communication and administrative systems. This infrastructure required ever-increasing taxes. High taxation often led to internal corruption, as the upper classes skimmed tax money for personal luxuries while the masses struggled for basic necessities. High taxes, corruption, and growing economic inequality led to increasing levels of social unrest, which required more domestic military policing and tighter social control, which were also increasingly expensive. Eventually, a shortage of soldiers required the empire to hire mercenaries who lacked loyalty to the regime. As a result, the cost of the military increased while its effectiveness declined. The spiraling cost of maintaining the Roman Empire at its peak level of complexity became too high and it began to falter. The collapse was hastened by fragmentation, invasion and looting by outsiders, insurrection and rebellion among insiders, and a declining population.

Past collapses have sometimes unfolded quickly, but often the process has been agonizingly slow, depending on a variety of internal and external factors. How much damage is the civilization doing to its environment and energy sources, eroding or degrading its precious topsoil, cutting down its trees, depleting its groundwaters, or polluting its waters? How much is it exploiting and oppressing the poor and middle classes and distributing disproportionate wealth and power to those who need it least? How much is the society spending on its military and policing, and what is the return on its military investment? Socially, how deeply is the society's morale and shared identity being weakened by internal greed, decadence, corruption, distrust, resentment, and conflict? Is the civilization being further weakened by insurrections, coups, civil wars, mass migrations, financial crises, attacks and invasions, pandemics and plagues, climate change, and declining physical or mental health?

For our current global civilization to avoid a similar bumpy downhill Roman road to collapse, we would need a profound, massive, and unprecedented global transformation. The depth and breadth of this transformation would require great strength of spirit in individuals, local communities, and nations. It would require great creativity, imagination, collaboration, cohesion, character, and courage. But many of our spirit-strengthening institutions and movements are also currently in disarray, sharing in the division, corruption, and malaise of the civilization as a whole. Like a cancer patient who becomes less able to withstand chemotherapy as her cancer spreads, day by day our civilization grows nearer to a point of no return, where the possibility of transformation before collapse becomes less and less likely, and palliative care becomes more likely. Beloved children's singer Raffi captured the uncertainty shared by many: "[Climate scientists] say we can avert the worst-case scenarios of climate warming . . . if we act *now*. I've been at this since 1989, waiting for action commensurate with the threat. And [I'm] not seeing any, and so I go a little crazy. So I say, well, who's *we*? [. . .] And when is *now* over?"[5]

That diagnosis leads us to a disturbing prognosis: Our future will likely follow one of the following four scenarios, which will feature prominently through the rest of the book.[6] (I suggest a few imaginative depictions of each scenario in book or film at the end of each description.[7])

Scenario 1: Our current civilization will continue to destabilize the Earth's life support systems, and failing life support systems will

---

5 From an interview available here: https://substack.com/notes/post/p-125334569.
6 You may be interested in my methodology for creating these four scenarios. I am not a professional futurist, but I have great respect for the work of professional futurists like Cassidy Steele Dale, who explains professional futurist methodology here: https://cassidysteeledale.substack.com/p/how-to-predict-the-future/. (He offers a fascinating forecast regarding American democracy here: https://cassidysteeledale.substack.com/p/possible-futures-for-american-democracy.) In terms of the four scenarios presented in this chapter, scenario 1 represents a continuation of current trends. Current trends always have the benefit of existing momentum. They are also supported by the vested interests of people who depend on those trends to gain money and power, including people in the tech sector whose innovations are deployed primarily to keep current systems intact. As a result, scenario 1 may purchase short-term "regime continuation" at the expense of ballooning negative effects longer term. Those ballooning negative effects intensify the risk of harm in scenarios 2, 3, and 4. I follow a standard approach to risk assessment that balances two factors: the likelihood of a scenario and a scenario's severity of harm, both in the long term and short term. Scenarios with the most severe potential short- and long-term harm must be taken seriously, even if their short-term likelihood is relatively low. However, unlike most standard approaches, I do not assess harm solely in terms of our current economic measures or political categories, nor do I consider human well-being as independent of the well-being of the Earth as a whole, for reasons that will become clear in the chapters that follow.
7 Thanks to Kate Rae Davis for the suggestion to mention relevant fiction.

continue to destabilize civilization, creating a downward spiral in both the environment and in civilization. As we face this dangerous reality, enough of our citizens and institutional leaders will wake up and respond with sufficient urgency, unity, and wisdom to transform our civilization and learn to live within environmental limits, and thus avoid collapse. However, because the needed transformation process will be long, difficult, and messy, we will face many turbulent decades or even centuries before we reach a new, sustainable normal. We will call scenario 1 the Collapse Avoidance scenario. (This scenario is fictionalized in Kim Stanley Robinson's novels *New York 2140* and *The Ministry for the Future*.)

Scenario 2: Our civilization will not respond with sufficient urgency, unity, and wisdom to restabilize our environment and to live within environmental limits. Nor will our institutions be able to deal with the cascading effects of social turbulence and decline. As a result, our current global civilization will decline toward collapse, perhaps suddenly, but more likely gradually, like falling down a long stairway, one flight at a time. In the aftermath, some number of people—whether 50 or 10 or 2 percent of our peak population—will be able to regroup in a severely destabilized global ecosystem and rebuild new communities in various locations, retaining some elements of our current civilization. However, unless surviving communities learn what needs to be learned from our current civilization's multifaceted failure, in the longer term they will repeat our current civilization's trajectory of overshoot and collapse. If they gain needed wisdom from our collapse, they will rebuild with a new consciousness, spirituality, or value system that will begin a new chapter in the story of our species. We'll call scenario 2 the Collapse/Rebirth scenario. (Emily St. John Mandel's *Station Eleven* and Suzanne Collins's *The Hunger Games* unfold in this scenario.)

Scenario 3: Our global civilization will collapse and humans who survive will face a tenuous future on a decimated Earth. Many or most of the cultural and technological advancements of our current civilization will be lost, and many of the ugliest elements of our history—widespread violence, domination, desperation, brutality—will make a comeback. Survivors will live in post-industrial, post-capitalist ways of life that resemble pre-industrial, pre-modern ways of life, but under far harsher environmental and cultural conditions. They will look upon the ruins of our current civilization and experience shock at how much humanity squandered. We'll call scenario 3 the Collapse/Survival scenario. (This is the setting of Octavia Butler's *Parable of the Sower* and Cormac McCarthy's *The Road*.)

Scenario 4: As Earth's environment continues to deteriorate, human civilization will descend into a highly destructive collapse process. During this collapse, desperate nations, likely led by desperate authoritarians, will race to exploit remaining resources and eliminate their competitors, speeding up environmental destruction with war, perhaps including nuclear, chemical, and biological warfare. This catastrophic, mutually assured self-destruction of civilization will not only result in total or near-total extinction of humans, but it will also drive a significant percentage of land and sea life into extinction. We'll call scenario 4 the Collapse/Extinction scenario. (Adam McKay's film *Don't Look Up* and Alan Weisman's imaginative nonfiction book *The World Without Us* are portrayals of this scenario.)

Feel free to align yourself with one of these scenarios for the moment, but I encourage you to hold your current position lightly for now. You may wonder where I would place myself. For now, that's not important. (I'll tell you in the next chapter.) What is important now is to understand the key reason many people are moving up the scenarios. They are moving from assessing Collapse Avoidance (scenario 1) or Collapse/Rebirth (scenario 2) as our most likely future toward assessing Collapse/Survival (scenario 3) or Collapse/Extinction (scenario 4) as most likely.

In all of these scenarios, the primary problem is not the environment. The primary problem is us. Humans don't have an environmental problem; the environment has a human problem. (And, we might add, humans have an energy problem, as we'll see more clearly in chapter 20.) We have built a fast-growing, complex, expensive, unequal, resource-hungry, fragile, fractious, and weaponized civilization that is a threat to both the environment and to itself. As long as we suck resources from the Earth faster than the Earth can restore them, or pump out wastes faster than the Earth can detoxify them, we exist in a condition called "overshoot." Whenever our combined human footprint overshoots the Earth's long-term carrying capacity, we are living on borrowed time and jumping on thin ice. Unless we recalibrate fast, a doom scenario of some sort is inevitable.

Overshoot, we might say, is civilization's original sin. In the primal Genesis story in the Bible, when the original humans were told they could eat from all the trees except one, they were being warned (in the language of ancient storytellers) that they would lose their good lives in the primeval garden if they refused to live within environmental limits. They would become perpetually exhausted laborers in a field of thorns, leading to suffering and death. (We'll return to this ancient story in chapters 8 and 9.) This warning and its implied call to interdependence and interconnectedness with creation has been at the heart of religious insight and mystical experience for millennia. It has also been ignored, forgotten, minimized, or denied for millennia.

By the way, it wasn't just ancient religious texts that tried to warn us about collapse. The danger of overshoot was implicit in Charles Darwin's oft-misunderstood concept of "survival of the fittest."[8] Survival of the fittest did not mean survival of the most competitive, survival of the most aggressive, or survival of the most dominant. It

---

8 In *The Galápagos Islands: A Spiritual Journey*, I explain how both Marxists and capitalists, trapped in their industrial/colonial-era assumptions, twisted Darwin's biological insight to fit their economic assumptions. For both Marxists and capitalists, competing in the rising industrial economy was the focus. For Marxists, the focus was on competition among classes; for capitalists, it was competition among individuals and corporations. Neither understood the deeper ecological realities in which all competition took place. As a result, both systems perpetuate our predicament. Whether we are capable of reforming or replacing either economic system remains to be seen.

meant *survival of those who fit best* within their environment. In other words, *if we do not fit in with Earth's ecosystems, if we overshoot our environment's carrying capacity, we will go extinct.*[9]

Either overshoot or an unexpected disaster such as climate change, plague, or invasion has been an end-stage diagnosis for every major civilization in the past. Today, we spend vast amounts of money protecting ourselves from invasion and modest amounts protecting ourselves from plague, but until recently, we remained largely oblivious to overshoot and climate change.

If our current civilization collapses, we will face unique challenges because our civilization is global rather than regional. Putting fantasies of mass evacuations to Mars or Titan aside, we have nowhere left to go if we degrade our one and only planet. If we follow scenario 4 and unleash chemical, biological, and nuclear weapons in our bumpy ride to collapse, we could easily render the Earth not only uninhabitable for humans, but also for millions of other species.

Those who lean toward scenarios 1 and 2 (Collapse Avoidance and Collapse/Rebirth) believe that our governments, economies, religions, schools, scientific disciplines, media, and other social structures are wise enough, united enough, and strong enough to do enough—and to do it fast enough—to keep some sort of civilization or advanced society intact. Those who lean toward scenarios 3 and 4 (Collapse/ Survival and Collapse/Extinction) believe that our social structures are not wise or strong enough to do enough fast enough to keep our current civilization from destroying our environment, leaving Earth with little if any human presence. (I phrased those two sentences densely on purpose so that you will reread them two or three times, until you really get them.)

None of these scenarios are pleasant. Collapse Avoidance may look

---

9 Many feel that we are an exception to the evolutionary principle of fitness because of our ability to manipulate our environment. If our environment gets too hot or cold, for example, we simply build air-conditioned or heated refuges. This ecological exceptionalism is shortsighted in many ways, as we will see in later chapters. Left unchallenged, it will easily lead to a de-terraformed planet in which humans have destroyed Earth's beautiful and intricate web of life, leaving our descendants to survive only in engineered environments as if they were colonists on Mars.

the least unpleasant, but even it entails some very rough sledding. And it has unexpected risks and downsides, which we'll come back to in chapter 10.

All of these scenarios are especially disturbing to those of us who have prospered in this civilization. For the last five hundred years, as neighboring regional civilizations around the world were colonized and assimilated into one global civilization, the shared norm for the prosperous has been continual economic growth, political sophistication, and technological progress. We thought that our constant progress was largely the result of our own ingenuity. We didn't realize how much of our progress depended on the availability of cheap energy, energy derived first from animal labor and slave labor, then from the taming of wind energy by tall-masted ships, then from stolen resources from stolen lands, and finally from fossil fuels.

Today we excavate the ruins of collapsed civilizations from the past and display their artifacts in museums, but few of us ever take seriously the possibility that our civilization will follow their pattern of rise and fall.

People who think deeply about our current situation fear environmental collapse. But with no less urgency they fear the social collapse that will likely accompany the early stages of environmental collapse. Long before the last ice sheet has melted, long before the critical ocean currents have completely stopped their flow, long before the sea levels have engulfed our coastal cities, they imagine how the economies and governments of Earth's most powerful nations might cope with shock after shock. Fires, storms, floods, depleted aquifers, degraded soils, and droughts will lead to crop failures. Crop failures will lead to food shortages. Food shortages will lead to mass unemployment and mass migration, in turn leading to financial recessions and depressions, leading to supply chain disruptions, leading to un-insurability and debt defaults, leading to bank failures and currency failures.

They imagine how civil unrest would erupt and how governments would respond with increased crackdowns, which would increase civil unrest which would intensify government crackdowns. When governments can no longer keep the gas or electricity flowing, the grocery stores full of affordable food, the hospitals staffed with doctors and nurses and supplied with medicines, the banks functioning, the police and military forces maintaining order—and following orders, they imagine how civilization as we know it could quickly pass from stable to struggling to failing to fragmenting to collapsing.

In other words, long before the Earth destroys us, we destroy ourselves.

Right now, a lot of people can avoid thinking about scenarios like these. But over the coming years and decades, more and more of us will realize that the old norm is shaky. Inevitable progress and growth, perpetual prosperity and advancement will seem like a scam, and we will realize that our options are being reduced to four: Collapse Avoidance, Collapse/Rebirth, Collapse/Survival, or Collapse/Extinction. As the process unfolds, the experience of doom will tear like a cyclone through the nervous system of every person on Earth.

Every human will be rudely awakened from a longstanding sense of invincible normalcy and baptized into a hot, dangerous, and ugly new reality, a world falling apart.

Collapse Avoidance is still believed by many to be a viable option. Global coal use (one of our most harmful energy sources) has remained close to flat over the last decade. Solar energy and batteries are 90 percent cheaper than a decade ago; wind energy is 66 percent cheaper. Electric vehicles have grown to about 14 percent of new vehicle sales. The worst-case scenario predicted by scientists in 2014 is no longer likely in the short term.[10]

But growing numbers of knowledgeable researchers are afraid that

---

10 At least a few knowledgeable people are moving down the scenarios, from scenario 4 or 3 toward 2 or 1. They see progress in the environmental movement as sufficient to make scenarios 4 or 3 less likely than they looked a few years ago. But they are still deeply concerned about our future, and they acknowledge that we face a dangerous and uncertain path ahead, because the Earth of the foreseeable future will be much less hospitable than the Earth in which all human civilizations have evolved. See, for example, this August 2023 conversation between philosopher Robert Wright and journalist David Wallace-Wells, author of *The Uninhabitable Earth* (Tim Duggan Books, 2019), available here: https://youtu.be/MCC5LA2I-sk?si=iZd5ZHoL0jiHoXAp. And see the PBS *Weathered* episode "Have We Made ANY Progress on Climate Change?," available here: https://youtu.be/vFDnknU0h0s.

Collapse Avoidance is increasingly unlikely, even impossible, a casualty of "too little, too late." Environmental activist Derrick Jensen captured that sentiment powerfully in his article "Beyond Hope":

> The most common words I hear spoken by any environmentalists anywhere are, *We're f*cked*. Most of these environmentalists are fighting desperately, using whatever tools they have—or rather whatever legal tools they have, which means whatever tools those in power grant them the right to use, which means whatever tools will be ultimately ineffective—to try to protect some piece of ground, to try to stop the manufacture or release of poisons, to try to stop civilized humans from tormenting some group of plants or animals. Sometimes they're reduced to trying to protect just one tree. . . . But no matter what environmentalists do, our best efforts are insufficient. We're losing badly, on every front. Those in power are hell-bent on destroying the planet, and most people don't care.[11]

So here we are. As in the myth of Emperor Alexander (the Great) weeping because there were no more worlds to conquer, we sit with Derrick Jensen at an impasse.[12] We have raced through our planetary limits to sustainable growth, and none of our primary ideologies—political, economic, or religious—seem able to provide us a way out or a way through.

Some people think folks like Derrick Jensen have been working too hard and need a vacation. They're depressed. These poor, burned-out activists underestimate the power of technology or capitalism or the market or democracy or the indomitable human spirit to save us.

Isn't it possible, they ask, that a significant portion of Earth's eight-plus billion people are on the verge of waking up? Is it possible that as

---

11 Available here: https://orionmagazine.org/article/beyond-hope/.
12 In all likelihood, the story of weeping Alexander is a recent distortion of an ancient text. See: https://www.theparisreview.org/blog/2020/03/19/and-alexander-wept /. The power of the story, it seems to me, even if fictional, connects with a deep truth about colonizing civilizations: they can't survive unless they keep expanding and exploiting new lands. Without lands to conquer, they face overshoot, which signals their inevitable decline.

"normal" as we've known it disappears, our fractious and unfocused societies might tip in a positive way, moving under stress toward unity and collaboration? Might we be humbled and sobered, turning toward one another with wisdom, sanity, and solidarity, leading to the collaborative and transformational action required?

Might nuclear fusion solve all our problems? Or AI? Or bitcoin? Or a return to Puritan sexual norms and patriarchal family structures?

Maybe these optimists are right. Maybe Collapse Avoidance is still within reach. Maybe some combination of human technology, solidarity, skilled leadership, and good luck (or a divine skyhook) will help us dodge collapse.

But maybe, at the very moment we most need to come together, we will instead turn on each other and tear each other apart.

We could tip either way, or both ways at once. There's so much we don't know.

Welcome to reality.

That simple phrase has helped me immensely as I've done this research. It helps me slow down for a few moments and acknowledge that we do know some things with high levels of confidence. (For example, we know carbon dioxide and methane in the atmosphere trap heat; we know water melts at 32 degrees Fahrenheit or 0 degrees Celsius; we know several different ways to produce electricity.) But about other things, we have much less certainty.

When I say "welcome to reality," I am saying, "Welcome, self, to reality, both what I know and what I don't know." And I am also saying, "Welcome, reality, whatever you are, both known and unknown, into my awareness."

To hold both knowing and unknowing in a delicate, dynamic, and highly creative tension . . . that is one of the primary skills we will need if we want to live with courage and wisdom in an unstable climate, whatever scenario unfolds.

We need to face what we know. And we need to face what we don't know. Only what is faced can be changed. That is why I say, and I hope you will join me, *welcome to reality.*

Dear Reader,

I hope you made it through this chapter. For most readers, it will be the most challenging in the whole book, so you're through the worst of it already. If you are experiencing overwhelming feelings of depression and anxiety about our current situation, I encourage you to reach out to a mental health professional. You can find support in a number of places, including the Climate Psychology Alliance: (https://www.climatepsychologyalliance.org/index.php/find-support).

At the end of chapter 1, I suggested you read this chapter with dual curiosity: wondering about what I was going to say and wondering what your reactions would be. I encourage you to consider these questions or prompts in private to help in that reflection:

> Try to list (in writing, if possible) the emotions you felt as you read or listened to this chapter. Don't be afraid to admit that you hated some of what I wrote. I hate so much of this chapter too!

> You might want to go back and connect specific emotions with specific paragraphs and think more deeply about why those paragraphs elicited those emotions.

> If questions have arisen for you, please write those questions down before you forget them.

> If you pray, I encourage you to write a prayer in which you open your heart about how you felt reading this chapter, and about how you are processing it now, in retrospect. If you don't pray, consider writing a letter to yourself and tell yourself what you think you need to hear.

Here are some additional questions to journal about or discuss with friends:

> How does the phrase "welcome to reality" work for you? Can you think of other ways to say the same thing?

Summarize the four scenarios in your own words. Try to explain each one fairly, as if you thought it was the most likely to occur.

In this chapter, I mentioned your nervous system. What do you think reading this chapter did to your nervous system? What did reading it feel like in your body and in your conscious experience?

Practice saying, "Welcome, self, to reality," and "Welcome, reality, into my awareness." How does each intention affect you?

How successful do you feel in welcoming the reality of both what you know and what you don't know? Reflect on the word "unknowing."

These questions will be a good bridge to the next chapter when you're ready.

3

Mind Your Mind

The more we persist in misunderstanding the phenomena of life, the more we analyze them out into strange finalities and complex purposes of our own, the more we involve ourselves in sadness, absurdity, and despair.

—Contemplative Catholic monk Thomas Merton,
New Seeds of Contemplation

How much of this truth can I bear to see and still live unblinded? How much of this pain can I use?

—Womanist author Audre Lorde

Doctor, my eyes—tell me what is wrong. Was I unwise to leave them open for so long?

—Singer-songwriter Jackson Browne

Contemplation is meeting all the reality I can bear.

—Franciscan author Richard Rohr

I've been observing myself as I try to process the heartbreaking, mind-blowing, body slam of scenarios we considered in the previous chapter. You've probably been observing your reactions too. Asking our individual nervous systems to process disturbing scenarios like these is . . . a lot. In fact, you deserve sincere congratulations for making it this far in the journey. As a doctor might say after setting a dislocated joint, or a dentist might say after drilling out a decayed tooth, the worst is behind us.

I promised in the last chapter that I would tell you where I land regarding the four scenarios, and I think you can already predict the answer: *I don't land.*

The more I engage with the doom experience, the more I have decided that for me, at this point in my dance with doom, avoiding premature scenario elimination is the most honest and intelligent option I have—because I am welcoming the reality that there is much I know and much I don't know. I know with a very high degree of certainty that we are in serious trouble and that we have a long, bumpy downhill ride ahead of us. But I don't know—and can't know—what the end point of our bumpy downhill ride will be.

I know that scenario 1 comes with an expiration date: if sufficient action isn't taken soon enough, the "now" in "we must act now" will expire. At that point, Collapse Avoidance will be off the table. (Bill McKibben often says that our current situation is a timed test, and winning too slowly is the same as losing.) In the same way, I know that scenarios 2 and 3 also have expiration dates. But I don't know which possibilities are already off the table.

As I observe myself coping with what I know and what I don't know, I notice a consistent tendency to distort reality in an optimistic direction. "Things will work out," I say with strained cheerfulness. "They *have* to!"

Then I notice that the distortion swings in the opposite direction, toward despondency. I observe part of me whispering, "Forget it. We're defeated. It's fruitless to even fight for survival. We're screwed. Don't be a naïve fool and think otherwise." I notice that whichever extreme I swing to, I can find people who agree and reinforce that conclusion. Yet I suspect that this pull toward extremes is an expression of bias, a built-in glitch in my reasoning powers.[1]

If we lean either way, it seems to me, we can decrease our chances of survival and increase the likelihood of more catastrophic outcomes, because (as we'll consider in more detail in chapter 6) both optimism and despondency can lead us to complacency, and complacency is a poor survival strategy even in the best of times.

That's why one of my mantras for life after doom is "mind your mind." Pay attention not only to external evidence but also to the

---

1 For more on biases, see appendix 6, especially Certainty/Closure Bias and Cleverness/Deception Bias.

subjective internal dynamics that are constantly influencing your perspective as you evaluate and interpret that evidence.

When I say "mind your *mind*," I don't just mean your rational processes. Instead, I mean your whole nervous system, the hardware on which the software of your consciousness runs. It includes the brain, but really, it is much larger, comprising the network of nerves that extends through and is integrated with the whole human body. (It's worth noting that through all our media of communication, from speech and writing to the internet and social media, our individual nervous systems are linked as never before with billions of others too.)

One thing we know about our nervous system: it is far more complicated than we understand. That's why we reach for metaphors—each of which is admittedly limited and imperfect—to help us understand the system by which we understand.

My current working metaphor for my nervous system is "the board of directors of Me, Incorporated." This board of directors has three main committees. Each committee is composed of various arrangements of specialized cells that are located in various parts of my brain and body. Each of these committees has many subcommittees, but to keep the metaphor simple, I'll focus only on the three main committees.

First is the *survival committee*. This is the complex part of me that evolved long ago in fish and reptiles and has been passed up the evolutionary tree, further evolving through mammals and primates to humans. The survival committee's headquarters are in my brain stem and cerebellum. Its primary job is to keep me alive at least long enough to reproduce. That means it has to keep my heart beating, my lungs breathing, my digestive system operating, my need for sleep satisfied, my body temperature regulated. It makes me hungry and thirsty enough to stay nourished. It keeps me sensitive to pain and danger in the world around me so I can respond lightning fast to threats. It keeps me and my fellow humans sufficiently sexually stimulated so that we will reproduce. People often say it manages the seven *F*'s of survival for our species: our instincts or reflexes to feed, fight, flee, freeze, fawn, flock, or . . . mate.

People used to disparage this survival committee as the reptilian brain or lizard brain. They associated it only with fear, anger, lust, and other emotions they thought of as negative or primitive. But I think that's selling this survival committee short. First, it's an insult to lizards and other reptiles, fascinating masters of survival who have been around a lot longer than we have. Second, it's an insult to fear, anger, and sexual desire, each of which does essential work in our lives. Our survival committee is a wonder: it works so fast that we are not even aware of it until it's already engaged. Without a well-functioning survival committee, we wouldn't be here.

Think of the split-second negotiations that happen in my survival committee every time I cross a busy city street. I assess the speed of oncoming cars, my speed of walking or running, the width of the street, the height of curbs and the presence of obstacles that might trip me, the speed and presence of bicycles or pedestrians who might move into my path. What an amazing committee!

Second is the *belonging committee*. It is often associated with the limbic system of the brain. This essential part of me evolved among mammals (and also birds) whose survival depended on strong bonds of primal attachment between babies and their mothers, and sometimes their fathers and siblings, too, and often, the members of their herd, troop, flock, or pack. The belonging committee operates in constant communication and deep partnership with the survival committee, a relationship forged and fine-tuned over millions of years. It motivates me not only to care about my own survival, but also the survival of my family and herd. It motivates me to protect and be protected, to feel attachment and show affection, to be sociable and stay connected. Like the survival committee, it carries on constant, complex negotiations within itself, and works faster than I am even aware of. It's amazing.

Third is the *meaning (or understanding) committee,* often associated with the neocortex of the brain. It makes language possible and gives meaning to the word "meaning." It enables me to talk to myself and observe myself. It integrates current awareness with memory of past experiences and with the ability to imagine future scenarios (as we did in the previous chapter). It organizes my experience in stories with beginnings, middles, and ends. It helps me think critically, creatively, and independently. Without the meaning committee, there would be no

Bach or the Beatles, no Galileo or Einstein, nor Moses or Mary or Jesus or the Buddha or Mohammed. It is the most recently evolved part of me, and frankly, it still has a lot of bugs and glitches that haven't been worked out yet. (For more on these bugs and glitches, see appendix 6.) It is deeply integrated with the survival and belonging committees and never operates independently of them, although it often operates in tension with them.

Now this survival/belonging/meaning model approaches the brain vertically or evolutionarily, moving from the deepest parts of the brain that evolved in our early vertebrate ancestors to the more recently added outer layers that developed among mammals and higher primates. Like all models, it is a highly simplified version of a far more complicated reality. To add some complexity to this bottom-up or vertical model, we could add a horizontal dimension, looking at the left and right wings of each committee, each with its own strengths and weaknesses.[2] But even this simple three-committee model helps me understand my mind a little better so I can *mind* it, or guide and curate and manage it.

In each of us, all three committees experience and share constant observations, negotiations, arguments, deadlocks, and breakthroughs. I experience these interactions as thoughts, feelings, and decision-making processes. Sometimes, such as when I'm pondering the four scenarios we considered in the last chapter, those thoughts, feelings, and decision-making processes can feel like a noisy New York subway at rush hour, with crowded trains of tense travelers speeding in multiple directions and at various levels.

My survival committee hears these four scenarios and quickly assesses the risk of each to my own well-being. My belonging committee

2 According to some theorists, the left hemisphere appears to specialize in focused attention for analysis, problem-solving, exploitation, and control. The right hemisphere appears to specialize in open awareness and a sensitivity to connectedness, interdependence, beauty, and wonder. Centuries of cultural formation have favored left-hemisphere functions and silenced or sidelined right-hemisphere functions, contributing powerfully to our current situation. For more on these subjects, see Jill Bolte Taylor's *Whole Brain Living* (Hay House, 2021), Lisa Miller's *The Awakened Brain* (Random House, 2021), and the work of Iain McGilchrist, especially *The Master and His Emissary* (Yale University Press, 2009). You'll find a short video of McGilchrist's work here: https://www.youtube.com/watch?v=dFs9WO2B8uI.

thinks about my family and friends, my nation and religion, and other groups with whom I affiliate. My meaning committee assesses the gravity of the risk and starts strategizing responses to each scenario. It doubts this and affirms that, accepts this and rejects that, and wants further information so Me, Incorporated can be better prepared for whatever may come.

My survival committee seconds that motion for more information, so adds a sense of urgency, pushing me to keep reading this book and to seek further understanding.

Suddenly my belonging committee reminds me that many in my family and social circle have never given a thought to overshoot or collapse and don't even believe climate change is real. If I strengthen my belief that these dangers are real, I will be more out of sync with some of my family and friends, and my belonging committee is really afraid of being ostracized and alone. So it changes its vote. It drags its heels and makes me feel ambivalent about learning more. Then my survival committee may side with my belonging committee and remind me that I have more pressing issues to be worried about, and it prompts me to focus on them instead. After all, it says, doom is too big a deal for me to handle, so I would be smarter to focus on more manageable problems, like cleaning up the garage. My belonging committee joins in and pressures Me, Incorporated to avoid people and books who will intensify my feeling of doom, and to huddle with people who don't take overshoot seriously.

My meaning committee diagnoses this reaction as denial, and the debates and negotiations rage on so fast that I may not be fully aware of them. What I am aware of, though, is tension in my jaw and a sick feeling in my stomach, signs of stress in my survival committee. Even when I fall asleep, my dreams process the stress and keep the negotiations going in different ways.

When I think in this way of the internal board of directors of Me, Incorporated, I'm not so surprised by all the turmoil and conflict I feel as I dance with doom. In fact, I'm quite amazed at how well I—and we—are managing to get through another day!

To *mind my mind* is to be aware of what is going on inside me. To mind my mind is to seek to integrate my committees and all their subcommittees and members in the healthiest ways I can so I don't jump to premature closure, whether optimistic or despondent. To mind my mind is to keep waking up and welcoming myself to reality and welcoming reality to myself.

To mind my mind also means realizing that my mind is part of the reality I'm waking up to and welcoming, and it is the means by which I access that reality. Important work indeed!

In my experience, there are two primary ways we commonly mind our mind. Both are important.

The first way we mind our mind is social: we learn to *speak our mind* in *circles of trust*. We share our ideas with others who share our desire to wake up and welcome reality. We do so in an atmosphere of mutual respect, listening actively and without judgment, inviting constructive feedback and non-"gotcha" questions. We may seek out a trusted spiritual director or guide for a private conversation, or we may form a group with clear communication guidelines to keep the circle of trust free and safe.[3]

This is, in a sense, what scientists do with peer-reviewed papers. They write a paper, but before publishing it, they ask peers to look it over, to question its assumptions and methods, to see if it needs improvements, to be sure it's trustworthy when it's made public. Doing so helps researchers see where their own biases or limited perspectives might be distorting their thought process. Based on that feedback, they keep revising their papers until they reflect their own best intelligence, augmented by the collective intelligence of their peers. Informally, this is what many of us do around dinner tables or taking a walk with a trusted friend. It's not simply arguing, ego against ego, where I'm trying to attack or you're trying defend. It's conferring or seeking *clearness* (as the Quakers put it)—bringing multiple perspectives together to help us move closer to the truth together than we could have done alone.

The second way we mind our mind is personal: we practice

---

3 For excellent guidelines on establishing a circle of trust, see this resource from Plymouth Congregational Church in Minneapolis, MN: https://www.plymouth.org/wp-content/uploads/2020/11/Contemplative-Leadership.pdf/. See also the work of Parker Palmer.

contemplation. Here's how my friend and colleague, Father Richard Rohr, founder of the Center for Action and Contemplation, often defines contemplation: *Contemplation is meeting all the reality you can bear.*[4]

Through contemplative practice, I send my internal negotiations into a time-out. I disengage. I allow the habitual patterns of my three committees to be interrupted, suspended. I put them all into the awareness mode rather than the negotiation mode, without allowing any single one of them to call the shots and dominate the others.

And when I do that consistently enough, I stop being quite as dominated by fear, hurry, or anger (specialties of my survival committee), or by social obligations and expectations (specialties of my belonging committee), or by long-held beliefs and preferred narratives (a forte of my meaning committee). I open up the possibility for new patterns of relationship, where survival, belonging, and meaning are all important and all have a voice. And equally important, I step out of argument mode and decision-making mode into awareness mode so I can actually become curious about what reality—external and internal—is trying to tell me. In this awareness mode, my more mature values like wisdom, love, compassion, humility, and justice can change the atmosphere and set the stage for future negotiations.

Think back once more to how you felt as you read the previous chapter. Can you see why it was so intellectually, emotionally, and

---

4 Richard also defines contemplation as "a long loving look at the real." He often teaches that the practice of contemplation was deeply evident in Jesus' life and among the so-called desert mothers and fathers of the church. He offers quotes like these: "Until the mind is freed from the multitudes of thoughts, and has achieved the single simplicity of purity, it cannot experience spiritual knowledge" (Isaac of Syria). "Attention is the beginning of contemplation, or rather its necessary condition: for, through attention, God comes close and reveals Himself to the mind. Attention is serenity of the mind, or rather it's standing firmly planted and not wandering, through the gift of God's mercy" (Nicephorus the Solitary). "Some of the fathers called this . . . silence of the heart; others called it attention; yet others—sobriety and opposition (to thoughts), while others called it examining thoughts and guarding the mind" (St. Simeon). "Collect your mind from its customary circling and wandering outside, and quietly lead it into the heart by way of breathing" (The monks of Callistus and Ignatius). From *Daily Meditation*, February 27, 2023, available here: https://email.cac.org/t/d-e-zddiktl-tlkrjuydlj-s/.

viscerally unacceptable? Your survival committee wanted to pull the fire alarm and tell you to panic, or it was so afraid of panicking that it told you to throw this book in the trash so you wouldn't read another word. Your belonging committee thought of all the people you care about, and how helpless and unable to protect them you would feel if the chapter was true. That felt terrifying, which fired up your survival committee even more. Meanwhile, perhaps your meaning committee had never, ever thought about such dire possibilities before, so it instantly constructed a hundred arguments about why all four scenarios must be false . . . and then it may have constructed counterarguments against those arguments.

When you learn to mind your mind, you begin by allowing your thoughts and feelings to shout or cry, to throw a tantrum and have a meltdown. It's fruitless and ultimately quite harmful to perpetually beat down those feelings. So for some period of time, you let your inner committees express their distress and negotiate, firing up the subway for a frantic rush hour.

And then, at some point, you have to get off the train and exit the subway station and find a quiet place. Perhaps you'll meet with a circle of trust, processing with some friends what you're struggling with. Perhaps you'll find some solitude to practice private contemplation.

One of the most time-tested approaches to private contemplation could be called the focus/release method. Instead of letting my trains of thought and emotion take me where they will, I might turn my focus from my internal reactions and negotiations to my breath or my heartbeat. I might focus on a single, simple word.[5] I might focus on a phrase or mantra (like the chapter titles of this book). Sometimes, when simple breath, heartbeat, words or phrases aren't working, I might listen to music, dance, cook, or simply walk mindfully and focus on what I see around me . . . this, that, this, that . . . to disrupt my speeding trains of thought. Sometimes I focus on an image, a "happy place," or the face of someone I love (like Grandpa Smith or the faces

---

5 In my book *Naked Spirituality: A Life with God in Twelve Simple Words* (Harper-One, 2011), I offer guidance on single-word prayers that help focus the mind.

of my wife, children, and grandchildren).[6] I may go running, practice yoga, or play a game, so I have to shift my focus from inner turmoil to physical endurance and prowess.

Of course, whatever my focus is, I soon leave it and jump back on the trains of my internal subway whirring by. When I realize I'm on the subway again, I don't beat myself up (usually). Instead, I just step off the train and return to my chosen focus.

That act of returning to focus is the point of contemplation as a practice. Each return strengthens my ability to realize I'm on the subway again so I can disembark from its speeding trains. In a real sense, as long as I keep returning to focus, even my distractions serve the practice. It's a no-lose situation.

After I feel that I'm holding my focus with some steadiness, I let that word, phrase, or image go and let myself be present to a gentle stillness. This stillness feels like an unfocused awareness, a restful openness and receptivity, a soft fascination, a withdrawal into a secret safe place, or a breakthrough to a place so expansive that my trains of thought seem like tiny toys. Sometimes it feels good, restful, and serene, like I've been welcomed into the presence of all who have ever loved me. Sometimes it feels like a void, a darkness and emptiness, simultaneously a tomb and a womb. However it feels, I gain similar benefits (another no-lose situation).

I may remain in that stillness for only an instant, or perhaps a few minutes, or maybe even longer. When trains of interrupting thoughts and feelings return, I don't fight them; I welcome them gently—after all, those thoughts and feelings are part of the reality I am learning to meet—and then let them go whizzing away without me. Like returning to focus, returning to stillness is the point of the practice.

For many of us, contemplative practice is a form of prayer, while for others, it is simply a time-tested method of minding our mind. Either way, the no-lose practice of contemplation brings many benefits. Once I detach from the rushing subway system of racing thoughts and

---

6 Religious icons, rosaries, and prayer beads are longstanding ways of using physical action (eye movement, finger movement) to disembark from speeding trains of thought.

feelings, I realize how exhausting and in some ways addictive the rush can be. Contemplation liberates me from being a perpetual prisoner of my trains of thoughts and feelings; it helps me realize that I am not my thoughts and feelings. It helps me see that these inner reactions and negotiations happen to me and within me without my consent, like digestion, like sleep, like fatigue or laughter.

In the stillness, new insights, comfort, and ways of being often arise. If stepping off the train is *letting go*, and if dwelling in the stillness is *letting be*, receiving these gifts is *letting come*. When these new gifts come, I experience a kind of liberation, a *setting free*.

All of my best creative work seems to flow from this deep place of restful, receptive awareness beneath my mental subway system. You can see why I have chosen letting go, letting be, letting come, and setting free to shape the arc of this book.

What we experience in the letting-come phase some people describe as intuition. Many would call it the gentle voice of God speaking within them. Seasoned contemplatives like Thomas Merton describe letting go, letting be, letting come, and setting free as discovering the *true self*. Others call it becoming the best self. I tend to think of it as becoming the integrated, unitive, or connected self . . . as opposed to the fragmented or divided or separated self.

This connected self seeks to bring together smaller competing parts into larger harmonious wholes. It seeks to integrate the known and the unknown. It wants to help the parts of Me, Incorporated to live intentionally in relation to each other and to the reality outside of me. It seeks harmony and interdependence among parts, not domination, manipulation, exclusion, and oppression. It holds the both/and of part and whole. It sees both the forest and the trees. Recalling Joni Mitchell's iconic song, for the connected self, something is lost and something is gained in living each day, but at least we see *both sides now*.

In this light, let's go back to the experience we considered earlier, where part of you wants to meet reality, and part of you doesn't, or part of you wants closure on the most optimistic scenario and part of you wants closure on its opposite. A contemplative mind doesn't shut down those divisions, tensions, and arguments. But it isn't caught up in them either. Instead, in contemplation, you step down off this or that train and leave the subway via the nearest exit. For a few moments, you don't let yourself be overly attached to any of the speeding trains of feelings, thoughts, reactions, and negotiations that make up your internal subway. You take a time-out so the various committees or departments of You, Incorporated can welcome as much reality as you can currently bear.

It's OK if you don't feel you can handle very much reality yet. Just wanting to do so is an amazing start. If you keep learning to mind your mind; if you keep learning to let all the embodied parts of you do their job in an integrated way; if you keep learning to hold both knowing and unknowing, you will be in a far better place to face what is coming, whatever scenario unfolds.

In the next chapter, I'll share one specific practice that helps me mind my mind in unstable times like these.

Dear Reader,

As I mentioned earlier, if you're interested in learning some of the ways your "meaning module" struggles to deal with disruptive information, check out appendix 6. There I share how common glitches called biases often sabotage our desire to meet reality.

In this chapter, I offer the metaphor of three committees that make up the board of directors of You, Incorporated. Summarize the function of the survival, belonging, and meaning committees in your own words. If you're familiar with research on the left and right hemispheres of the brain, you can bring that understanding into play as well.

How does this metaphor or model sit with you?

Describe the idea of the connected or integrated self in your own words.

How do you experience the survival, belonging, and meaning committees when they're working against each other, and how do you experience them when they're integrated or connected?

I say that your mind is part of the reality you're waking up to and welcoming. Why do you think I felt it necessary to emphasize the need for integration of your different committees or mental modules?

If you feel that your levels of inner anxiety or despair are overwhelming, again, I encourage you to share your distress with friends or family in a circle of trust, or to seek support from a mental health professional. You can consult organizations like the Climate Psychology Alliance to find professionals who take these concerns seriously: https://www.climatepsychologyalliance.org/.

4

Send in the Poets

Grief is a cruel kind of education. You learn how ungentle mourning can be, how full of anger. You learn how glib condolences can feel. You learn how much grief is about language, the failure of language and the grasping for language. . . .
—Nigerian author Chimamanda Ngozi Adichie, *Notes on Grief*

It is the nature of poetry and art to be paean and praise heard above all the wails of lamentation. . . . The happiness of contemplation is a true happiness, indeed the supreme happiness; but it is founded upon sorrow.
—Catholic philosopher Josef Pieper,
Happiness and Contemplation

What is a poet? An unhappy person who conceals profound anguish in his heart but whose lips are so formed that as sighs and cries pass over them they sound like beautiful music.
—Danish philosopher Søren Kierkegaard

There must be those among whom we can sit down and weep, and still be counted as warriors.
—Feminist poet Adrienne Rich[1]

What is grief if not love persevering?
—The AI/synthezoid character Vision in
the TV series *WandaVision*[2]

When I wake up, welcome reality, and mind my mind in the presence of doom, an intense emotion greets me every morning. It walks

---

1 Quoted in Ayana Elizabeth Johnson, Katharine K. Wilkinson, *All That We Can Save* (One World, 2020).
2 Thanks to pastor/entrepreneur Donny Bryant for this epigraph.

with me through the day and even after I fall asleep, it appears in my dreams.

Grief, the feeling of loss, has a thousand dimensions in this time of doom—grief for the simplicity of the old life before doom moved in, grief for the old normal when we assumed that our economy was innocent, benevolent, and sustainable, grief for the loss of confidence in politicians, institutions, technology, or even democracy being able to protect us . . . grief for paradises paved to put up parking lots, grief for beautiful creatures becoming endangered or extinct, grief for the loss of wild and green places, grief for our children because of the unstable climate we are leaving them . . . grief for what we could have done but didn't . . . grief for all the beauty that will be desecrated between this point and the end point of any one of the four scenarios we have considered. So much grief.

Biblical scholar Walter Brueggemann captures the relevance of grief in a time of doom: grief, he says, is the counter to denial.[3]

I mentioned earlier the well-known stages of grief first articulated by Elisabeth Kübler-Ross: when faced with current or anticipated loss, our brains are frequently jolted by waves of shock and denial, bargaining, anger, and depression. Ideally, depression eventually recedes and leaves us in a place of acceptance. (Sometimes *meaning* is added to the original list, or it is included as part of acceptance.) In my years as a pastor, I often shared these stages with grieving people in my congregation. Knowing what to expect during the turbulent grief journey helped people not be so confused and afraid.

Some years later, I found myself in a seven-year grief journey of my own, accompanying first my father and then my mother through their dying process. The stages-of-grief model helped me just as it had helped so many others.

But there was something that nobody prepared me for in my parents' dying process, like a side stream that was largely untouched by shock and denial, bargaining, anger, depression, and acceptance. It was the *sweetness* of grief, the *purity, meaning,* and *love* I found in

3 Walter Brueggemann, *Reality, Grief, Hope: Three Urgent Prophetic Tasks* (William B. Eerdmans Publishing, 2014).

grief. I recently discovered that Susan Cain has written a whole book on this bittersweetness, aptly describing it as "a quiet force, a way of being, a storied tradition, dramatically overlooked, brimming with human potential, authentic, elevating."[4]

If you could have offered me an anesthetic that would have taken away the bitterness of grief, perhaps it would have been tempting at times. But if you told me the anesthetic would also numb the sweetness of grief, I would have turned it down in a second. This bittersweetness in the grief experience, I knew, was humanizing me, deepening me, and making my life better and fuller than it would have been without it. If I shut grief down, I would also shut love down.

Sometimes, the very personal ache of grief inside me seemed to expand outward, like rings of compassion for everyone everywhere who had been or ever would be touched by loss. This sense of universal compassion carried another kind of sweetness that invited me to drop into something deeper and healthier than shock and denial, anger and blame, bargaining and frenzy, anxiety and depression, and even deeper than acceptance. It dropped me into *appreciation,* or its close cousin *praise.*

I felt this sweetness one morning near the end of my dad's life as I pushed him in a wheelchair around a nearby lake, a blanket on his lap as he sang (literally!) to the strangers walking by. I recalled how he had pushed me in a stroller six decades before. The feeling of participating in the cycle of generations was at once sad and sweet, sorrowful and beautiful. For a few moments, I felt a depth and breadth of appreciation beyond words: appreciation for my father, appreciation for the strangers who smiled and waved as he sang to them, appreciation for the cycle of life, appreciation for life itself, for being itself, for this one eternal moment into which I felt I had dropped unexpectedly.

I felt it when he whispered in my ear near the end, his mind reeling from delirium, asking me for help in an imaginary situation in an imaginary hospital where he was still practicing medicine. I felt it listening to my mother near the end of her life, as she would tell me the same story again and again, almost every time I saw her. She was a little girl.

---

4 *Bittersweet* (Crown, 2022).

Her dad came home from work. She ran to greet him. He knelt on one knee in the doorway between the hall and the living room, and she sat on his knee to tell him all about her day. Such a sweet and tender story. I felt it the day she forgot how to use her computer, and a few months later, when she forgot how to use her cell phone. It was a feeling of loss, yes, but it was also a deep, sweet appreciation of the treasures I had always had in my mother without fully recognizing them, because they were so constant they could be easily taken for granted. It felt like I was hearing the beautiful echo of a song I had not fully appreciated when it was being sung.

Do you see what is happening to me right now, as I write these words? It is only in grief, in loss, that I am fully appreciating the beauty in the lives of my parents. It is only in grieving their loss in their absence that I more fully experience the sweet meaning of their presence. It is only in grieving their loss that I more fully feel my undying love for them, and their undying love for me. As I feel that sweetness tinged with grief, or that grief tinged with sweetness, I recall the wisdom of Catholic philosopher Josef Pieper in his beautiful book *Happiness and Contemplation*. Having counts for little or nothing, he explained. The rich man can *own* ten fast new cars, but *appreciate* none of them the way a poor child appreciates her one hand-me-down bicycle. It is not having that brings deep joy, but *appreciating*.

Over the course of my life, I so often took my parents for granted. I so easily saw them as supporting cast members in a story that was about me. Then, in the grief of watching them weaken, fade, and die, the spotlight was on them. I gradually saw, knew, and appreciated them as protagonists in their own amazing stories . . . my dad's unconquerable cheerfulness and affability, his deep devotion to the practice of medicine, his love of picnics and hikes and sledding and swimming and all things outdoors, his childlike, uninhibited delight even as an old man . . . my mom's exquisite kindness, her love of writing letters and checking in with her family, her deep bond with her father—a bond that was being transferred to me as her primary caretaker, as she was in the liminal space between one room and another. It's true to say that my experience of my parents' lives was only completed by the experience of grief in their loss: without grieving their absence, I would have missed so much of the richness of their presence in my life. This is a precious gain that comes with loss. This is a tender sweetness that comes with grief: appreciation.

So, once again, let's continue *waking up* and *welcoming ourselves to reality*. Let's continue *minding our mind*: the world that we so love is ending, dying, being murdered by ignorance, being killed for convenience and profit. Shock and denial, blame and anger, anxiety and bargaining, and exhaustion and depression are the inevitable responses of our internal board of directors to the loss we face. Then, as these powerful emotions wash through us or over us, we can learn to drop down into the sweet current of deep grief that helps us appreciate—to know, to praise, and more fully to love—all that we are losing, all that may soon be lost.

I think of a wetland I used to explore as a boy growing up in Maryland, part of the Rock Creek watershed. I spent hours exploring that wetland in every season, sometimes barefoot, sometimes in boots that nearly always overflowed and filled with cold water because I ventured in a little too deep. How could I stay dry when trilling toads and wriggling tadpoles moved among cattails in the spring? How could I stay away in summer and miss a chance to see that single great blue heron or mammoth snapping turtle who both hunted there, resident dinosaurs to my boyhood imagination? How could I not search for newts and crayfish in its cold waters in autumn, its sky-mirroring surface dappled by yellow tulip poplar, red maple, and orange-amber sweet gum leaves? How could I not return in the winter to slide on the ice and peer through to see painted turtles moving in slow motion along the leafy bottom? How could I not return again as soon as the ice melted to search among the brown soggy layers of decomposing leaves where spotted salamanders gathered for mysterious, slow-motion mating rituals, while red-winged blackbirds called *conk-la-ree!* from the nearby willows?

Several years ago, I was in the old neighborhood again, and I parked my car at the same dead-end street where my friends and I used to follow a narrow trail to the swamp fifty-some years earlier. The trail was still there, but now it was broad and paved for bicycles. The wetland had disappeared. In the place where I remembered it, I found a shiny green tractor parked, its operator taking a rest from mowing the grass between metal picnic tables and park benches in the now-civilized public park. As I sat on one of the benches and looked around, I was overcome by sweet grief for the delight I once enjoyed as a boy, a lost magic boys and girls today will never know, at least, not there.

In writing these words, do you see what I'm doing? I'm returning to this precious place in my memory, this sacred swampy ground. I'm appreciating it, praising it for what it was, all the more because it has been lost. Once again, my echoing experience of the place, my love for it—my life interwoven with it and its life interwoven with mine—all are being intensified through the conscious experience of grief. I recall the words attributed to William Butler Yeats: "Things reveal themselves passing away."

You have your lost places unknown to me. I have mine unknown to you. We could not protect them. But we do not let these good creations disappear only to be forgotten, unappreciated, unpraised, unlamented. Our love for them outlasts their existence. So together, we remember them in grief. We feel them more fully revealing themselves to us in their passing away. In the years ahead, we will feel these losses by the thousands, millions . . . beautiful places, delightful creatures, scraped away by bulldozers, incinerated in flames. E. O. Wilson once captured the tragedy in cool, abstract prose. It is "the ultimate irony of organic evolution," he said, that "in the instant of achieving self-understanding through the mind of man, life has doomed its most beautiful creatures." In that wording, he successfully cooled the grief into tragic irony. By hiding human agency in the grammar, so to speak, he also softened the tragedy, feeling, I think, that it would be too great to bear unless we glance at it sideways and only for a moment.

There is a place for that sideways glance, I know. But there is also a place for the poets and other artists who help us feel the grief and stay with it without intellectualizing it. We feel it in Bruce Cockburn's song "Beautiful Creatures," when he sings of "the knot in my gut," because "we create what destroys," and as a result, "the beautiful creatures are going away, going away." We feel it in Mary Oliver's poetry. "To live in this world," she says, "you must be able to . . . love what is mortal; to hold it against your bones knowing your own life depends on it; and, when the time comes to let it go, to let it go."

In the first of her two poems about geese, "Wild Geese," she captures the delight of the way the world "offers itself to your imagination," the way it "calls to you like the wild geese, harsh and exciting," the way it "over and over" announces "your place in the family of things." Then, in "Snow Geese," she begins, "Oh, to love what is lovely, and will not last! What a task to ask of anything, or anyone, yet it is ours." Then she describes something lovely that will not last, a flock of geese passing overhead, snow white but rendered golden in the angled autumn sunlight. "They flew on," she says, but it doesn't matter whether she will ever see them again, because "when I saw them, I saw them."

We feel it in Mark Nepo's poem "Adrift." It offers these haunting lines: "In the very center, under it all, what we have that no one can take away and all that we've lost face each other. It is there that I'm adrift, feeling punctured by a holiness that exists inside everything. I am so sad and everything is beautiful."

When we resist intellectualizing the grief into irony and explanation, the poets can guide us to make our grief sacred by taking it seriously and reverently, processing it deeply and slowly. We experience it as sharp, penetrating, breathtaking. If we stay with grief long and with intention, if we don't suppress it or escape it, if we humbly gesture with words toward a lost beauty too big for words, we feel both our own grief and the poignant sweetness of what is being lost. The pang of loss is like a blow to the chest, but poetry and all the other arts help us keep breathing, breathing out soulful sadness for all we lost and breathing in the beautiful sweetness of all we loved. Each breath brings deep and bittersweet joy.

When I was a pastor, I was often asked to perform funerals for people I didn't know. Whenever possible, I would try to gather the family before the memorial service. I would ask them to share stories about the loved one they had lost. I told them their stories would help me to honor their loved one in my eulogy, which was true, but I had another purpose as well. Almost without exception, before long, as one story would pour out and invite another and another, tears would mix with laughter. The bereaved would remember the unique beauty of the person they had lost, and as they celebrated the loved one through stories, their sense of loss transformed, at least momentarily, into a sense of awe and gratitude that they had known and loved such a wonderful human being. The sadness of bitter grief was mixed with the joy of sweet gratitude.

Whatever scenario unfolds in the years ahead—Collapse Avoidance, Collapse/Rebirth, Collapse/Survival, or Collapse/Extinction—feelings of grief will fill us as smoke fills air during a wildfire. Grief will unleash wave upon wave of shock and denial, anger and blame, anxiety and depression.

I can promise you there will be grief. But I cannot promise you there will be sweetness. To go there takes practice, intention, desire. That's when poetry will help you, whether you read it or write it, sing it or draw it, sculpt it or dance it. It will even feel like prayer if you pray, or something very much like it if you don't.

Yes, the latest statistics will shock you tomorrow morning, then put you into a panic, and then infuriate you. Next week, new record-high temperatures here and there and everywhere will depress you. Corporations and oligarchs will fill you with disgust and fury as they externalize death and internalize profit. Politicians will compete to see which one can impress you as most shrunken, most craven, most insipid. There will be no sweetness in the headlines, no sweetness in the cool prose of peer-reviewed scientific papers, no sweetness in the latest prediction from this panel or that agency or that would-be prophet.

Meanwhile, geese will pass by overhead, and you may not see them because the weight of grief won't allow you to lift your eyes. Or you may notice them momentarily, but not really see them, certainly not "secretly, joyfully, clearly." That's why you need, during this flight through doom, to invite a poet to sit to your left, and a songwriter to sit to your right. That's why you need a painter and photographer and filmmaker and sculptor and potter and landscape architect and novelist and dancer and playwright and architect to sit at your table and share your bread and tears.

Poetry and the arts—like the right kind of prayer—can help us to stay with grief long enough to feel its sweetness, long enough for the sweetness and grief to deepen our sensitivity to the exquisite agony and ecstasy that we call appreciation, praise, love . . . and life. We will find or write and recite the poems and prayers that resonate most deeply within us. We will revere and honor the beauty that has already been lost or is being lost at this moment. We will find poetic ways to lovingly describe it and lament it so it does not pass away unpraised.

We will do it out loud together when we can, weaving poetry and song into liturgies of lament and love. We will do it silently and alone when we must.

Perhaps, in our poetry, in our praise, in us, as beautiful creatures die and beautiful places are destroyed, the beauty itself lives on, deathless.

And perhaps, as we are inspired by grief to eulogize what is being lost, we will also be inspired by love to save all we can still save.

Dear Reader,

Here are some questions to consider—alone or in a reading group—to go deeper in your reflection:

What role does poetry currently play in your life?

If you're like most people these days, it probably doesn't play much of a role. Why do you think poetry—which has been a primary art form throughout human history—seems so much less important now?

Compare and contrast the experience of reading a poem with watching a TV show or movie, and consider why shows and movies are so much more popular these days than poetry.

Then talk about the role TV shows and movies can play in helping us wake up, welcome reality, mind our minds, and grieve. Can you give any specific examples?

Choose one of the poems or song lyrics mentioned in this chapter. Look it up and spend some time with it. See how it affects you.

Consider how other art forms—dance, photography, film, painting, sculpture, architecture, landscape architecture—help you taste the inexpressible bittersweetness of love and grief.

I begin the next chapter with an experience from my religious up-bringing. Be prepared for it to strike you as really strange (unless you grew up in a similar background). Later in the chapter, I'll turn from my unusual religious background to something that almost all of us share.

5

When the Story Does Harm, Step Away

When I criticize a system, they think I criticize them—and that is of course because they fully accept the system and identify themselves with it.
—Contemplative monk Thomas Merton[1]

The deepest crises experienced by any society are those moments of change when the story becomes inadequate for meeting the survival demands of a present situation.
—Catholic "geologian" Thomas Berry, *The Dream of the Earth*

I was nine years old, sitting in church on a Saturday night, mesmerized.

The previous Sunday morning, I had attended our communion service, our preaching service, and Sunday School (three hours total). Then my dad, mom, brother, and I came back Sunday night for a preaching service. We were back again Tuesday night for prayer meeting, and then, Wednesday through Saturday evenings, we were back to hear a visiting preacher who was in town to lead what other denominations called "revivals," but we just called "special meetings." (Why would we need to be *revived*, when we were doing just fine, thank you very much!)

Considering how much time I spent in church as a child, the fact that I became a pastor was either a miracle or inevitable.

My parents were wonderful examples of what Christians should be. But the tradition in which they were raised (and in which they raised me) was a little more . . . tricky. You've probably never heard of the Plymouth Brethren, but if you've ever heard of "the Rapture," you

---

1 Quoted in John Howard Griffin, *Follow the Ecstasy* (Orbis, 1993).

have our heritage to thank. (You're very welcome.) The Rapture was the Plymouth Brethren's gift to Christendom way back in the 1830s. Just as the Mormons and Millerites (later the Seventh-Day Adventists) were getting their start in the US, the PBs (as they're called by the few people who know about them) were getting organized, albeit loosely, in Ireland and England. Like the Mormons and Millerites, they felt that standard Christianity had lost its plot, and they aimed to restore it to its intended glory, down to the last detail.

Some of them to this day think they succeeded.

Among their many obsessions, the PBs were determined to map out the future using the Bible as their divinely inspired crystal ball.

That Saturday night, little nine-year-old me was staring wide-eyed at a huge timeline draped across the front of the chapel. I had never seen anything like it before. The preacher was using that timeline to explain all of past history and all of future history in one majestic hour. A Chart of the Ages depicted everything from "Eternity Past" to "Eternity Future," featuring the Seven (literal) Days of Creation, the Seven Dispensations, and the Seven Churches of the Church Age. (We *really* liked the number seven.) Along the way, the preacher taught us about the Rapture, the Great Tribulation, the Millennium, the New Heaven, the New Earth, and the Lake of Fire.[2]

I was just a kid. So, of course, I believed what my religious leaders were telling me, especially when they had a huge chart to prove it. I didn't understand that the chart conveyed a peculiar theological sidetrack called Dispensationalism. I believed it was God's truth. How cool is it to understand everything that will ever happen—past, present, and future—at the age of nine!? Needless to say, I bought that Chart of the Ages hook, line, and sinker. I stayed hooked for a while.[3]

---

2 You can see it here: https://www.bbusa.org/books/evangelism/prophecy/chart-of -the-ages-a-chart-large-size-2009-new-edition-detail.

3 I experienced some downsides of the chart, to be sure. For example, not long after the chart sermon, I returned home from school one day to find the doors unlocked but my mother and little brother not there. I quickly assumed that the Rapture had happened: Mom and Peter had been beamed up to heaven and I had been left behind. (My brother was nicer than me, so I wasn't surprised.) I sat on the back porch, pondering my fate as an orphan, unsuccessfully trying to hold back tears, until my mother and brother cheerfully returned home from visiting a neighbor. I quickly dried my tears and never told anyone . . . maybe until now?

In the years ahead, the end-times theology of the Chart of the Ages was further promoted in bestselling books like *The Late Great Planet Earth* and *This Present Darkness*. They suggested that the end-times would climax in the 1980s or in 2010 or shortly after that, following a long tradition of failed predictions.[4] These books led to some shabby, manipulative movies too, like *A Thief in the Night* (1972) and *A Distant Thunder* (1978). I had no idea at the time how harmful these books and movies would be to conservative Christians of my generation: not only did they theologically misinform us if not traumatize us; they were also grooming readers for acquiescence to authoritarian politics.[5] But that's another story for another time.

By the end of that night in church, nine-year-old me was certain of this: throughout my lifetime, the Earth would get worse and worse. Then, when things looked absolutely hopeless, my fellow Bible believers and I would be beamed up to be with Jesus through something called the Rapture. After that, the Antichrist would come and make things on Earth even worse, until Jesus came back to make things much worse than that, ultimately destroying the whole Earth in the worst battle ever, the Battle of Armageddon. (We raptured Christians would watch all this horror unfold from our safe and air-conditioned box seats in heaven.)

The preacher said there was a guaranteed happy ending in heaven for us and a guaranteed torturous ending elsewhere for everyone else. Part of the obscene weirdness of this kind of teaching was that we were supposed to feel happy about it. Our "unsaved" friends and relatives (not to mention billions of strangers) were only getting what they deserved when they suffered eternal conscious torment in hell, we were taught. And we who were Bible believers weren't getting what we deserved . . . we were getting what *Jesus* deserved. Streets of gold! No more crying or pain! An eternal feast (with no weight gain)! Golden crowns! Rewards for every good thing we ever did, and

---

4 See Festinger, et al., *When Prophecy Fails* (Martino Publishing, 2009, originally published in 1956).
5 They led to even worse apocalyptic fiction like the Left Behind books and films. For an investigation of where this Rapture porn led, see the 2023 documentary *Praying for Armageddon*, directed by Tonje Hessen Schei and Michael Rowley (https://www.imdb.com/title/tt27009795/).

especially for lost souls we led to the Lord! An eternal heavenly church service where we would sing unending praises to God! (Admittedly, to a squirmy young boy in a clip-on tie and uncomfortable leather shoes, that eternal church service thing didn't sound completely great, except in contrast to the alternative eternal destiny depicted in fiery orange and red on the Chart of the Ages.)

Later that Saturday night, I left church understanding that earthly doom was the foyer to heaven. The worse things got, the more it proved that our theology was right.

Looking back, I feel so sad for nine-year-old me being subjected to this teaching. What does it do to a child morally, to be told to rejoice in my individual eternal destiny, singing about being saved week after week, thanking God for salvation in prayer after prayer, and yet remain so numb to the destruction and damnation of all my fellow human beings who were not saved, redeemed, justified, elect, born again, orthodox, or otherwise exempt from damnation, however described? How was I supposed to consider all the beauties of the Earth, all the forests, mountains, rivers, and oceans, all the creatures who live within them, creatures that as a nine-year-old boy I already loved . . . and then think that their entire reason for existence was to serve as cheap, disposable props in a drama whose only stars were God, angels, and the members of my religion?

But that's what I believed, because that's what *we* believed. And that's how I felt (or tried to feel), because that's what *we* felt. Nobody seemed to care that our religious profit came at the expense of the Earth, her creatures, and all our fellow humans. God said it, the Bible taught it, we believed it.

Looking back, the Chart of the Ages narrative sold to nine-year-old me feels downright abusive, like a case of mass brainwashing.

That brainwashing, however, was highly profitable to the religious industrial complex, because people scared as hell of hell will cough up a hell of a lot of money.

Eventually, I couldn't buy it anymore. I explored beyond the narrow hall of my religious tradition and discovered that there were better ways to interpret the Bible than I had been taught. I migrated from fundamentalism to more open and thoughtful forms of faith, forms that encouraged me to welcome truth wherever it was found, including in other faiths.

But that same old theological story from the Chart of the Ages is still going strong today, upheld by churches, radio networks, cable TV empires, websites, and publishing houses. I know this, because when I write or speak about our need to care for the Earth, I still get a flurry of emails and social media replies from its current devotees: "Jesus is coming back and it will all burn anyway! So drill, baby, drill," they say. "Live like a child of the King! We were meant to prosper! Only souls matter, and only humans have souls—not polar bears!" They'll condemn me for being a "woke leftist" among "social justice warriors," who are foolishly trying to make the world a better place. "You just don't understand," my old fundamentalist friends still say, "that the world is *supposed* to be a deteriorating unsalvageable mess until Jesus returns. In fact, if things got better, it would prove our theology is wrong!"

And then I see it—an insight into why my religion tried to instill so much joy about so much destruction. I have written elsewhere about a "cult of innocence."[6] There is a related phenomenon we might call a "cult of correctness." It works like this: Our individual identities as true believers are woven into the corporate ego of our religious group, and that corporate religious ego is fused with our theology. If our theology is criticized, we are criticized. If our religion is labeled misguided or wrong, then we are so labeled. If we are misguided or wrong, then our whole identity is threatened, since we are taught that we are nothing without our faith, which means our correct doctrine. At all costs, as a matter of identity, belonging, and survival, *we must be right.* If it takes the destruction of everything and everyone everywhere to prove us right, then bring it on!

If that sounds absurd to you, you should thank God (or whoever or whatever you thank) that you have never been this kind of true believer. But understand this: there are billions of people around the world who are being raised within this kind of religious framework

---

6 See *Do I Stay Christian?* (St. Martin's Essentials, 2022).

today. There are Protestant versions of it, Catholic versions of it, and I'm sure parallel versions in other traditions as well.

It seems to me that this kind of theology poses a bigger threat to human survival than coal-fired power plants and gas-guzzling cars, because wherever people have fused their identity with this kind of theology, they will vote, spend, and pray for something very close to scenario 4, Collapse/Extinction, believing it is God's will, perfectly foretold in the Bible.[7]

Because I was such a true believer and good soldier of this kind of theology, I was only able to disentangle from it through a long and painful process, detailed in many of my books. What I jokingly call my inner fundamentalist still perks up from time to time, showing how a childhood of indoctrination can be healed, but scars remain.

Somewhere along my journey through life, I realized that what I called "theology" was really a story, a narrative . . . a cosmic narrative. That story made sense of our lives and gave us a sense of meaning, purpose, and belonging. It made life matter.

And here's what is striking about the theological narrative I and billions of Christians have inherited: *It is both socially disengaged and anti-ecological.* It says little or nothing about our need to be engaged with movements for social justice, anti-racism, poverty reduction, violence reduction, and the like. The story is about other things entirely. And when it comes to ecological overshoot and its consequences, this popular theological narrative says those consequences don't matter, because salvation gives us believers a "get out of ecological jail free" card via the Rapture, and because God can't wait to destroy the whole damned world anyway, extracting the only thing of value: disembodied human souls. (We'll consider a radically different telling of the biblical story in chapters 8 and 9.)

Equally striking: *The same is true of the narrative of capitalism—it is utterly anti-ecological.* Conventional capitalism—by which I mean

---

7 In fact, their story has a worse ending than Collapse/Extinction, because after collapse comes something worse than extinction: eternal conscious torment in hell. I wrote a work of instructive fiction on this subject, the third in the New Kind of Christian trilogy, called *The Last Word and the Word After That* (Fortress Press, 2019, originally published in 2005).

the economic story that upholds our current global civilization—acts as if the economy is the ultimate reality, the invisible hand that guides human history. It tells us who we are: abstracted *consumers* with wants and needs that the economy can fulfill. It provides ultimate justice, rewarding the hardworking and punishing the lazy. It either ignores social injustice or promises that its own invisible hand will resolve it. It takes no account of the environment. (In fact, it has a subdiscipline called environmental economics, as if the environment were a subset of the economy!) Capitalism-induced environmental blindness, aided and abetted by distorted Christian end-times theologies, made it possible for us to race through overshoot without even noticing.

I used to think that theological struggle was the deepest level of our struggle, because I believed that our spiritual identity was the deepest level of our identity. But that began to change when I attended a conference back in 2004, along the shore of Chesapeake Bay. The Sandy Cove Conference was organized by a small group of Evangelical leaders to educate their peers about climate change. Few considered me an Evangelical anymore, but I was invited anyway because the organizers knew I cared about the environment. At the conference, Sir John Houghton spoke. A brilliant climate scientist, head of the main scientific organization studying climate change, and an Evangelical Christian, he gave a presentation that was majestic, his evidence irrefutable. But the leading Southern Baptist at the conference said he could not accept the evidence. Someone asked why. He replied something to this effect: "A problem of this magnitude requires big government solutions, and our denomination is committed to the conservative principles of small government and free enterprise. For that reason, I can assure you that the Southern Baptist Convention will oppose your efforts."

I was stunned. It wasn't simply theology that would keep the Southern Baptists from signing. It was theology coupled with political and economic ideology (small government conservatism and free market capitalism). It was a perfect example of what Kevin Kruse was soon to detail in his book *One Nation Under God: How Corporate America Invented Christian America*.[8] I was livid. I could barely contain myself

---

8 Basic Books, 2015.

until the next coffee break. I found Sir John Houghton, vented my frustration, and asked how he could remain so calm and patient. I'll never forget his reply.

As long as the Republican Party was in power, he said (this was during the George W. Bush administration), the US wouldn't address climate change. And Republicans wouldn't address climate change until Evangelical Christians were on board. But Evangelicals would not be on board until Southern Baptists were on board. "So you're saying that the climate of the entire planet, and the future of the entire planet, is being held hostage by the Republican Party, and in particular by American Evangelicals, and in particular Southern Baptists?" I asked, incredulous. Sir John nodded. I can still hear his charming accent: "I'm afraid so. So I have no choice but to keep working with both urgency and patience."

Watching how religious institutions have behaved in the years since, I've come to see the degree to which the religious industrial complex is a wholly owned subsidiary of the global capitalist economy. I now suspect that our spiritual or religious identities take shape within an even deeper frame, our economic identity. It doesn't have to be this way, and I wish it weren't this way, but my seven decades of life have led me to believe that these days, economics more often shapes theology than theology shapes economics.

Simply put, the theology so many of us inherited was perfectly designed to render us obedient drones, doing our part to extract natural resources, put them through industrial processes, and produce two things: waste and profit (a little profit for most of us, and a lot for those above us in the economic pyramid). We didn't ask questions about the long-term consequences of how we made a living. We didn't raise ethical objections when we heard the cries of the Earth and the cries of the poor. Instead, we let our theology conveniently turn our attention to what happened after we died, seldom interfering in all the rampant political and economic violence in this life, violence that was harming billions of people, all of our fellow creatures, and even the physical systems of the Earth.

I've come to see that the religious elite and the corporate elite are part of the same cabal, knowingly or unknowingly. Right up to this moment, they share together in the short-term profits of ecological overshoot and plunder. Together they discount the long-term costs, one in the name of God and the prophets, and the other in the name of corporate profits. To the degree religious leaders make parishioners into compliant workers, obedient voters, and enthusiastic consumers in the economy, corporate profiteers can exploit both human labor and the Earth's resources with religious protection. To the degree that the profiteers are happy, they can make donations to their religious accomplices. These donations are called charitable, but to me they have the smell of payoffs.

If that sounds like an overstatement, then I invite you to imagine a history textbook written about this period in one or two hundred years (if we avoid scenario 4, that is, and if honest history textbooks are still being written). Students will read how, in our lifetimes, scientists realized that we humans would have to budget our future use of fossil fuels to avoid throwing the Earth's climate system dangerously out of balance. (The remaining budget in 2012 was 2.795 gigatons of carbon dioxide, to be exact.[9]) But the fossil fuel industry continued to gain the rights to drill, sell, and burn more and more fuel, until it had enough drilling rights to produce ten times more than the budget allowed. To avoid the collapse of the ecosystem, and our civilization with it, the fossil fuel executives would have to leave 90 percent of their assets stranded in the ground. That would be a loss of about $100 trillion. (I've tried to avoid numbers and statistics in this book; these paragraphs are a rare exception.)

Our descendants will have to ask why over eight billion of us were willing to let a tiny group of oligarchs make $100 trillion for themselves at the expense of . . . everyone and everything on Earth, present and future. Why weren't we organizing a worldwide strike? Why weren't we laying our bodies down on the driveways of oil company headquarters? Why weren't we voting do-nothings out of office? Why weren't we acting like our children's lives depended upon urgent action? How could sane people allow such a thing?

The only rational explanation for our inaction, future historians

---

9 See Bill McKibben's article in *Rolling Stone*, "Global Warming's Terrifying New Math" (July 19, 2012), available here: https://www.rollingstone.com/politics/politics-news/global-warmings-terrifying-new-math-188550/.

will conclude, was that we are all victims of brainwashing—a combination of religious and economic brainwashing. We have stopped acting as rational creatures, Homo sapiens. We have been inducted into a religious money cult, a civilizational death cult; we have evolved into Homo theocapitus, people who worship the big bronze bull of Wall Street with his shiny, pendulous testicles.[10] We have become consumers who would rather die than disrupt the economy. We have fallen prey to our own crazy capitalist Chart of the Ages, which is a GDP growth chart. If you feel that I'm being too hard on capitalism, listen to American farmer/sage Wendell Berry:

> No amount of fiddling with capitalism to regulate and humanize it can for long disguise its failure to conserve the wealth and health of nature: eroded, wasted or degraded soils; damaged or destroyed ecosystems; extinction of biodiversity, species; whole landscapes defaced, gouged, flooded, or blown up; thoughtless squandering of fossil fuels and fossil waters, of mineable minerals and ores; natural health and beauty replaced by a heartless and sickening ugliness. Perhaps its greatest success is an astounding increase in the destructiveness and therefore the profitability of war.[11]

Let me say it as plainly as I can: Capitalism tells a story no less alluring and destructive than the Chart of the Ages. In its current form this story will destroy the Earth, just as certainly as the story told by conventional religious fundamentalism will. Neither can pull us back from the ledge of scenario 4 to scenarios 3 or 2 or 1. Working together, religious and economic fundamentalism will push us over the ledge, singing a hymn and counting corporate profits as we go. If you want to withdraw your consent from ecological overshoot, you will need to disidentify with the stories told by both religious fundamentalism and economic fundamentalism. You will need to break up with the ideologies and narratives that have intimately shaped you.

---

10 For more on capitalism as religion, see David Dark's *Life's Too Short to Pretend Your'e Not Religious* (IVP, 2016).
11 From his interview with Bill Moyers, available here: https://www.youtube.com/watch?v=2ejYAfcjJmY.

Over recent centuries, more and more people have found their old religious narratives to be unbelievable . . . and dangerous too.

Relatively few people have seen the folly and danger of their economic narrative. All they can see are the profits it keeps adding to their investment accounts, for now at least. Even those who have been exploited by the capitalist narrative keep buying it, like a lottery ticket, hoping they'll get lucky and win big . . . tomorrow.

Those who lose faith in their religious and economic framing stories face a shared problem. What new story will replace the old one?

For many, the only alternative story to conventional Christianity and capitalism is nationalism, or white supremacy, or hedonism, or narcissism, or nihilism, a belief that meaning and morality are delusions.[12] Those stories have one thing in common: they are equally careless about justice and the Earth, and they do not support the virtues and values needed to help us constructively face the times of turbulence that lie ahead.

If we're going to evade the Collapse/Extinction scenario, it's going to require a lot of people making a break with the old religious and economic stories that aid and abet ecological overshoot. We're going to have to step away from the harmful stories that brought us here, the stories that give us a self-righteous "our lives matter and to hell with everything else" spirit. Deconstructing failing stories and reconstructing new ones, we might say, is not just a matter of personal spirituality or ideology; it's now a matter of planetary survival.

You will know you have *not* dismounted from the destructive stories of the current theo-economic system when someone criticizes conventional theology or conventional economics and you feel that they are criticizing you, as Thomas Merton so aptly observed.

---

12 Donald Trump eloquently illustrated nihilism when asked how he handled stress during a TV interview in 2004: "I try and tell myself it doesn't matter. Nothing matters. If you tell yourself it doesn't matter—like you do shows, you do this, you do that, and then you have earthquakes in India where 400,000 people get killed. Honestly, it doesn't matter." See "It Doesn't Matter, We'll See," *Washington Post*, October 19, 2018. https://www.washingtonpost.com/lifestyle/style /it-doesnt-matter-well-see-the-trump-doctrine-is-sounding-more-fatalistic-every -day/2018/10/18/218d3b8a-d14d-11e8-83d6-291fcead2ab1_story.html

You will know you *have* dismounted from the stories of the current system when you can voice the critique yourself.

When we dismount from our civilization's current framing narratives, we will feel that although we are still *in* the civilization, we are no longer *of* it. It no longer defines us.

When we disentangle our identities from the civilization's dominant story, we can begin imagining, embodying, and telling a new story, a story that gives us a deeper sense of meaning, belonging, and purpose, one that helps heal the Earth, our fellow humans, and our fellow creatures rather than destroying them. Having faced various scenarios of doom, we find ourselves ready to live for something bigger than personal wealth in this life or personal salvation after it. In this new story, our life is not about *us*. It is not about us as individual humans, nations, religions, civilizations, or even as a species. In this new story, we are about life; life that is bigger than us, life that goes on after we're gone.

A new and better story may catch on. It may even help us avoid scenario 4 and land in one of the other scenarios. (We'll return to this idea of a new story in coming chapters, especially 8, 9, and 17.)

But even if it doesn't turn things around, a new and better story will help us do our best to live well while we still have the chance. It will help us, in a time of fear and insanity, to live with a measure of insight, serenity, and hope.

Ah, but hope is complicated, as we'll see in the next chapter.

Dear Reader,

I felt I took a risk in inviting you down the theological rabbit hole of eschatology, the study of the future and the end of the world according to various religious traditions. I felt it was a worthwhile risk, in hopes it would ease you into an insight you may have found offensive if I had said it from the start: that capitalism functions as a kind of religion, and that it can easily have cultic tendencies. Here are some questions for your personal reflection and group conversation:

How did you respond to my childhood story of the Chart of the Ages? How does it affect you when you realize that millions of people are still being taught this view that the past, present, and future are already mapped out by God?

How do you respond to this conclusion I drew after attending the Sandy Cove Conference: "Economics more often shapes theology than theology shapes economics"?

How do you respond to the idea that capitalism, like a religion, tells a story that frames our lives and determines what has value?

Offer any additional reflections you have on how religion and economics are contributing to our current situation.

If we step away from the framing stories or narratives told by conventional religion and conventional capitalism, where might a new story arise?

6

Hope Is Complicated

Losing hope is not so bad. There's something worse: losing hope and hiding it from yourself.

—Southern novelist Walker Percy,
The Moviegoer

Hope is not the same thing as optimism. It is not the conviction that something will turn out well, but the certainty that something is worth doing regardless of how it turns out. . . . [This] hope . . . gives us the strength to live and continually to try new things, even in conditions that seem as hopeless as ours do, here and now.

—Former Czech president and playwright Václav Havel,
Disturbing the Peace

People are always asking me where I find hope, and I tell them I don't think of things that way. . . . I believe in the truth and in doing the right thing because it's the right thing to do, let the chips fall where they may.

—Anthropologist/author/podcaster Sarah Kendzior

We don't have a right to ask whether we're going to succeed or not. The only question we have the right to ask is, "What's the right thing to do? What does this earth require of us if we want to continue to live on it?"

—Kentucky sage Wendell Berry[1]

You may have noticed that over the first five chapters, I have mentioned hope only rarely and in passing. That was intentional, and it will change in this chapter, where hope takes center stage.

I've always been a big fan of hope.

---

1 From "Wendell Berry on His Hopes for Humanity," an interview with Bill Moyers, available here: https://www.youtube.com/watch?v=2ejYAfcjJmY/.

That's probably because I had my first brief but intense affair with depression when I was still a teenager. "I never want to go there again," I told myself. But depression in its various forms has come back to sit on my chest several times over the years. So throughout my adult life I've felt that I need to lean hard into hope as a matter of emotional survival.

As a result, I was surprised, as this book began to take shape, to realize that hope can be a problem. In fact, in the presence of doom, hope (at least a common and superficial kind of hope) can be downright deadly.

I felt this the other day as I was listening to a lecture by theologian and activist Miguel De La Torre. He captured one of the downsides of hope like this: "Hope is what is fed to those who are being slaughtered so they won't fight what is coming." This insight came to him, he explained, as he toured Auschwitz, one of the horrific death camps where the Nazi regime enacted genocide against Jews, Soviet and Polish POWs, Roma, and others. All who entered the gates of the death camp passed under a large inscription at the entrance: ARBEIT MACHT FREI, which means "work sets you free." The inscription was intended to inspire the hope of freedom, which rendered prisoners more willing to work and less likely to resist.[2]

In other words, malevolent forces often use hope to manipulate us, rendering us compliant to their continued oppression. Hope can be a false promise, not just a lie, but a dangerous, delicious lie. And the lie becomes all the more appealing when the only alternative we see is despair.

Thich Nhat Hanh, writing from a Buddhist perspective, addressed another danger of hope. Hope has some value,[3] he said, "because it can make the present moment less difficult to bear." But when we "cling to our hope in the future, we do not focus our energies and capabilities on the present moment." We bypass the present to dwell in a better imagined future, and in so doing, we bypass the joy, peace, and other

2 I heard Miguel De La Torre at a conference called Evolving Faith in 2022. See his book *Embracing Hopelessness* (Fortress, 2017).
3 See Joanna Macy and Chris Johnstone, *Active Hope* (New World, revised edition 2022).

gifts available to us here and now—including the sweetness of grief we considered in chapter 4.

Another contemporary Buddhist teacher, Joan Halifax, offered an additional critique of hope: Nobody actually knows for certain what the future holds. In Buddhist thought, there is "no independent origination." In other words, the future constantly arises from conditions we, together with all sentient creatures, help create in the present. Because current conditions are impermanent and constantly changing, the future is unknowable, and our actions matter. This is why Joanna Macy, another Buddhist teacher, argues not simply for hope, but for *active hope*.

Karl Marx anticipated many of these insights when he wrote in 1844, "Religion is the sigh of the oppressed creature, the heart of a heartless world, and the soul of soulless conditions. It is the *opium* of the people" (italics mine). In context, he was not attacking religion, as many people interpret this quote. Instead, he was expressing sympathy for the working classes who suffer oppression and exploitation by the economic system in which they labor. Their pain is so great, he said, that they naturally seek an anesthetic to numb it. The opiate offered by religion is the hope of a pain-free heaven. By dealing this drug of hope—many today call it "hope-ium"—religion offers palliative care to the oppressed between now and their death.[4]

But hope-ium also aids and abets the oppressors by pacifying the labor force, as Miguel De La Torre so powerfully saw at the gate to Auschwitz. If the oppressed can muster the courage to put away the opium, they will feel the pain of their current condition, and that pain may make them desperate enough to take collective action toward their own liberation. It's counterintuitive to many of us—to see hope as dangerous and desperation as necessary. But you have to admit that

---

4 I have deeply mixed feelings about the term "hope-ium." I understand why many use it. But by mocking hope, or by treating the various kinds of hope as if they were nothing but forms of denial, people risk discrediting one of the most powerful psychological experiences shared by healthy people. A wide array of research shows the life-saving, health-promoting fruits of cultivating hope. See, for example, research by Dr. Daniel Gutierrez, available here: https://psycnet.apa.org/record/2019-29454-001.

Karl Marx and Miguel De La Torre had a point, as did Thich Nhat Hanh and Joan Halifax.

I felt the dangerous side of hope in my own religious upbringing. We were taught two attractive ideas: that God was in control, and that God guaranteed us a happy ending in heaven. We had an army of Bible verses to defend this pair of beliefs, and we quoted them a lot. (We ignored the many other Bible verses that contradicted our beliefs.) As a result, rather than feeling the pain of our current situation and translating that pain into action, we took a long draw from our religious hope-ium pipe, sang songs about the coming joys of heaven, and fell into a pleasant dream of blissful indifference.

You can see why environmental activist Greta Thunberg has thundered: "I don't want your hope. I don't want you to be hopeful. I want you to panic . . . and act as if the house is on fire. Because it is."[5]

In my public speaking, I often feel what Greta feels. People are willing for me to speak some hard truths, as long as I am sure to end on a hopeful note, reassuring them with a few happy-ending anecdotes that everything will be OK. They need me to leave them at least as happy in their relative complacency as they were when I found them. But here's the catch: happy and complacent people don't change. And people who don't change are sitting ducks for doom.

To put it in Darwinian terms, unchanging people are unfit for a changing environment.

Of course, dangers, we learn as we age, often come in pairs. So if hope can lead to complacency and even paralysis, so can despair.

Because of the way our internal board of directors works, both hope and hopelessness can have a surprisingly similar appeal. First, both relieve us from the uncertainty of an unknown future. For one, a happy ending is assumed; for the other, a tragic ending is inescapable. Either way, at least we know what's coming. Second, both promise us a future that asks nothing of us.

Because things are going to turn out fine, you don't have to do or change anything.

---

5 Panic, of course, has its downsides too, which Greta, I'm sure, fully understands. It sometimes takes dangerous language to wake people from their slumber.

Because there's nothing you can do to avert doom, you don't have to do or change anything.

Just as hope can give you permission to return to your previously scheduled complacency, so can despair.

Professor and ethicist Sharon D. Welch proposed an apt name for despair-supported complacency: "cultured despair." She noticed that many affluent, middle-class, and privileged activists are quick to give up on their cause when results don't come quickly and easily enough to suit them. Their "inability to persist in resistance" and their susceptibility to "cynicism and despair when problems seem intransigent" arise from the fact that "it is easier to give up on long-term social change when one is comfortable in the present." "Becoming so easily discouraged," she writes, "is the privilege of those accustomed to too much power, accustomed to having needs met without negotiation and work, accustomed to having a political and economic system that responds to their needs." She concludes that for those "cushioned by privilege and grounded in privilege," for whom "the good life is present or within reach," it is tempting to "resort to merely enjoying [the good life] for oneself and one's family."[6]

I think you can see it clearly now: hope is complicated, and so is despair. If you've always thought hope was nothing but good and despair was nothing but bad, listen to environmental activist Derrick Jensen turn things upside down:

> When we stop hoping for external assistance, when we stop hoping that the awful situation we're in will somehow resolve itself, when we stop hoping the situation will somehow not get worse, then we are finally free—truly free—to honestly start working to resolve it. I would say that when hope dies, action begins.
>
> People sometimes ask me, "If things are so bad, why don't you just kill yourself?" The answer is that life is really, really good. I am a complex enough being that I can hold in my heart the understanding that we are really, really f*cked, and at the same time that life is really, really good. I am full of rage, sorrow, joy, love,

---

6 *A Feminist Ethic of Risk* (Fortress, 2000).

hate, despair, happiness, satisfaction, dissatisfaction, and a thousand other feelings. We are really f*cked. Life is still really good.

Many people are afraid to feel despair. They fear that if they allow themselves to perceive how desperate our situation really is, they must then be perpetually miserable. They forget that it is possible to feel many things at once. They also forget that despair is an entirely appropriate response to a desperate situation. Many people probably also fear that if they allow themselves to perceive how desperate things are, they may be forced to do something about it.

Jane Goodall has been one of my lifelong heroes. Her 1999 book *Reason for Hope* had a profound influence on me over twenty years ago. More recently, she published *The Book of Hope: A Survival Guide for Trying Times.*[7] There Goodall offers four reasons for hope: the amazing human intellect, the resilience of nature, the power of youth, and the indomitable human spirit. (Her four reasons, I think, can be simplified to two: the resilience of both humanity and nature.) She still believes that it is not "too late to do something to put things right" and that "we still have a window of time during which we can start healing the harm we have inflicted on the planet."

"[B]ut that window is closing," she adds, and soon it will be "too late." She acknowledges that already "we have not just compromised but stolen [the future of today's children] as we have relentlessly plundered the finite resources of our planet with no concern for future generations." She is not giving up, but she is no Pollyanna. She offers no guarantees.

A careful reading of her book demonstrates that even today's great apostle of hope isn't always optimistic. In fact, she admits that she often feels that what we're calling scenario 3 or 4 is inevitable:

On many days I admit that I feel depressed, days when it seems that the efforts, the struggles, and the sacrifices of so many people fighting for social and environmental justice, fighting prejudice and racism and greed, are fighting a losing battle. The forces raging

---

7 Jane Goodall and Douglas Abrams (Celadon, 2021).

around us—greed, corruption, hatred, blind prejudice—are ones we might be foolish to think we can overcome. It's understandable that there are days we feel we are doomed to sit back and watch the world end "not with a bang but a whimper" (T. S. Eliot). . . . Like all people who live long enough, I have been through many dark periods and seen so much suffering.

Goodall knows the odds are not in our favor, and that we are in for "trying times," as her subtitle admits. When she clings to hope and refuses despair, what she is really refusing is the paralyzing complacency of defeatism: "And why would you bother to take action if you did not truly hope that it would make a difference?" For Goodall, as for so many, hope is essential because without it, we will give up. Hope is, in this sense, a synonym for the will to live.[8]

So there's the paradox. According to people I respect and trust, hope is essential because it motivates. According to other people I respect and trust, hope is dangerous because it keeps you from facing how bad things really are and responding appropriately.

Good people promoting hope and good people critiquing hope are both against the same thing: foolish complacency. And both are for the same thing: wise action. That's why Miguel De La Torre says that the best alternative to hope is not despair, but desperation, "because desperation propels me toward action." He explains, "When I have no hope, when I realize I have nothing to lose, that's when I am the most dangerous" to the supporters of an unjust status quo. With nothing to lose, I can risk everything.

As I wrestled with this tension around hope, I had to admit two things to myself, and now I admit them to you. First, no matter how many encouraging stories I am told—about this amazing technological breakthrough, about that social movement, about these brave young activists, about that amazing progress in decarbonization or

---

8 Research psychologist Dr. Daniel Gutierrez studies hope in therapeutic situations. He describes hope as a combination of will and way. When people feel "I will strive to survive this challenge" and "There can be a way through this challenge, even though I don't see it now," that combination of will-power and way-power increases the likelihood of positive outcomes. (Personal conversation, September 18, 2023).

anti-racism—I am not optimistic about our situation. If hope means optimism—a sense that we can "win"—*I often feel that I have lost hope.*

It's not that I'm certain of Collapse/Extinction; I am not certain of any scenario. My problem is that even Collapse Avoidance doesn't feel like a win. At this point, I feel that we have left the domain of conventional hope because we are no longer fighting to win, but rather to avoid the most tragic scenarios of loss.

For those with theological interests, this space beyond the domain of conventional hope may be what St. Paul refers to as "hope against hope" (Romans 4:18). We see something similar in the Hebrew prophets like Habakkuk. The Judean prophet warned of inevitable defeat and doom for his people in the late seventh century BCE (Habakkuk 2:2–3). But his prophecy ends with a bold declaration of his vibrant will to live, with a note of defiant joy (3:17–19). Similarly, Jesus conducts much of his ministry with the assumption that he will be killed (Luke 13:33), yet he trusts that his work will carry on in others who will do "greater things" than he had done (John 14:12). This "hope against hope" seems to be empowered by a refusal to give up the will to live even though the way to do so is not at all clear.

Perhaps the idea of "hope against hope" helps explain my second realization: *Even without optimism, I still have motivation. I still have no interest in giving up.* For a while, of course, I was too devastated to know whether I had motivation or not. But gradually, I began to feel arising in me an even more invincible motivation than before. When I was largely energized by hopeful optimism about outcomes, my motivation was dependent on receiving a continual flow of encouraging anecdotes and keeping discouraging evidence at bay. And now, here I am, feeling that the discouraging evidence far outweighs the encouraging evidence. But rather than slumping into an easy chair of despair or paralyzed resignation, I am still on my feet, brimming with defiance and creative energy. For a while, I couldn't figure out why I was still standing.

Then I came upon a paragraph from historian Howard Zinn that intrigued me and seemed to beckon me beyond my paradox of hope and despair:

To be hopeful in bad times is not just foolishly romantic. It is based on the fact that human history is a history not only of cruelty, but also of compassion, sacrifice, courage, kindness. What we choose to emphasize in this complex history will determine our lives. If we see only the worst, it destroys our capacity to do something. If we remember those times and places—and there are so many—where people have behaved magnificently, this gives us the energy to act, and at least the possibility of sending this spinning top of a world in a different direction. And if we do act, in however small a way, we don't have to wait for some grand utopian future. The future is an infinite succession of presents, and *to live now as we think human beings should live, in defiance of all that is bad around us, is itself a marvelous victory* [italics mine].[9]

When I considered Zinn's word "victory," it was as if the categories of my struggle, the terms of my inner debate, began to shift. Zinn wasn't presenting me with a choice between Team Hope that thinks we can win and therefore stays in the struggle, and Team Despair that walks off the field before the game is over because it has concluded that victory is impossible.[10] Zinn presents me with a different notion of victory and a different choice entirely. My real choice is between Team Cruelty (or Team Apathy or Team Selfishness or Team Indifference) and Team Wisdom, Courage, and Kindness.

Reflecting on Zinn's words today, I feel a powerful inner invitation to live *magnificently* in this present moment, to live "as human beings should live" . . . *whatever the outcomes might be,* whatever scenario

---

9 From his autobiography, *You Can't Be Neutral on a Moving Train* (Beacon, 2002).
10 As I studied the scientific and sociological data related to ecological overshoot and civilizational collapse, I felt a high degree of stress. Some researchers made a strong case that collapse is inevitable or extinction likely, so activism is irrational, foolish, and naïve. Others told me that there are still ways through our current situation to a livable outcome, so defeatism is misguided and premature. But none of the actions they advocated seemed to match the magnitude of the threat. I felt that I was faced with two unsatisfactory options: one was rational but defeatist and the other was hopeful in mood but unconvincing rationally. That helps me understand why Zinn's words were so helpful and catalytic for me. He reframed the issue as a moral choice I could make rather than as an intellectual assessment I could not make.

unfolds. This detachment from desired outcomes makes my response to doom feel less like a matter of intellectual risk assessment and more like a free moral choice. It feels so right that Zinn uses the word "defiance," because that is what I feel: the energy of fierce defiance. *All that is bad around us* motivates me to resist, to defy, to refuse to comply, and that very defiance feels like *a marvelous victory*.

I would like to invite you into a thought experiment to understand the power of defiance. It won't be easy, but I think it will prove worth the discomfort.

Imagine that scenario 4, Collapse/Extinction, becomes as inevitable as the incoming asteroid at the end of the movie *Don't Look Up*. Imagine that in 5, 25, 75, or 250 years, our centuries of ecological overshoot will catch up with us. Imagine that sea levels rise and forests burn and crops fail and vast parts of the Earth become uninhabitable because of heat. Imagine that refugees flee, markets fail, and nations go to war over the last fossil fuels. Imagine that two small men in expensive suits simultaneously press red buttons on opposite sides of the world, and within minutes, nuclear bombs fall on a hundred cities in both hemispheres. Imagine that the wind carries a mushroom cloud that rains deadly radiation across the land. Imagine the cloud drifts toward a city where people you dearly love are living.

And now imagine that they have twenty-four hours before the cloud reaches them. Obviously, it is too late for them to organize an anti–nuclear weapons rally or do anything else to avert the inevitable. So how would you want them to spend those last twenty-four hours? On their last day on Earth, would you want them to go out in a blaze of gunfire, venting their rage on every living thing? Would you want parents to curl up into a ball of catatonic agony or drink themselves into oblivion, leaving their children to die alone in terror? Or would you want people you love to be as brave and good and kind to each other as they possibly could on the last day of the world?

Would you want a young mother to sit at a table with her child and fill page after page with brightly colored paintings? Would you want a young boy to play with his dog, to throw a stick and take a walk, to tell him what a good dog he is and how much he loves him?

Would you want a little girl to invite her friends out into the field and play ball and tell jokes and make their last day a good day? Would you want neighbors to come out into the street and thank one another for being good neighbors? Would you want the family to cook and share their favorite foods for their last meal together at dinner, and maybe plant a tree in the back yard at sunset? Late that night, would you want this family to hold one another tight and tell each other how much they love each other, and maybe even pray together in gratitude for every moment of life they have shared together? Would you want them to make their last day a day they really *lived*? Would you see the way they spent their last day in that horrible situation as an expression of wisdom and courage? Would you consider their last day lived in that way a marvelous victory?

Or would you say it didn't matter, that it was meaningless, because they were going to die anyway? Isn't everyone going to die anyway, sooner or later?

This thought experiment helps me understand that there is a motivation that goes deeper than hope as commonly understood. This "hope against hope" inspires "the energy to act" when all hope for a good outcome is gone. Derrick Jensen gives us a name for this motivation. In response to the question "Why am I an activist?" Jensen answers,

Because I'm in love. With salmon, with trees outside my window, with baby lampreys living in sandy stream bottoms, with slender salamanders crawling through the duff. And if you love, you act to defend your beloved. Of course results matter to you, but they don't determine whether or not you make the effort. You don't simply hope your beloved survives and thrives. You do what it takes. If my love doesn't cause me to protect those I love, it's not love.

Choctaw elder and retired Episcopal bishop Steven Charleston similarly invites us to orient our lives around the axis of love in this beautiful passage:

The signs are all around us. We can see them springing up like wildflowers after the prairie rain. People who had fallen asleep are waking up. People who had been content to watch are wanting to join. People who never said a word are speaking out. The tipping point of faith is the threshold of spiritual energy, where what we believe becomes what we do. When that power is released, there is no stopping it, for love is a force that cannot be contained. Look and see the thousands of new faces gathering from every direction.

[. . .] Sometimes, in this troubled world of ours, we forget that love is all around us. We imagine the worst of other people and withdraw into our own shells. But try this simple test: Stand still in any crowded place and watch the people around you. Within a very short time, you will begin to see love, and you will see it over and over and over. A young mother talking to her child, a couple laughing together as they walk by, an older man holding the door for a stranger—small signs of love are everywhere. The more you look, the more you will see. Love is literally everywhere. We are surrounded by love.

So I trust it is becoming clear: in the words of spiritual educator Cynthia Bourgeault, "Our great mistake is that we tie hope to outcome."[11] If we can see a likely path to our desired outcome, we have hope; if we can see no possible path to our desired outcome, we have despair. If we are unsure whether there is a possible path or not, we keep hope alive, but it remains vulnerable to defeat if that path is closed.

When our prime motive is love, a different logic comes into play. We find courage and confidence, not in the likelihood of a good outcome, but in our commitment to love.[12] Love may or may not provide

---

11 Cynthia Bourgeault uses the term "mystical hope" for this "hope against hope." See her video "The Roots of Hope Run Deep," available here: https://www.scienceandnonduality .com/video/the-roots-of-hope-run-deep-1.

12 This approach might be considered an example of virtue ethics, as opposed to consequentialism (the philosophy that our actions should depend on desired outcomes) and to deontology (a duty- or rule-based approach to ethics). In philosophy, virtue ethics are typically associated with Plato, Aristotle, and Confucius. In my Christian

a way through to a solution to our predicament, but it will provide *a way forward* in our predicament, one step into the unknown at a time. Sustained by this fierce love (as my friend Jacqui Lewis calls it[13]), we may persevere long enough that, to our surprise, a new way may appear where there had been no way. At that point, we will have reasons for hope again. But even if hope never returns, we will live by love through our final breath.

To put it differently, even if we lose hope for a good outcome, we need not lose hope of being good people, as we are able: courageous, wise, kind, loving, "in defiance of all that is bad around us."

When we subtract from conventional understandings of hope all comforting optimism about future outcomes, the "hope against hope" that remains looks even larger, even more beautiful and more powerful. Standing "on the brink of oblivion" (to use Ernest Becker's phrase) we feel arising within us this sustained declaration: We will live as beautifully, bravely, and kindly as we can as long as we can, no matter how ugly, scary, and mean the world becomes, even if failure and death seem inevitable. In fact, it is only in the context of failure and death that this virtue develops. That's why Richard Rohr describes this kind of hope as "the fruit of a learned capacity to suffer wisely and generously. You come out much *larger* and that *largeness* becomes your hope."[14]

My friends have been asking me lately about the title of this book. When I tell them, their next question is almost always, "Do you have hope?" What can I say?

Here's what I'll say going forward: *It depends on how you define hope. Hope is complicated. But writing this book is helping me to see that even if hope fails, something bigger can replace it, and that is love.*

---

tradition, virtue ethics are rooted in Jesus' teaching of the primacy of love. Obviously, virtuous character, considerations of consequences, and duties and rules are all important considerations. But in a situation like ours, fraught with many unknowns, I find that virtue ethics provides a way where there was no way.

13 Her most recent book, *Fierce Love* (Harmony, 2021), is a call to loving resistance and creative defiance.

14 From *A Lever and a Place to Stand* (Hidden Spring, 2011), p. 104.

Dear Reader,

When I felt the impact of the central idea of this chapter—that hope is complicated—I felt that I had a book that needed to be written. Here are some questions for you and your reading group to consider.

Was Miguel De La Torre's observation—"Hope is what is fed to those who are being slaughtered so they won't fight what is coming"—new to you? How do you respond to it?

Put in your own words why hope is complicated, and why fierce, courageous, defiant love may be better words for what we need in our current situation.

Choose one of the definitions or quotations about hope in this chapter and explain what you appreciate about it.

This chapter marks the end of part 1: Letting Go. What do you feel you are letting go of at this point in your reading experience? If this were the end of the book, what would be your main takeaway?

We'll return to the subject of hope in a later chapter. Now, we turn to the subject of seeing, and we'll question an assumption many of us share about what is going on in the world.

PART 2

LETTING
BE

A Place of Insight

7

Learn to See

Those who do not have power over the story that dominates their lives—the power to retell it, rethink it, deconstruct it, joke about it, and change it as times change—truly are powerless, because they cannot think new thoughts.

—Novelist Salman Rushdie

[It] is not a matter of proving the existence of the light, but of blind people who do not know that their eyes could see. It is high time that we realize it is pointless to praise the light and preach it if nobody can see it. It is much more needful to teach people the art of seeing.

—Swiss psychiatrist C. G. Jung[1]

The universe is a system of sacred circles, all related to each other, all needing each other. We are never alone.

—Cherokee author Randy Woodley[2]

You're waking up. You're welcoming all the reality you can bear. You're minding your mind. You're inviting the poets and artists to help you grieve. You're dismounting from the unhelpful narratives you have ridden through life, and you're transcending simplistic notions of hope. That means you're ready to open your eyes a little wider and learn to see a little deeper into what's going on.

When I say "see," I mean "understand." Not just to see with eyes,

---

1 The passage begins, "Christianity must indeed begin again from the very beginning if it is to meet its high educative task. So long as religion is only faith and outward form, and . . . not experienced in our own souls, nothing of any importance has happened. . . . The man who does not know this from his own experience may be a most learned theologian, but he has no idea of religion and still less of education." From *Collected Works*, vol. 12. Thanks to Michael Petrow for this quote.
2 From *Becoming Rooted* (Broadleaf, 2022).

but to see with insight. It begins, yes, with the same animal seeing that we share with a herd of deer gazing out across a meadow, scanning for danger as they chew on grass. But insight goes beyond eyesight. It involves our whole internal board of directors, so that our seeing is enriched with hindsight, foresight, and insight.

If you're of a certain age, for most of your life, you have seen the world through a set of rose-colored glasses that were placed upon you, metaphorically speaking, at birth. A few centuries ago, only babies born in the Western world received these glasses, but more recently, anywhere people drink Coke, go to the movies, or use cell phones, many if not most newborns receive them. Equipped with these glasses, we perpetually see the world in a golden-hour glow, full of optimism. These are the glasses of progress.

With these glasses, progress is not simply *what* we see: it's *how* we see.

We develop this way of seeing, this deep faith in inevitable progress, through a thousand channels—in the way we're taught history in school; in the way we experience technology as we buy cars, TVs, computers, and smartphones; in the way our investments nudge ever upward (in the long term); in the way our theology draws the arc of history (especially if we're Christian); in the way political candidates make their pitch for our votes; in the way activists invite us to march; in the way banks give us credit; even in the seemingly objective way we're taught physics, chemistry, and biology. Because nearly everyone around us also sees the world tinted rose and gold, it's almost impossible for us to imagine seeing any other way. Scientists call this way of seeing a paradigm, philosophers call it a world view, and sociologists call it a social construct, but whatever we call it, it is, to us, simply common sense. It's the way we see.

Our cultural lenses are, in effect, augmented reality glasses. Through them, we look at a mountain and see how many board feet of lumber or tons of coal it can produce, yielding a handsome profit. Our progressive lenses give us X-ray vision to see oil reserves waiting beneath the soil and ocean, worth billions. Our magic glasses give us miraculous powers. Behold! A miracle! Where others see only a forest or mountain or plain or seafloor, we see money! Wherever we turn our gaze, our cultural lenses transform everything, Midas-like, into profit, and profit means progress, and progress means leisure, pleasure, power, safety, and fun!

But those very glasses make our current situation invisible. Whatever we can't see, we can't accept, process, talk about, or change. To the degree we wake up, welcome reality, mind our mind, grieve, and question our old stories and the false hope they promised, our old way of seeing stops making sense. It's as if those tinted augmented reality lenses bequeathed by our culture have filled up with oily smudges, annoying scratches, and deep cracks. Eventually we wonder, "Maybe we could see better without the damned things?"

Perhaps scenario 1, Collapse Avoidance, can coexist (albeit uneasily) with our old way of seeing. Perhaps that's why it's so popular. But as soon as scenario 1 becomes untenable, or when its full costs become clear, more and more people will realize that the world they thought existed is a fantasy world, a cult-induced delusion. A world of constant progress? A world with no environmental limits? A world where the economy owns and controls the environment, where our fellow creatures and future generations deserve no say in how we treat our one and only planet, where infinite economic growth is possible? A world of stable institutions that always solve our biggest problems? A world where the arc of history bends toward ease and plenty? That world no longer exists. For a long time, we bought it, just like nine-year-old me bought the Chart of the Ages. We believed it because people we trusted believed it. But now, in the fading light of doom, we see through it.

That may be a gift that nobody was asking for, but it is a gift nonetheless.

When we look at the world without those glasses, the invisible hand of the market no longer looks like the hand of God. Our civilization no longer looks collapse-proof. Our species no longer looks extinction-proof.

Before writing this book, I thought I had taken off my modern-Western-capitalist-world-view glasses of guaranteed progress. But as I've been doing this research, I've realized that, zombie-like, the old world view keeps being undead. I imagine your experience will be like mine, if you're of a certain age.

But if you're younger than that certain age, I suspect that even though you were given the same modernist, capitalist lenses I was, you're less attached to them. You see things differently, because the old world view was already collapsing when you were coming of age. The way you see things is more the way those of us who are older need to see things. The words of the old folk song "Teach Your Children" captures our situation: the parent generation needs to learn from the younger generation, because the parents' world of inevitable progress is passing away.

The experience of doom invites us—and requires us—to see in many new ways. Let's consider just two of those new ways of seeing: first, the ability to see change as more real than things, and second, the ability to see systems within systems within systems. In a previous book, I described how I experienced that first change in seeing by recalling an experience I had while fly-fishing in Wyoming one afternoon.[3] As I cast my fly (a lure made of feathers and thread) to a seam in the water, a place where fast-flowing water meets slower or still water, I wondered: What is a seam, anyway? It certainly was not a set of atoms; every second, one set of atoms was replaced by new ones. If we suddenly froze the stream to stop the atoms from moving, capturing the seam as in a photograph, the seam would no longer exist. That's because the seam, we might say, wasn't a fixed and static thing. It was a pattern of things, a relation and flow of things. It was temporary, contingent, more of an event than a thing.

I looked upstream and saw a hump of water in front of a rock: another pattern or event. I saw the stream itself . . . also an event. I looked at the rounded rocks beneath my feet: before the stream smoothed them, they were jagged boulders on a mountain, and before that, bedrock under the mountain, and before that, fluid magma deep beneath the earth, and before that, space dust drawn into orbit around the sun. What I saw as a solid round rock was just one event in a long, long story. Then I looked down to see my reflection in the water, and behold! I realized that I too am an event, a flow, a pattern

---

3 The fly-fishing story is adapted from chapter 7 of *Do I Stay Christian?* (St. Martin's Essentials, 2022).

of relationships! I had always seen *things* as most real or fundamental, and change was merely something that happened to them over time. I was coming to see change as most real and fundamental, and things were events that happen over time. Change became the constant in which things come and go, appear and disappear, form and fade away.

Then I recalled how Einstein's breakthrough discoveries supported this new way of seeing. Einstein proposed that energy and matter were less like oil and water (two things that normally don't mix) and more like water and ice (two manifestations of the same thing). One could, in fact, be turned into the other. If you "freeze" energy, you experience it as matter. If you accelerate matter enough, you experience it as energy. Matter and energy were no longer fundamentally different things, but rather, they became different expressions and experiences of the same . . . thing. Ah, but there my language throws me back into the old universe, because what do I mean by "thing"? Now, everything—a rock, a mountain, a government, a star, a flower, a person, a civilization—looks less and less like a thing that exists and more and more like an event that is happening, one part of uncountable other events and processes over time. This is the unfolding, ever-changing universe I now live in. It is a universe of constant motion, becoming, evolving, participating in relationships, decomposing, recomposing.

When we see change in this way, we take time more seriously. So-called timeless human institutions (like monarchy or democracy), timeless economic systems (like feudalism or capitalism), and timeless authority structures (like patriarchy or oligarchy) lose their golden glow. You realize that just as the tallest mountain can be eroded by millions of years of weather and wind, things you were taught to trust as timeless can and do change . . . average temperatures, the availability of cheap fossil fuels, the inevitability or desirability of economic growth.

In our current situation, our heightened sensitivity to change over time helps us see phenomena like tipping points and lag time, phenomena that were previously so easy to miss that they often became invisible.

You probably understand tipping points already. Imagine you're cutting down a huge tree that is four feet in diameter. Your chainsaw bites through the wood . . . one inch, five inches, ten inches. The tree is still standing, visibly unchanged. Inch by inch you cut, and you see no change at all, except that a small mound of sawdust accumulates at the foot of the tree. The sawdust seems harmless—a by-product—and it is easily ignored. Then, say, at thirty-two inches into the tree, you hear a slight crack. But the tree doesn't fall. At thirty-six inches there's another crack, but still it stands. Then at thirty-seven inches, you hear a series of loud cracks and the tree begins to lean ever so slowly for about a second, and then it crashes suddenly with a ground-shaking thud. You realize that the inches you cut beyond thirty were qualitatively different than every inch you cut before, because the tree began giving evidence that it was reaching its tipping point. The inch between thirty-seven and thirty-eight was the tipping point itself, beyond which there was no going back; the tree would keep falling whether you kept cutting or not.

Our civilization has been cutting the metaphorical tree of Earth's ecology for millennia. And inch after inch, we got away with it. Those operating the chainsaw could see no significant negative consequences at all beyond some sawdust to sweep away, and the more they cut, the richer and more comfortable we all felt. We naïvely concluded that we could keep cutting forever with no consequences. Then there was a crack. But nothing else happened, so it was soon forgotten and we kept cutting. Then came another crack, and another . . . but there were no obvious consequences. The tree was still standing, whatever we did. We grew confident—overconfident—that it would stand forever. Those rose-colored glasses helped us see some things, but they blinded us to others, like the possibility that our profit-making activities could eventually lead to a tipping point of ecological collapse, after which what had been profitable would bankrupt us completely.

That is where the idea of *lag time* comes in. Let's say that we chainsaw through the tree on a calm day, but stop after the first crack. Then, a week later, a strong wind comes, snapping the tree. Or imagine that no strong wind comes for many years, and that the tree keeps growing even with a deep slice through its trunk. Can you imagine how the tree would eventually grow so much taller and its canopy would spread so much broader that even a tiny breeze would cause its weakened trunk to snap?

Here's just one way that lag times affect our current situation: we know that two-thirds of the Earth are covered by water. So when sunlight heats and warms the Earth, more than half of the warming is held by our oceans. Over time, a whole lot of water holds a whole lot of heat.

Now imagine that we get our act together and stop adding carbon to the atmosphere tomorrow, so we stop trapping solar heat within the blanket of our atmosphere and we reach "net zero" emissions by this weekend. Problem solved, right?

Not quite. Remember all the heat that has already been absorbed by the oceans? It will be slowly released upward, into the air. (You'll recall that heat rises.) So even if we "solve" our carbon problem at its source tomorrow, we haven't changed the reality that the oceans will continue to release stored heat for a long time. When you put tipping points and lag times together, you can see why humans find it so hard to see the danger we are putting ourselves in. Inch after inch, crack after crack, our actions produced few obvious negative consequences and many positive, enjoyable ones. We got away with murder.

Until now. Now we face the cascading lag times and self-reinforcing cycles of consequences labeled "doom loops" by experts.[4] Those experts are helping us understand more every day about where tipping points and lag times have brought us.

For example, we know that ice reflects solar energy back into space, keeping the Earth's overall temperature relatively stable. When the ice melts away, ice-free land and water absorb even more heat, which further accelerates the rise in temperatures, pushing ice to melt faster and faster and faster. We know that we are either very near or slightly past the tipping point for the planet's ice.

We also know that as ice melts and oceans warm, seawater expands and sea levels rise. A large percentage of the human population

---

4 See https://insideclimatenews.org/todaysclimate/whats-a-climate-doom-loop-these-researchers-fear-were-heading-into-one/.

lives along coastlines that will be affected by rising seas. In addition, as ice melts, we know that huge quantities of methane held in permafrost on land and under shallow seas will be released, supercharging the overheating process, which speeds up all the other systems toward their tipping points.

We also know that one of the most powerful ocean currents that redistributes heat in (and beyond) the Atlantic has already been slowing and weakening because of melting ice flowing into the North Atlantic. We know that when ocean currents change, weather patterns change. Predictable weather patterns become unpredictable. Extreme and unseasonal droughts, floods, freezes, hurricanes, tornados, and heat waves kill crops, animals, and people.

Many experts believe it is already too late to stop these interrelated tipping points, based on the amount of carbon we have already pumped into the atmosphere and the lag time in accumulating effects. We don't know for sure which tipping points have already been crossed, but we do know that if we burn all the fossil fuels that Exxon, Shell, Chevron, and other oil companies already own, we will turn our lag times and tipping points into doom loops, forcing us into scenarios nobody would ever willingly enter.

We know that the carbon we are burning into the atmosphere is already mixing with seawater and making our oceans more acidic, not to mention hotter. More acidic and overheated seawater causes plankton and coral to die, which leads to massive die-offs of small fish that depend on plankton and coral. That leads to die-offs of the big fish that depend on small fish. In addition, many of those same plankton absorb carbon dioxide and produce oxygen, so without them, carbon dioxide levels increase and oxygen levels decrease, speeding up acidification and die-offs in a vicious cycle.

We know that when temperatures rise past a certain tipping point, trees from the Amazon rain forest to the boreal forests of the far north will burn or sicken and die of disease, releasing millions of tons of carbon instead of absorbing them as they would normally do.[5] Grasslands also burn and die with a similar result. Then, deserts and dry

---

5 For an insightful and poignantly written exploration of forests and their future,

savannas replace the dead forests and prairies, and eventually, the deserts themselves become uninhabitable for many hardy creatures that currently survive there. Very quickly, the amount of land suitable for agriculture drops below what is needed to feed humanity. We can measure how these processes are already happening in many places, and are rapidly approaching their tipping points, if they have not already passed them.

Although there is much we don't know, we are constantly learning more about these tipping points and lag times and the dangers they pose, because scientists around the world—whose job is to pay unflinching attention to reality—are diligently gathering data every single day.

As we learn in the presence of doom to see more clearly and more maturely, we are also learning to see how changing things participate in dynamic systems. This is a relatively new skill for us as a species. The scientific revolution helped us see big things and take them apart into smaller and smaller components. It helped us dissect a frog and see its organs, cells, and cell components. We could design a complex machine and then disassemble its component parts, down to each individual bolt, gasket, and gizmo. We could even peer into molecules and atoms. We became experts at analysis, at breaking big, complex things down into smaller, simpler parts and tracing back big, complex effects to smaller, simpler causes.

It takes a lot of practice for people with highly analytical minds to retrain ourselves to put parts together again and see the larger wholes or systems in which they participate. We are still clumsy when it comes to seeing things whole and forecasting patterns of change in larger systems. Through newer scientific disciplines like field theory and systems theory, network theory and complexity theory, chaos theory and emergence theory, we are venturing into new frontiers in our ability to see in these new ways. Our field of vision pops out from simple, two-dimensional lines of cause and effect to three-dimensional, dynamically interacting spheres of relationship.

Let's start with four of those spheres, beginning with our individual

---

see Ben Rawlence, *The Treeline: The Last Forest and the Future of Life on Earth* (St. Martin's Press, 2022).

embodied lives (the personal sphere), which includes the 100 trillion (!) cells that constitute the survival, belonging, and meaning committees that make up our internal board of directors. Our *individual spheres* interact within the many layers of the *social sphere,* from friendship circles to family circles to communities and cities and nations and international alliances, all of which are part of our global civilization. The human social sphere is part of the larger interdependent community of living things, the *biosphere.* And the biosphere is part of the larger sphere of the Earth itself, the *geosphere.* Our planetary home, the geosphere, exists within the solar system (or heliosphere), which exists within the spinning disc of the Milky Way galaxy, which exists along with billions of other galaxies in the expanding sphere we call the cosmos or the universe. Each of these spheres is porous, in the sense that each interacts with the other spheres.

Now we can see our current situation unfolding across all four of our local spheres:

1. Geosphere: The Earth's physical systems have already been dangerously disrupted by human activity. Additional disruption is on the way in the form of higher temperatures, changing oceanic currents and wind zones, more extreme storms and droughts, melting ice and rising, acidifying oceans, drying, eroding, and deteriorating soils, depleted aquifers, and disruptive anomalies in familiar regional weather patterns.

2. Biosphere: Physical disturbances in the geosphere pose a threat to all plants and animals in the web of life, a web that connects every living thing to every living thing, a web that includes us.

3. Social sphere: As our geosphere and biosphere become increasingly unstable, our civilization will also grow increasingly unstable, setting in motion unprecedented disturbances that will affect every dimension of society—all our economic, political, educational, agricultural, recreational, religious, and other shared activities. At some point, unless we change our shared way of life profoundly and rapidly, our current global civilization will reach a period of collapse during which civilization shrinks in both population and

complexity. Such a descent toward and through collapse will be ugly and scary for every community.

4. Personal sphere: Turmoil in the geosphere, biosphere, and social spheres will create turmoil within each of our individual nervous systems. It will take a new set of habits and practices to sustain personal well-being during this disruptive time.

Our rose-colored glasses put us in a golden hour for the last four or five centuries, a golden hour in which our civilization stored up a lot of gold. Blinded by ever-increasing prosperity, prosperous citizens of our civilization didn't see how the Earth itself was being damaged by human actions. Nor did they see how millions of their human neighbors were being exploited for the comfort, pleasure, and profit of the prosperous. Nor did they see how human civilization itself was becoming unsustainable. Nor did they see how ecological instability would reach a tipping point in which their dreamworld could become a nightmare. Nor did they see how much they didn't see.

The experience of doom takes a lot from us. But yes, it does bring certain gifts, one of which is a new clarity and insight. Seeing may be easy, but learning to see with clarity and insight is not. It takes time and practice. If we take off our rose-colored glasses, we can learn to see more truly.

This world of green valleys and blue oceans and white clouds, this world of red rocks and iridescent feathers and orange salamanders, the countless amazing shades of human skin (not just black and white!); this precious shimmering and radiant world that has immeasurable value that transcends small human constructions of money, profit, and GDP—this world will become more visible, more beautiful to us than it has ever been before. The green of dollars and the gold of coins will look tawdry compared to a mound of moss or a field of autumn grasses.

In the coming chapters, we will try to develop this gift of insight. But learning to see will require us to ask for help from people our civilization has pushed aside for a long, long time.

Dear Reader,

We're deep enough into this shared journey together that I felt you would be ready to grapple with some deep ideas . . . about time and change, for starters. But I imagine that some of you may have felt that you showed up in a philosophy class you didn't sign up for. I hope I didn't lose you, and that you felt not just that you saw some new things, but that you could see everything in some new ways.

Here are some questions to reflect upon, write about, and consider with friends.

How do you respond to this passage: "I had always seen *things* as most real or fundamental, and change was merely something that happened to them over time. I was coming to see change as most real and fundamental, and things were events that happen over time. Change became the constant in which things come and go, appear and disappear, form and fade away."

I introduced the ideas of tipping points and lag times. Try to summarize them in your own words.

I talked about *rose-colored glasses* and *the golden hour,* referring to a way of seeing the world that assumed that progress was inevitable. How attached do you feel to the idea of inevitable progress? Can you name some upsides and downsides to this way of seeing?

I explored a shift in seeing, from seeing in analytical lines (cause and effect, whole and part) to *seeing things whole*—spheres or fields or systems of complex interaction. Try to describe *seeing things whole* in your own words.

I offered a way of seeing our lives as four concentric and permeable spheres: personal sphere, social sphere, biosphere, and geosphere. How did you feel as you tried to see in this way?

Respond to this statement: "The experience of doom takes a lot from us. But yes, it does bring certain gifts, one of which is a new clarity and depth of sight."

You'll have an opportunity to practice new ways of seeing in the next two chapters.

8

Seek Indigenous Wisdom

Upon suffering beyond suffering, the Red Nation shall rise again and it shall be a blessing for a sick world. . . . I see a time of seven generations when all the colors of mankind will gather under the sacred Tree of Life and the whole Earth will become one circle again. In that day, there will be those among the Lakota who will carry knowledge and understanding of unity among all living things, and the young white ones will come to those of my people and ask for their wisdom. I salute the light within your eyes where the whole universe dwells. For when you are at that center within you and I am at that place within me, we shall be as one.

—Lakota war leader Crazy Horse[1]

Humans, as a species, have been around for approximately 10,000 generations, and the human genus has been around for more than 100,000 generations. For all but the last 600 generations, our ancestors were hunter-gatherers.

—Harvard paleoanthropologist Daniel Lieberman[2]

It feels like we are living in a time of apocalypse, an age when everything we take for granted is starting to collapse around us. It feels like the end of the world. . . . This situation is nothing new for me as a Native American. My ancestors already lived through an apocalypse. . . . Native American culture in North America has been through the collapse of civilization and lived to tell the tale.

—Choctaw elder / retired Episcopal bishop Steven Charleston[3]

---

1 Quoted in Sherri Mitchell, "Indigenous Prophecy and Mother Earth," in *All We Can Save,* edited by Ayana Elizabeth Johnson and Katharine K. Wilkinson (One World, 2020).
2 From his *New York Times* article, available here: https://www.nytimes.com /roomfordebate/2011/05/12/do-we-want-to-be-supersize-humans/we-still-have-the -bodies-of-hunter-gatherers.
3 From *We Survived the End of the World* (Broadleaf, 2023), p. 2–3.

To accept our place as simple human beings—beings who share a world with every seen and unseen creature in this vast community of creation—is to embrace our deepest spirituality.
                    —Cherokee author and theologian Randy Woodley[4]

I grew up in the 1950s and 1960s, and starting in elementary school, we were introduced to Christopher Columbus, Hernán Cortés, and Francisco Pizarro as great heroes to admire. We called them "explorers." Those who followed in their footsteps, we called "pioneers" and "settlers." If we used words like "conquistadors" or "colonists" (funny how we didn't say "colonizers"), they were roughly synonymous with "winners." They were the good guys of history, with whom we were proud to be associated.

In my young adulthood, I began to see all things colonial in a new, non-rose-colored light. I read books like *Bury My Heart at Wounded Knee; Things Fall Apart; 1491;* and later, books like *Shalom and the Community of Creation; Neither Wolf nor Dog; The Poisonwood Bible; Unsettling Truths; Native;* and *Braiding Sweetgrass.* These and other resources taught me—gradually and powerfully—to see colonialism more from the point of view of the colonized.

My elementary school world view was flipped upside down.

Even through all those changes, though, concepts like *development, progress,* and *civilization* went largely unchallenged in my thinking. It was only when I arrived on the doorstep of doom that I took off the rose-colored, golden-hour capitalist glasses that I had been issued as a so-called *progressive, civilized* member of the *developed* world.

I've come to see that the conquest, domination, land theft, exploitation, and genocide of indigenous peoples that I associate with colonialism is one side of the gold-plated coin of our current civilization. On the other side is the conquest, domination, land theft, exploitation, and ecocide of the Earth and all her creatures. Both sides of the coin involve a group of people who see themselves as exceptional, superior, chosen, and supreme. They give themselves permission to dominate, exploit, and destroy whoever and whatever they desire.

---

4 From *Becoming Rooted: One Hundred Days of Reconnecting with Sacred Earth* (Broadleaf, 2022).

Their habits of mass extraction and mass pollution lead inevitably toward mass destruction and extinction.

To put it bluntly, our civilization is colonialism, and colonialism is our civilization. Our civilization is supremacy (racial, religious, ideological, national, or human), and supremacy is our civilization.[5] Our civilization is land, resource, and labor theft, and land, resource, and labor theft are our civilization. Look closely at our civilization and you'll find the short-term prosperity of some group of people being purchased at the long-term expense of other people, other creatures, and of the Earth itself.

Sometimes our civilization has pressed harder on the exploitation of humans and other living creatures. Sometimes it has pressed harder on the exploitation of the Earth and its air, land, and water. But either way, like so many civilizations that rose, declined, and collapsed over history, our current global civilization lives by a story of domination and exploitation.[6]

You are probably wondering if there could be an eco-civilization, one that is post-colonial, post-industrial, non-exploitive, and just, one that lives wisely, compassionately, and sustainably as part of the Earth. Perhaps. Some civilizations in the past were far more sustainable than others, but our current civilization is decidedly not one of the more sustainable ones, and humans like us who have been so deeply shaped by this civilization will find it virtually impossible to even imagine an alternative civilization, much less build it. Our civilization has embedded so many unconscious assumptions in our brains, and those assumptions have so deeply formed us—even brainwashed us—that unless we experience some kind of external intervention, we won't ever

---

5 What is said here of colonialism in general could also be said of capitalism in particular. Can people alive today develop a new, less harmful form of capitalism or some entirely new economic system in time to avert catastrophic destruction of the Earth and human civilization? Can something so different from our current consumptive capitalism still be called capitalism? Can capitalism be decolonized and rendered regenerative? The answers to these questions will be up to people alive today. But first we must ask the questions.

6 That story of domination sets in motion other stories that I have explored elsewhere: in a collection of essays called *The Seventh Story: Us, Them, and the End of Violence*, and in a children's book called *Cory and the Seventh Story* (See theseventhstory.com/), both coauthored with Irish peace activist and author Gareth Higgins.

see or imagine what we can't now see. In other words, to experience the healing of our rose-colored, golden-hour nearsightedness, and to begin imagining an ecological civilization, we will need insights, values, and perspectives from outside our industrial/colonial civilization.

So where might we find some outside consultants and guides who have not been shaped by our self-defeating economic assumptions? The natural answer would be among indigenous peoples who lived for millennia on their lands without overshoot and collapse.[7] But here we face two problems. First, over the last five hundred years, our expanding industrial/colonial civilization stole their lands, shamed and suppressed their cultures, and either mass-murdered indigenous peoples, assimilated them, or moved them into concentration camps, at every turn seeking to suppress and eradicate their ancient ways of life. It's a miracle that indigenous wisdom survived such a vicious and sustained assault.

Second, even when citizens of modern civilization like me consult indigenous sages who have survived the colonizers' attempted genocide, we typically approach them in an industrial/colonial way. We might re-exploit indigenous people for a patina of misappropriated wisdom, pasting indigenous epigraphs on industrial chapters just as we might hang pseudo-indigenous tourist jewelry around our stiff industrial/colonial necks. (Even this chapter could be written or read in this exploitive way.) To explore this subject appropriately is delicate, like surgery, so easy to botch, yet it is a matter of mutual liberation and survival.[8]

---

7 I am not saying that indigenous people made no mark on the land. The fossil record suggests that wherever ancient humans went, they entered new ecosystems as competitive megafauna whose growing biomass replaced some percentage of the biomass of the megafauna they encountered. As a result, shortly after the arrival of humans, species like the glyptodon, the ground sloth, the Eurasian cave bear, the moa, and the thylacine went extinct. Such a loss of food sources would have forced human populations to change their way of life and learn to adapt to the land without overshoot, requiring them to develop ecological values that contribute to sustainability rather than colonizing values that contribute to conquest and expansion. For more on this subject, follow this conversation between bio-ecologist Bill Reese and journalist Rachel Donald on the *Planet: Critical* podcast, available here: https://youtu.be/ID-P1 _AwczM?si=xTs4l2Ot4RQLeuPf.

8 Many well-meaning people try to repair harm done to indigenous people by romanticizing and even fetishizing them. It is essential to make it clear that is not what

As people like me, who are the descendants of the colonizers, are humbled by the suicidal trajectory of our current civilization, as we face our past, unclench our fists, and let go of the arrogant, short-sighted folly of the whole colonial project, as we reach a place of letting be, we finally begin to see what was formerly invisible to us. We begin to honor and cherish the people our ancestors misjudged and mistreated so mercilessly. We realize they hold a legacy of eco-logical insight that our civilization did and does its best to wipe out. They maintain ways of holistic seeing and long-term thinking that we desperately need—such as the Seventh Generation Principle of the Haudenosaunee Confederacy, or the Cherokee concept of *eloheh*, or the Lakota vision of *mitakuye oyasin*.[9]

So descendants of the colonizers come, at long last humbled by the disaster we have unleashed, asking indigenous friends, elders, and authors for guidance in facing our current situation. These indigenous leaders have every right to be suspicious after such devastating harm has been done to them and to the land they love (which, to them, are not two separate things). They've seen our civilization's duplicity for centuries, its arrogance, its ignorance. They have every reason to wait until the doom more and more of us feel consumes our civilized arro-gance and our arrogance consumes our haste and our haste consumes our presumption and lack of self-knowledge.

They are wise when they tell us to do our own homework, part of which is to learn from books and other resources by indigenous leaders to help us see just how deeply our own civilization has brainwashed

we are advocating in this chapter. What Rabbi Danya Ruttenberg says about Jews can be applied (with care) to indigenous people: "Philosemitism is antisemitism, too. Fetishization of Jews and Judaism is also an objectification of us and a denial of our humanity, and also often comes with a side of appropriation." For more on this subject, see Jonathan Lear, *Radical Hope: Ethics in the Face of Cultural Devastation* (Harvard University Press, 2008). And see Philip J. Deloria, *Playing Indian* (Yale University Press, 1998), and Vine Deloria, *Custer Died for Your Sins: An Indian Mani-festo* (University of Oklahoma Press, 1988).

9 For more on this Seventh Generation Principle of the Haudenosaunee Confederacy, see https://www.ictinc.ca/blog/seventh-generation-principle/. For more on *eloheh*, see Randy Woodley's multifaceted work: https://www.randywoodley.com/eloheh/, and especially *Indigenous Theology and the Western Worldview* (Baker Academic, 2022) and his up-coming book with Edith Woodley, *Journey to Eloheh* (Broadleaf, 2024). For more on *mi-takuye oyasin*, see Richard Twiss, *Rescuing the Gospel from the Cowboys* (IVP, 2015).

us, dehumanized us, and shrunk our imagination. They know, as all wise teachers do, that unless we are sufficiently humbled by the consequences of our shortsighted folly and longstanding arrogance, we will not be ready to learn anything new.

I might have expected these wise teachers to send us away, to wish upon our culture the same tragic end our civilization visited upon theirs. But in my experience, when we do our homework and come in a humble, teachable, honest spirit, we are often treated with unexpected compassion, great mercy, great graciousness. Our teachers know (from their wisdom) that we are all relations and our futures are interwoven in one web of life. They reflect the gracious spirit of the Shoshone elder who said, "Do not begrudge the white man for coming here. Though he doesn't know it yet, he has come to learn from us."[10]

In this light, I can't help but recall Jesus' words about the meek inheriting the Earth. The word "inherit," of course, evokes what survivors receive after someone else has died. In that light, we could understand Jesus to be saying that even though aggressive and ruthless civilizations rule the Earth in the short term, in the longer term their violent and arrogant project will fail and they will go down with their overloaded pirate ship of stolen cargo. Then, when arrogant civilizations self-destruct and die, the meek—those with indigenous wisdom, those with a wise and humble spirit, those who pursue deep communal well-being rather than shallow individual happiness—will have their opportunity to live by a different vision, different values, a different story.

I shouldn't be surprised that Jesus would see things this way. After all, he was an indigenous man, part of a people rooted in the land who had resisted arrogant tyrants and colonizing civilizations since Pharaoh.[11] From childhood, he had been raised on the origin stories of the twelve tribes of Israel. He knew of their trails of tears to Egypt

---

10 From Randy and Edith Woodley's forthcoming book, *Journey to Eloheh* (Broadleaf, 2024).
11 Thanks to my friends at T'ruah for this brilliant turn of phrase: https://truah.myshopify.com/.

and Babylon, their journeys into the wild and their encounters there with the Creator. He had been shaped by stories of burning bushes and vision quests, of tents of meeting and rituals of purification, of his ancestors' great exploits, great errors, and great recoveries. He learned his peoples' more recent history as well, as wave after wave of invaders colonized, dehumanized, oppressed, and exploited his people and their land.

I have spent most of my career as a Christian pastor and as an encourager of pastors and church leaders. All of my life I have been exposed to the Bible. For over fifty years, I have been a serious student of the Bible. For over forty years, I have taught and preached the Bible. It's rather odd that it is only in the writing of this book that I feel I have begun to see what the Bible actually is and has been all along: the collective diary of an indigenous people who saw what the colonizer mindset was doing to humanity, to the Earth, and to her creatures.

The Bible has something in common with fossil fuels. Fossil fuels are concentrations of chemical energy, derived from the decomposition of living creatures. They were laid down over millions of years in the solid, liquid, and gaseous forms we know as coal, petroleum, and natural gas. Our civilization learned to exploit them over the last few hundred years. The Bible, like other sacred indigenous literary artifacts, is a concentration of wisdom . . . what we might call intellectual or spiritual energy. This spiritual energy is the concentrated residue of many generations of indigenous wisdom, laid down in the genres of story, poetry, law, proverb, and prophecy, augmented by gospel and epistle. Like fossil fuels, the Bible has been exploited, often as fuel toward harmful ends, and often without attention to its harmful side effects. And like fossil fuels, the Bible has been exploited to make certain people a lot of money and bestow upon them a lot of power to do a lot of harm. In fact, when many people today hear the word Bible, they think of it as the tool of the colonizers, not the literature of the colonized.

Ponder this for a moment: The Bible begins to take shape as colonizer civilizations are taking over. It is written and preserved by indigenous leaders who want nothing to do with any kind of exploiting civilization and its idols. (Idols could be seen as the mascots or branding logos of a civilization.) The very notion of God to the ancient Hebrews is anti-empire, because God sees the dignity of those the empire exploits for cheap energy. God feels their pain and is willing to disrupt the empire to set them free. Again and again, the Bible warns of collapse if the Hebrew people abandon indigenous ways and adopt exploitive civilization's values and ways. The Bible, we might say, is a set of documents perfectly designed to disempower the very imperial religion that currently uses it to support its supremacy.

I have come to see the Bible and all its major characters—God, Adam, Eve, Moses, Abraham, Sarah, Hagar, David, Isaiah, Mary, Jesus, Paul, the Holy Spirit, and all the rest—as victims of a kidnapping. They have been taken hostage by colonizing captors who parade them out in public for propaganda purposes. We think we know these characters, but to a great degree, we only know the cartoonish distortions of them that their captors have manipulated like puppets in front of us.

When the "civilized" people of the Roman Empire encountered the Bible in the early centuries of Christianity, it attracted them in some ways and it terrified them in others.[12] They domesticated and co-opted it by reinterpreting it in light of their own colonial assumptions. Then they taught their misunderstanding to everyone as dogma. They threatened with death, banishment, or damnation those who didn't comply with their interpretations, just as colonizing civilizations typically do.

If we take off the interpretive glasses we were given by colonizers, we begin to see what the actual indigenous Bible has been saying all along: that trying to live like gods leads to doom. Living by the love of money and the love of weapons leads to doom. Living by taking more than you give leads to doom. Living without care for the Earth and the vulnerable leads to doom. Living by the ethic of dominating civilization leads to doom.

---

12 Notice how the businessmen of the Roman colony in Philippi react to Paul and Silas in Acts 16:19–24, after Paul and Silas show concern for a slave woman.

Again and again, the Bible shows itself to be the work of indigenous and oppressed people resisting exploitive civilization. When they capitulate to civilization's values and strategies, things do not turn out well, again and again.

I wish this weren't true, but the Bible also shows that again and again, dominating civilization wins. Money, power, corruption, and exploitation win. Doom wins. This sad trajectory even occurs in the religion that takes shape in Jesus' name.

"Wait," you might be saying. "I thought the Bible is a book of hope!" And that's where I'd remind you that *hope is complicated*. Yes, the Bible is a book of hope for the oppressed and meek. But their hope of liberation is inseparable from the defeat or collapse of the civilizations that oppress them! (Take, for example, Mary's famous Magnificat. She did *not* say, "The rich and poor will be sent away full, fat, and happy, and a good time will be had by all." She said, "God has filled the hungry with good things and sent the rich away empty." See Luke 1:53.)

The Bible offers little hope to the arrogant oppressors, beyond the escape clause that if they repent—if they rethink their dominating overshoot project and defect from it, if they learn to live in humble, generous harmony with one another and the Earth—they can begin again, if they do so in time. In fact, that is the best framework for understanding familiar terms like "repentance" or "salvation" or "redemption" or "being born again." These words were not intended to evoke an individual forgiveness transaction with a free trip to heaven as a bonus; instead, they issued a call for the privileged and powerful to rethink the deep and unrecognized assumptions of their civilization. They challenged colonizers to see afresh, with new eyes, eyes that have been freed from the "civilized" distortions that trained them to see certain things, miss other things, and imagine they saw things that weren't really there. This new vision can help repentant colonizers live with a new identity in a different story than before, so the Earth and the poor no longer groan under the marching boots of dominating civilizations.[13]

---

13 The many biblical sayings and stories regarding blindness and sight take on new importance in this light, especially those in the Gospels.

We might say that the only hope of the oppressed and meek is the doom of the arrogant civilizations that oppress them. The only hope of the Earth and its creatures is the doom of the arrogant human civilization that crushes and exploits everything it encounters. Do you see why, even in the Bible, both hope and doom are complicated?

The Bible seems to raise, as I see it now, two probing questions. First, how do we learn a good and loving way of life—*shalom* for the ancient Jews, the kingdom of God for the indigenous Jewish prophet Jesus, *eloheh* for the Cherokee, *amahoro* and *ubuntu* for many African peoples—when we are dominated by a death-dealing civilization that is winning its way toward collapse? And second, how will we live *after* the end—in the aftermath of the current dominating civilization's inevitable collapse? How might future generations make a new beginning after the collapse of the current civilization, if humans survive at all?

Let me state it as clearly as I can: The real horizon in biblical literature is not the end of an individual life at death. Nor is it the end of the space-time universe. It is the end of whatever shortsighted and small-hearted civilization currently dominates the world.

This indigenous library, like all indigenous wisdom, tells victims and perpetrators, colonized and colonizers, oppressed and oppressors the same message that combines doom and hope: The end of the world as you know it is near, but the end of the world as you know it is not necessarily the end of the world itself. To the elites at the top of a civilizational pyramid, the collapse of their civilization will truly feel like the end of the space-time continuum. They cannot imagine surviving apart from it. But to those of our species and other species who suffer under our civilization's domination, our civilization's collapse could feel like liberation. It would be, for them, not the end of the world, but their only chance for a new beginning.

In this way, a story that looks like doom can actually be a story of liberation.

We'll go there next.

Dear Reader,

How did you relate to my childhood education about Christopher Columbus, Hernán Cortés, and Francisco Pizarro? Were you taught similarly, or did your teachers have a different approach?

Sometimes, authors risk being misunderstood to make a point boldly and bluntly. How did you respond to these two sentences: Our civilization is colonialism, and colonialism is our civilization. Our civilization is supremacy (racial, religious, ideological, national, or human), and supremacy is our civilization.

If you are a descendant of or beneficiary of colonizers, have you ever considered colonialism in this way? How did you begin to see history from the point of view of the indigenous, the colonized?

Respond to my interpretation of Jesus' words, "The meek shall inherit the Earth."

There's a complex tradition in colonial history of romanticizing indigenous people, often called the "myth of the noble savage." It stands alongside another myth, the "myth of the brutal savage," which was used to justify enslaving or eradicating indigenous peoples as inferior. I hope you can see that I'm not interested in perpetuating either of these myths. Instead, I'm trying to help us grasp that the current dominant way of seeing—through the eyes of colonizers—is not the only way to see, that there is a longstanding "minority report" that resists colonizing assumptions. Are you curious about seeing the Bible as an example of that minority report?

9

Don't Read the Bible (in the Same Old Way)

The Potawatomi people originated in the Great Lakes region of Turtle Island. We tell stories of Skywoman, who fell to the Earth from Skyworld and created land on the back of a turtle. We also tell the story of Original Man, brought to Earth by *Gitchie Manitou* or *Kche Mnedo,* the Great Spirit. Original man walked the Earth and named all the creatures, living in harmony with all things in the Earth. His companion was the wolf, given by Creator to help him. . . . Our origin stories come from the land because she is our teacher. So our very connectedness to God, Sacredness, Mystery, and to our identity is in the land.

—Potawatomi poet and author Kaitlin Curtice[1]

If you make victims and survivors the ones who are most responsible for reconciliation, you're harming them again. The people who are most responsible for reconciliation are the people responsible for creating the harm in the first place.

—Irish author and peace activist Gareth Higgins[2]

I'd like to take you on a very brief guided tour of the treasury of indigenous, ecological wisdom available for us in an unexpected source, the Bible, if we have eyes to see. I'm focusing on the Bible not to show its superiority over other indigenous wisdom (which in itself would be a supremacist, colonial approach), but rather to situate it in the genre of indigenous wisdom, the tribal wisdom of the Hebrew people. The Bible is the sacred text most often used today to buttress civilization's

1 Kaitlin Curtice is a gifted writer, poet, storyteller, and songwriter from the Potawatomi people. This quote is from her book *Native* (Brazos, 2020).
2 From his newsletter to the *Porch* community. For more information on Gareth and the *Porch,* see https://www.theporchcommunity.net/.

dominating world view; it is my desire to show how the Bible actually subverts that world view, page after page.

Have you ever noticed that in Genesis, as the Bible begins, the icon of human dignity, freedom, and goodness is not a priest offering sacrifices, a pharaoh enthroned in a gilded temple, a conquistador seated on a horse with his sword held high, a rich white man in an expensive suit sitting in a boardroom or standing in a pulpit, or an angry religious zealot (in the US or the Middle East) holding high an AK-47 or AR-15? No, it's a couple of naked indigenous people living in a garden, in harmony with each other, with themselves, with all their fellow creatures, and with the Earth itself. They don't even get a creation day of their own: they are created on the same day with "living creatures of every kind: cattle and creeping things and wild animals of the earth of every kind." They are made from earth. In fact, the name Adam means "child of red earth."[3] These Earth children are one beautiful, wild species among many.

Yes, Earth children are given "the breath of life," but so are all the other animals. Yes, they are given *dominion* (Genesis 1:28), a fraught word to be sure, but why should we let the colonizers define that word in their own image, as if it meant *domination*? Why assume that dominion in Genesis means a license to kill, exploit, torture, or drive to extinction? Why not assume that dominion means "to exercise the same tender, loving responsible care the Creator has, as the Creator's image bearers"? In this light, the text is suggesting that these humble Earth children bear kingly dignity and responsibility to care for the well-being of every creature in the realm that has been entrusted to them. Just as a good king must preserve justice and safety for every citizen, the primal humans must cherish and protect each bird of the air, each fish of the waters, each creature that moves across the ground, each tree, each wildflower, each unfurling fern.

That ecological interpretation is reinforced in a second creation narrative a few verses later (2:15), when in place of "exercise dominion," humans are instructed "to work with the Earth and care for it," not "squeeze every penny of profit you can from it!"

---

3 Interestingly, the English word "human" also shows a connection to soil—*humus*.

In this context, we encounter the first prohibition (Genesis 2:16): "Eat of any tree except one: the tree of knowledge of good and evil." Through this prohibition, humans retain broad freedom ("enjoy the fruit of every single tree") but they also must live within limits ("except one tree"). Refusing to honor that one limit is, in a sense, refusing to live like Earth children, refusing to respect one's ecological niche, demanding to suck out more resources than the garden can replenish, demanding to pump out more waste than the garden can detoxify and recycle. The tree's name suggests its purpose: *Follow the prohibition and you will know good. Violate it and you will know evil.*[4]

Can you see how grasping for godlike knowledge and power would be a way of rejecting our place as human creatures who must live as part of our environment, within its limits? Can you see how refusing to live within limits, playing Creator rather than creature, would lead to dominating civilization as we know it?

The prohibition comes with a warning, a consequence: in the day you eat of it, you will die. In other words, if you leave your place as one beloved creature among other beloved creatures in a sacred creation, you will experience suffering, sweat, tears, violence, and, in the end, extinction. You will no longer fit in with your environment. You will compete with it, to master it. In your bid to live as immortal gods, the story suggests, you will die like dogs (no insult to dogs intended).

As a side note, with the Egyptian empire posing a constant threat just to the south of the Hebrew people, might the tempting serpent in the archetypal story evoke, not a literal snake or even a metaphysical devil, but the *ureas,* the golden cobra that symbolized divine power on the crown of the Pharaohs?[5] Might the temptation of the serpent be the temptation of civilization's exploitive values?

In this light, the primal couple's banishment from the garden would reflect the bitter realization that humans can't have it both ways: they can't live harmoniously as Earth children in the garden, "walking with

---

4 I am not arguing that this interpretation is the only possible one, but rather that it is a plausible one to be taken seriously. Like other sacred narratives, this story invites a wide array of interpretations. It is, as one rabbi put it, "a bottomless well of meaning."
5 See https://en.wikipedia.org/wiki/Uraeus. The Genesis serpent also evokes its counterpart in the Gilgamesh epic.

God in the cool of the day," naked and not ashamed—while at the same time violating wise creaturely limits. They can't live a life of ecological overshoot and still have access to the tree of life.[6]

The descent into an unsustainable and suicidal civilization continues in Genesis as humans "progress" from life as hunter-gatherers tending the Creator's sacred Earth (like Adam and Eve) to life as nomads tending their own herds (like Abel) and to life as settled farmers tending their own fields (like Cain). Cain's and Abel's two ways of life are expressed in two different forms of religion, hunter religion (that offers meat in worship) and farmer religion (that offers crops in worship). Their religious tensions lead to violence, as the more "advanced" settled farmer (from civilization's perspective) kills the more "primitive" nomadic herder. Just as we'd expect, the following generation of humans takes the next natural step toward civilization by building cities (4:17).

Cities multiply, and soon, more people are living, but their lifespans are shorter (Genesis 6:3), reflecting declining environmental health. The desires and actions of civilized humans are twisted, and violence is everywhere. God—I'm speaking here of a literary character named God in the story—is so distraught about the violent mess humans are making that God responds to violence with violence, flooding the Earth to wash the evil away. (By the way, might this story be an ancient memory of the kind of flooding that ancient farmers would experience as they concentrated their populations in fertile but vulnerable river valleys?) After this disruption to normal climate patterns, God feels terrible. He feels that he (our male pronoun is fitting here) has made a terrible mistake and promises he has learned his lesson and will never do such a thing again.

The human survivors of the catastrophe are not so smart. They quickly repopulate the Earth and by Genesis 11, they are developing a new technology (using bricks for building rather than stone). This new technology speeds up the building process and makes it possible to build taller dwellings, which makes it possible to concentrate more

---

6 I am not a fan of the traditional Christian doctrine of "the fall." But if there is a fall in the Bible, this is it: a fall from sustainable living into overshoot.

people in the same space, which speeds up economic growth. They build a tall tower to celebrate the magnificence of their great civilization, Babel. The fact that everyone in Babel speaks the same language makes it easier to consolidate power, which means that the budding civilization will be able to do more harm. So God disrupts this centralization of power and suppression of difference. Babel collapses and its peoples scatter and preserve their independent identities through a diversity of languages. But soon, new Babels arise. One of them is named Ur.

One of the Bible's star characters, Abraham, begins as a citizen of Ur. But he has a dream—a common guiding force in indigenous cultures—that inspires him to leave civilization and become a nomad, a step down in the ladder of social advancement by civilized standards. He seeks what all indigenous people cherish: a land to call home for generations to come, a land to till and protect, a land to belong to. Abraham has other dreams which together inspire a coherent vision for his descendants: not to be members of a civilization or empire, but to be members of a people, a tribe, rooted sustainably in its land with its own distinctive culture and language . . . never to be conquered by another Babel or Ur. This new Abrahamic tribe will not be a threat to other nations, but will instead be a blessing to them. This anti-colonial, anti-imperial vision of deep tribal identity, ecological sustainability, and intertribal solidarity and mutuality becomes one of Abraham's great gifts to humanity.

Toward the end of Genesis, Abraham's descendants face the second major episode of climate disruption found in Genesis. This time, it's not a flood, but rather a drought. Famine predictably follows, and Abraham's tribal descendants have to flee for their lives, crossing the border into the prosperous and powerful civilization of Egypt.

As Genesis ends, Abraham's tribal descendants settle in Egypt as climate refugees. But as Exodus begins, the hospitality of the Egyptian empire proves as fickle as that of later empires: the civilization turns the refugees into slaves. After centuries of enslavement, the great Exodus saga unfolds as a supremely anti-imperial tale. God is not impressed with the pomp and pyramids of Egypt. Instead, God hears the groans and cries of the enslaved at the bottom of the economic pyramid and disrupts the empire to liberate its oppressed underclass.

What happens to the newly liberated Hebrew children? They become hunter-gatherers again, refugees from Egypt's exploitive civilization, going back to an earlier stage of development, as it were, to start over. Each morning, they gather a mysterious food substance (the word manna means "what is it?"). The wild becomes their ecological school, teaching them to live reverently with the Earth rather than controlling it, trusting it rather than taming it.[7] In a sense, they go back to Genesis 1 again and have yet another chance to learn the most fundamental of lessons: to live as interdependent creatures, walking softly and traveling light upon the Earth, taking no more resources than the Earth can replenish, pumping out no more pollutants than the Earth can detoxify.

Before they are allowed to settle again, they are given laws, laws that protect both the people and the land from human exploitation. In the Torah, especially the books of Leviticus and Deuteronomy, we see detailed instructions about letting fields go fallow, not destroying forests, respecting the rights of animals, canceling debts, taking sanitation and waste disposal seriously, reversing the concentration of wealth and power in the hands of a few, and so on.[8]

The Torah offers no belief in an afterlife. All the positive or negative consequences of living by or against the Tribal Law pertain to this life. Live wisely and you and your descendants will live and thrive in the land, the Torah says. Break the Tribal Law and God promises that "the land will spit you out" (see Leviticus 18:28).

---

7 To people brought up with civilized/colonial interpretations of the Bible, as I was, the word "wilderness" is typically used to describe the place of reorientation after liberation from the Egyptian empire. The term connotes a *dangerous wasteland,* something so terrible that many liberated Hebrew slaves would rather go back to slavery than have to survive there. I propose that an indigenous reading of the text should not be reduced to that perspective. The wild, the land, the Earth itself becomes their teacher for a generation, to help them deprogram from the brainwashing and miseducation of Egypt and its pyramidal economy.

8 See Nigerian theologian Solomon Olusola Ademiluka's article "An Ecological Interpretation of Leviticus 11–15 in an African (Nigerian) Context" in *Old Testament Essays,* available here: http://www.scielo.org.za/pdf/ote/v22n3/01.pdf/.

The most famous of the Torah's 613 tribal laws, the Ten Commandments, can be read as a how-to manual for a sustainable society.[9] First, the people must revere as supreme only the god who liberated them from enslavement; they must resist all theologies that legitimize exploitation. Second, they must not turn God into a talisman or tool to justify human domination: they must not copy the civilizations that surrounded them by erecting "graven images." Third, they must avoid trivializing the name of God, since God-talk can also be used to claim exceptionalism for *us* and to impose domination on *them*. Fourth, in contrast to the 24/7 economies of empires, wise communities need to assure time to rest, to enjoy life, so that work and profit don't become absolute values.

Fifth, the generation in power needs to honor older generations and not cast them off simply because they no longer are profit centers. Sixth, they need to reverence the rights of their fellow humans as equal to their own by refusing to kill them—a clear prohibition against the careless attitude toward human life that is characteristic of colonizers and enslavers. Seventh, they must respect the marriages of their neighbors as they reverence their own, and not violate them. Eighth, they must respect the property rights of their neighbors as equal to their own, and not steal. Ninth, they must not corrupt and twist the legal system that is intended to protect the innocent and vulnerable, thereby harming the innocent and vulnerable. And tenth, they must go to the heart of the matter and deal with the deepest human problem, the problem that we saw illustrated in the Garden of Eden narrative: unlimited desire, the desire to play God and live without limits.

By the time they cross the wild expanse and come to their ancestral lands, they justify the slaughter of its new inhabitants by saying their God gave them a mandate to do so, an episode in the biblical story full of moral contortion and travail.[10] But even within that violent man-

---

9 I am grateful to David Bodanis for this insightful approach to the Ten Commandments (unpublished manuscript).

10 The slaughter of the Canaanites has been used often by colonizers to justify their own brutality. I explore this issue of religious violence in several of my books, including *A New Kind of Christianity* (HarperOne, 2010) and *Why Did Jesus, Moses, the Buddha, and Mohammed Cross the Road?* (Jericho, 2012). I should add that contemporary biblical scholarship raises a wide range of questions about the historical

date, they are told repeatedly that if they don't live within wise limits, they will not be protected from the consequences of their actions. For example, if they don't treat refugees as equals to citizens, if they neglect the vulnerable widow or orphan, if they oppress the poor, if they let justice be corrupted by prejudice, if they fail to give their people, their animals, and their land the dignity of rest, they will go the way of every other civilization. They will become refugees, widows, and orphans, impoverished, oppressed, and exhausted by hard labor. Just as they have conquered, so they will be conquered.

Anyone who has read the creation and founding narratives of other indigenous people will recognize many literary elements that are shared with Genesis, Exodus, and other texts from the Hebrew library.[11] The resonances are stunning: Edenic gardens, banishments due to wrongdoing, long migrations, animal interventions, the giving of laws or rules for living, the rise of great warriors and prophets, promises of hope, proverbs and parables, and remembrances of going astray.

As the Biblical story continues to unfold, we watch the loose confederacy of Hebrew tribes gradually centralize power and become a kingdom, a morally ambiguous achievement. Soon after, King Solomon builds a huge temple using slave labor, showing that even an understanding of God as slave liberator can devolve into a more conventional theology of empire, with God as slavery legitimizer. Movement leaders known as prophets arise to call out dangerous developments like these. Along with their warnings, they share a wide array of visions (another common element of indigenous literature), inspiring

---

accuracy of many biblical stories, including Egyptian slavery, the Exodus, and the violent conquest of Canaan. Many scholars also raise the question of whether historical accuracy is a category that is appropriate to apply to ancient texts like these, texts that may have emerged long after the events they describe to help a group of tribes coalesce in a stronger sense of shared indigenous peoplehood, and to help them address the questions and challenges of their own time.

11 You can read versions of a number of indigenous Native American / First Nations creation stories online, including Cherokee and Salinan (https://www.americanyawp.com /reader/the-new-world/indian-creation-stories/); Haida, Gwi'chin, Piikani, Anishinabe, Inuit, and Mi'kmac (https://www.historymuseum.ca/history-hall/traditional-and-creation -stories/); Potawatomi (https://www.mpm.edu/content/wirp/ICW-137); and Haudenosaunee (https://www.oneidaindiannation.com/the-haudenosaunee-creation-story/).

people to imagine a better way of life. Sadly, predictably, the prophets are most often ignored, mocked, imprisoned, banished, or killed.

Within a few generations, the kingdom experiences civil war and is eventually conquered by a series of superpower civilizations: the Assyrians, Babylonians, Persians, Greeks, Syrians, and Romans. As in Egypt, the survivors experience the discontents of civilization as they are trampled by the imperial horse's hooves.

Into this situation of domination, Jesus arises in the tradition of the prophets before him. One story claims he is born completely apart from the violent patriarchy of earthly civilization: God bypasses patriarchy and produces a new kind of human being through a woman alone.[12] When Jesus comes of age, he speaks of an alternative civilization that operates by radically different values: the kingdom, empire, or civilization of God, or perhaps (translated into our current situation) the alternative economy or regenerative ecosystem of God. To help us understand this new way of life, Jesus advocates an indigenous ethic of biomimicry, counseling us to learn creaturely wisdom from birds and wildflowers, growing seeds and resilient trees. He flips the script of civilization, trading the imperial love of power for the primal power of love. He calls people to nonviolent resistance against violent imperial powers, and invites them to model an alternative set of values as a "city on a hill."[13]

At the core of his message we encounter a shocking ultimatum (Matthew 6:24): You will either love God and hate money, or you will love money and hate God. Why this binary? Why is money the

---

12 I explore this literary (or nonliteral) interpretation of the virgin birth narrative in my book *We Make the Road by Walking* (Jericho, 2014).

13 The values found in Jesus' teachings closely parallel the ten shared indigenous values Randy Woodley identified in his in-depth interviews with eight native elders, his survey of over one hundred indigenous people from over thirty tribes across North America (Turtle Island), and his study of key texts written by native people. Here are the ten Harmony Way values that emerged: *respect* for the Earth and all creatures as sacred; *harmony* with people and nature; *friendship; laughter; equality; authenticity; history; work/rest balance; generosity;* and *accountability/interconnectedness/relatedness.* From his lecture "Growing Our Roots: Understanding the Indigenous Worldview." Also see his upcoming book with Edith Woodley, *Journey to Eloheh* (Broadleaf, 2024). More here: https://www.eloheh.org/about.

ultimate danger in the eyes of this indigenous teacher? Is he too naïve to understand how important and necessary money is? Or might he see what no typical civilized person can see?

For Jesus, money is the currency of the Roman civilization that is oppressing the poor and vulnerable. Money is the empire's symbolic language by which it shapes people to live by its unsustainable and unjust values. Money is the admission ticket. Money is the measure of value. Without money, to the empire, you're nothing.

The civilization of God, according to Jesus, runs on a different currency altogether: love. Whatever God loves has value, from wildflower to sparrow to the most forgotten, marginalized, and vulnerable human. Being loved by God—not wealth, social status, religion, gender, sexual status, or citizenship—confers sacred value. If you are learning to love, you are entering God's alternative civilization, family, or ecosystem. If you're rich in money but bankrupt in love, you're not a success: you're a fool. For Jesus, the civilization of God is a civilization of love where love is the prime directive. First, you love God, who could be defined as the transcendent loving presence in whom every creature is beloved. If you love God, you love what God loves . . . which includes the fish of the sea, the birds of the air, and the wildflowers in the field, and you.

God's love also includes all your neighbors, no exceptions . . . including your neighbor of another gender, social class, ability level, culture, race, nationality, or religion. In a particularly provocative challenge to the Roman Empire's demand for absolute loyalty, Jesus claims that love should even extend to enemies. In teachings like these and especially in his parables, he consistently pokes the unconscious assumptions of dominating civilization with a sharp stick. By our wincing reactions we begin to realize that those assumptions are still there, beneath the surface, inside us.

When it is clear that his contemporaries will not accept his message and instead will remain actively or tacitly loyal to the values of the dominant Roman civilization, Jesus speaks harsh words about what is coming. An unjust, unwise, unloving civilization, he says, will not stand. Collapse is coming. Those who can flee it should flee it. Those who can't flee should prepare to endure very difficult times. Many should expect to die, and he reminds them that death isn't the worst thing that can happen to a person. In fact, it would be better to be misunderstood, misjudged, imprisoned, or even die as a witness to nonviolence and love than to survive as a violent conqueror or cowardly collaborator.

This indigenous prophet underscores this last point by engaging in bold acts of nonviolent civil disobedience at the center point of contemporary religious and political life, the Temple in Jerusalem. He knows that his actions will lead to his imprisonment, torture, and death . . . because, well, that is what dominating civilizations do to those who challenge their supremacy and legitimacy. But before his death, he assures his followers that he will live on in them if they keep faith with his way of love. He gives them a ritual meal in which they dramatize taking his body and blood into their body and blood so they can live on as the ongoing embodiment of his spirit in the world.

The movement continues with the early Christian thinker/movement builder Paul who preaches a radical message of life *in Christ* rather than *in the Empire* or *in this present age* (which is roughly equivalent to a phrase I am using repeatedly in this book: our current situation). He speaks of the Spirit of God as the Spirit of love, joy, and peace. The nonviolent and unifying divine Spirit does not eradicate or homogenize diversity, but rather celebrates it and harmonizes it in concern for the common good. Paul and his team dare to preach this liberating message even in imperial centers of power like Philippi, Athens, and Rome. Wherever the message goes, its messengers lift up love, unity, solidarity, and interdependence as their core values . . . rather than domination, retaliation, exploitation, accumulation, us-them exclusion, and isolation. Within the empire and its structures of domination, followers of this new way of life set up little tribes where they re-indigenize. They share rather than hoard wealth and they live in deep simplicity, solidarity, and humility.

The letters of Paul and others read like entries in a diary, helping us see the struggles of these tribes or communities of creative resistance who are *in* the Roman Empire, but not *of* it. In one letter (Romans 8:19–23), Paul writes that all creation is groaning, waiting for a new day when human beings will stop destroying the Earth and start behaving like true human beings, true children of God. In the same letter (Romans 5) he speaks of Jesus as a second Adam, a second "child of red Earth."

At the end of the Christian Bible, an old mystic, banished to an island, writes a work of apocalyptic fiction in which civilization collapses in an orgy of economic desperation, religious corruption, desperate political violence, and ecological catastrophe—the same macabre mixture of environmental and social collapse that produce our sense of doom today. In one passage, a third of the Earth is ecologically decimated: trees, grass, seas, fish, rivers. In other passages, huge numbers of people die during horrific wars and plagues (the two often go hand in hand, because where war goes, infection and disease follow). In the chaos, people are subjected to new levels of social and economic domination. Whereas Paul could call the Roman Empire a "minister of God" in Romans 13,[14] the writer of the Book of Revelation calls empire "the Beast" and he calls the religious structures that support it "the Whore."

After the collapse, a new ecological civilization becomes visible—in a visionary way: the New Jerusalem (not the New Rome) descends from the sky in the last chapters of the Bible. The city is compared to a beautiful young bride, and in it both God and humanity are at home and at one. Interestingly, unlike the historic, literal Jerusalem, this New Jerusalem has no temple . . . no trappings of traditional religion. Religious structures are not necessary because the light of God enlightens everyone. Its main features are a protective wall with gates that never close, suggesting safety and security. The names of the gates evoke Israel's tribal past, and at the heart of the city are a spring-fed river of life and a tree of life, evoking Eden. The tree's fruits bring healing to all nations. Religious structures are no longer necessary in this vision because the light of God enlightens everyone. This vision combines the original garden with a new kind of city, perhaps suggesting a

---

14 Paul's attitude toward the Roman Empire is not simple or dualistic; it is highly nuanced. For example, in the previous chapter of his letter to the Romans, he tells people, "Do not be conformed to the world, but be transformed by the renewing of your mind." "The world" refers to the culture of the Roman Empire, and "the renewing of your mind" means engaging in the kind of decolonizing work we are doing in these chapters. Paul does not see the empire as stable or invincible: he warns people in another letter (1 Corinthians 7:29) that "the time is short," suggesting that normal life will soon be disrupted.

new kind of ecological civilization. The injustice, evil, and suffering of the old civilization are gone forever.[15]

This brief overview skips over a lot of juicy details, but I think you can see what looks inescapably clear to me. The conventional approach to the Bible generally interprets the Bible in service to our current civilization's power and profit. It does so by distracting readers from the Bible's indigenous roots and this-worldly message of embodied life on this side of death. Instead, it shifts our focus to a disembodied life after death. As a result, conventional Christianity has too often been little more than a pious religious bumper sticker or hood ornament on the gas guzzler of our unsustainable civilization. To the degree it continues in this role, providing moral cover (and even superiority) for a suicidal project, it has become one of Earth's primary forces of doom.

So here is an alternative to the conventional way of reading the Bible, and this alternative reading leads to an alternative orthodoxy (as my friend and colleague Richard Rohr calls it, or a new kind of Christianity, as I have called it, or the harmony way of *eloheh*, as Cherokee theologian Randy Woodley calls it). This alternative approach, rooted in indigenous values and narrated from the vantage point of those who have been oppressed and marginalized by extractive and exploitive civilizations, could help create the conditions in which we might imagine a new arrangement, a post-colonial and ecological society, a new beloved community that learns what the old arrangement wouldn't or couldn't accept.

If you were to ask me how to read the Bible in this alternative way, I would say first of all, *please don't. Don't read the Bible at all*—at least not in the same old way. *Don't read the Bible* with your civilized, industrialized, supremacist assumptions unchallenged. *Don't read the Bible* from the vantage point of the colonizers and oppressors. You'll see

---

15 I want to say clearly that I do not believe biblical texts like these should be taken literally; they should be read literarily, with maximum sensitivity to the nuanced and varied ways literature works to convey meaning. This is surely one of the saddest tragedies of conventional biblical interpretation: that teachers who should have known better didn't help readers approach the Bible with literary rather than literalistic sensibilities.

only what an exploitive civilization in overshoot has already trained you to see![16]

Instead, I recommend that you take a break and disrupt your colonial/civilized thinking with some indigenous thinking. Immerse yourself in Robin Wall Kimmerer's *Braiding Sweetgrass,* Randy Woodley's *Becoming Rooted* or *Journey to Eloheh,* Kaitlin Curtice's *Native,* Steven Charleston's *Spirit Wheel* or *We Survived the End of the World,* Mark Charles and Soong-Chan Rah's *Unsettling Truths,* and other books and resources by indigenous authors.

Once you feel your allegiance to the currency of colonizing civilization being broken (you'll know, because the break will hurt), then you can go back to the Bible on your own, and maybe, through the cracks in your civilized armor, some of the light you need will begin to shine through. Perhaps your first reintroduction to the Hebrew Scriptures should be from a rabbi (after all, it's a library of indigenous Jewish literature), or at least from a scholar who privileges Jewish readings of their texts. And perhaps your first reintroduction to the New Testament should be from an indigenous point of view by reading from the new *First Nations Version* (IVP, 2021). And perhaps, you can start listening to indigenous, womanist, Black, liberation, ecofeminist, and queer theologians and biblical scholars like Steven Charleston, Dr. Wilda Gafney, Julie Faith Parker,[17] James Cone, Leonardo Boff, Ilia Delio, and Dale Martin, so they can reorient you to how the biblical text works from a fresh perspective. Once you are able to see the Bible from a new vantage point, then by all means, read it!

I'm sure that my Muslim, Hindu, Jewish, Sikh, and other friends can give a wealth of examples of ways their sacred texts and traditions

---

16 In this light, the right wing of civilization can be seen as not conservative enough. It seeks to preserve the values of the recent past, epitomized by Adam Smith, Margaret Thatcher, or Ronald Reagan, when they should have gone further back, to preserve essential values of Crazy Horse and Black Elk of the Oglala Lakota, or Chief Seattle of the Duwamish, or Sun Bear of the Chippewa, or Big Thunder Wabanaki of the Algonquin, or the Great Law of Peace of the Haudenosaunee (or Iroquois) Confederacy. Similarly, the left wing of civilization can be seen as not progressive enough. It promotes values that are still limited by current economic assumptions, assumptions that indigenous peoples were not bound by.

17 Her *Eve Isn't Evil: Feminist Readings of the Bible to Upend Our Assumptions* (Baker, 2023) is an accessible and insightful new resource.

are equally full of deep indigenous wisdom. And I suspect they could also point to tragic examples of members of their own communities explaining away, twisting, and corrupting that indigenous wisdom for power and profit. I've only focused on the Bible because it is the sacred text in my tradition . . . and also, because it is currently being abused to inflict the most harm on both people and the planet.

I can hear a rumbling out there, a stir of people saying, "Wait. Aren't you being unfair to civilization? Are you saying there's nothing good about civilization?" I hear you. We'll talk more about this subject in the next chapter. But for now, I hope you'll resist trying to rescue our current civilization, and instead, linger here, in the liberating presence of indigenous wisdom, because it may be the only thing that can rescue our planet from our civilization.

Dear Reader,

You may have been surprised by this chapter's provocative title, "Don't Read the Bible." Why do you think I put it so provocatively?

I recommended a number of books by indigenous authors. Have you ever read a book by an indigenous author, or watched a movie by an indigenous filmmaker, or listened to a lecture by an indigenous speaker? If yes, what did you learn, and if no, what book by an indigenous author might you like to read—either now, or as soon as you complete this book?

Choose one of the paragraphs where I offer a reading of the Bible as an indigenous text, and explore it more deeply. Perhaps go back and read relevant passages in the Bible, or compare what I've suggested to a commentary that offers a conventional interpretation. Or read through the notes to this chapter and do some further research.

Can you imagine a post-industrial and post-colonial civilization that is truly ecological? Is civilization without overshoot possible? Why or why not? What would it look like?

10

Maybe It's Good. Maybe It's Not.

Out beyond ideas of wrongdoing and rightdoing,
There is a field. I'll meet you there.
When the soul lies down in that grass,
The world is too full to talk about.
Ideas, language, even the phrase "each other"
Doesn't make any sense.

—Sufi poet Rumi[1]

Blessed be you, mighty matter, irresistible march of evolution, reality ever newborn; you who, by constantly shattering our mental categories, force us to go ever further and further in our pursuit of the truth. . . . Blessed be you, mortal matter: you who one day will undergo the process of dissolution within us and will thereby take us forcibly into the very heart of that which exists.

—Jesuit priest/paleontologist Pierre Teilhard de Chardin,
The Heart of Matter

All deeds are right in the sight of the doer . . . the violence of the wicked will sweep them away . . . the upright give thought to their ways.

—Proverbs 21

After letting go, in the place of letting be, we feel like castaways who have washed up on a new shore. Surprised to still be alive, we wake up. We blink. We open our eyes wide but everything looks different. We feel we need to learn to see all over again. We who thought our civilization was superior and exceptional begin to see its downsides, and so

---

1 This is the popular Coleman Barks translation. Ari Honarvar offers a very different translation here: https://medium.com/@arihonarvar/beyond-right-doing-and-wrong-doing-cb6eddbcc7e4.

we turn to indigenous peoples for the treasuries of insight that colonial civilization tried to destroy. We realize that our sacred texts are actually repositories of that indigenous wisdom, and we understand why our civilization's authority figures trained us not to see that wisdom. If we open our eyes wide enough and long enough, we hear echoes of the Sufi poet Rumi's most famous poem. We realize that "Out beyond ideas of wrongdoing and rightdoing" doesn't mean a field of amorality where right and wrong don't exist or don't matter. Rather, Rumi's field is a place where we see that our *ideas* of right and wrong are simply that—*our ideas*. Whatever right and wrong really are, they may not correspond to our simplistic ideas as people shaped by a civilization that has proven itself wildly successful, amazingly arrogant, and deeply unjust and unsustainable.

There's a story that helps me begin to see what can be seen in Rumi's field. I've heard it told in a variety of ways, sometimes as a Chinese folktale, sometimes as a Buddhist parable.[2] It goes like this:

Once there was an old Chinese farmer who sat in front of his house each evening to watch the sun set.

Just after dark one evening, his son came home leading a beautiful stallion. "Father, I have wonderful news. I found this horse today wandering near our fields. We never could have afforded such a wonderful creature. Such good fortune!"

"Maybe it's good," the old farmer said to his son. "Maybe it's not."

The next day just before sunset, the old man heard a commotion. The neighbors came, carrying his son on a stretcher. "Sir, we have terrible news! The stallion threw your son and ran away. And worse still, your son's leg is broken. This is terrible fortune!"

"Maybe it's bad," the old farmer said. "Maybe it's not."

A few days later, a group of soldiers came to the old man's village, drafting all young men to go to war. The farmer's son couldn't walk, so he alone was spared from going to war. His neighbors came to him again. "It's such good fortune that your son had that accident. Now

---

2 I understand that Alan Watts popularized this story in the US. You can hear his version, in his own voice, here: https://youtu.be/sWd6fNVZ20o?si=31B9a_Zhg2YLYZmn.

he doesn't have to go to war and even if he walks with a limp, at least he can take care of you in your old age."

"Maybe it's good," the old farmer said. "Maybe it's not."

The story goes on and on, with various twists of fortune, and each time, the old farmer's refrain is the same: maybe . . . maybe not.

The old farmer saw enough unexpected consequences through the years that he had learned not to rush to judgment as quickly as his neighbors. The story invites us to follow his example and brings to mind another of Rumi's beautiful poems:

> What do we do?
> We love life.
> This is our full-time job.
> Like diligent farmers,
> we sow seeds of kindness wherever we go.
> Please don't ask us to be
> accountants of wine cups.
> We are worshippers of the Wine.[3]

The binary accountant's mind, counting wine cups and sorting everything into this or that profit-loss category, is important when your focus is wine cups. But when you are worshippers of wine, you develop the ability to hold back from binary or dualistic thinking. You develop the wine worshipper's fine art of the "maybe" . . . the Chinese farmer's keen ability to restrain himself from shallow, binary judgments . . . the depth of vision to see both short- and long-term . . . these non-dualistic capacities will serve us well in a turbulent time.

Back in the previous chapter's consideration of our current civilization, we could easily have slipped into shallow either/or thinking. Perhaps we did. Now we have an opportunity for second thoughts.

Many of us, perhaps all of us, feel deeply grateful for the amazing gifts given to us by civilization: aspirin, showers, the ideal of equal human

---

3 Available here: https://medium.com/@arihonarvar/what-do-you-do-rumi-s-answer -4ea926979a7e.

rights for all people, anesthesia, appendectomies, antibiotics, Bach, air travel, birth control, smartphones, Aretha Franklin, public education, the beautiful game of soccer/football, the internet, Bob Dylan, remote work, butter pecan ice cream, an average life-span that climbs past forty, fifty, seventy, even over eighty in some places.

And we could go much deeper: we could look at the rich philosophical and moral conversations that have been going on for thousands of years. Without these conversations, you and I wouldn't be thinking together right now. These conversations began in the West with the pre-Socratic philosophers and in the East, with Confucius and Lao-Tzu and their contemporaries in China, and with the early Vedic sages in India. Each philosophical lineage was the product of a civilization that created enough security and prosperity for philosophy to begin and develop. Along with these philosophical conversations, civilizations supported traditions of artistic exploration, political theory, religious reflection, and scientific inquiry. These traditions within a civilization often stood up to critique their civilization, helping it become more just, more humane, more wise. In so doing, civilizations supported the well-being of billions of human beings. So we have good reason to celebrate civilization and exclaim, "Isn't civilization good?"

But then, we look at the cost of bringing those accumulating benefits from the past to us today. We think of past human costs—centuries of colonization, land theft, enslavement, torture, war, corruption. We think of present human costs—children mining coltan for our smartphones in the Congo, farm workers picking tomatoes and watermelons for low pay in abusive conditions, people suffering from asthma and cancer because factories legally externalize the cost of air pollution, farmers committing suicide because the climate and the economy squeeze them from both sides, billions scrambling for necessities while the 1 percent are floating in a hot tub of luxuries.

We think of future human costs . . . what will eight or ten billion people face in the next several decades as our world overheats by two, three, five, seven degrees? Imagine if ten billion of us have a short life or a long and miserable dying process during several decades of dueling demagogues, riots, gangs, terrorism, civil war, and economic meltdown, with or without mushroom clouds. At some point might we have second thoughts about something that seemed so good for some for a while, something that may conclude so badly for all in the end? Then imagine, added to the heartbreaking human costs, the staggering costs inflicted upon this precious, rare, living planet. Can we bear to mourn the coral reefs, plankton, whales, dolphins, sea turtles, tuna, gulls, puffins, seals, redwoods, old-growth forests, prairies, and just a few miles from where I sit, the majestic Everglades? Might we groan, "Isn't civilization terrible?"

"Maybe it's good, maybe it's not" is another way of saying *maybe good and bad aren't the best or only categories to lump everything into.* Yes, some plans are good first steps, but they're bad long-term strategies. Yes, some solutions are better than the problems they address, but they're not as good as new solutions that could soon replace them. Yes, some developments are a step in the wrong direction, but sometimes, a step in the wrong direction takes us quickly into trouble, so we look for a better direction.

Maybe in the end, our simplistic binaries like good and bad, right and wrong, wonderful and terrible have been calibrated by the habits, values, and structures of our current civilization. (Again, maybe that's part of what the Genesis story of the tree of knowledge of good and evil was trying to tell us.) Maybe our idea of common sense is only common or sensible in our kind of civilization. Maybe, more than we realize, good means good for civilization at this moment, or good for our economic ideology or political party, or good for business. But maybe things judged good for us now will be harmful down the road, for us or for other people or creatures.

Maybe we need to join the old farmer at sunset. Maybe we need to crawl up from the beach where we awakened as castaways, and make our way inland to Rumi's field, lying in its grass and feeling in the world a fullness too deep for superficial accounting.

Are profitable quarters and big returns for shareholders always good? Is a declining GDP always bad? Is the growth of the number of billionaires always good? Is a major increase in taxes always bad? Is it always a good thing for my country or party or religion or profession to prosper? Or might there be times when my country, party, religion, or profession deserves to falter?

Might a severe disruption of our current civilization be necessary to avoid something even worse? Might its full collapse be necessary to avoid something even worse? Brace yourselves for an even more disruptive question: Might there be circumstances under which the extinction of our species would be necessary to avoid something even worse?

Normal people don't entertain such questions in normal times. But in a time of doom, you feel less like a wine cup accountant and more like the old Chinese farmer at sunset. The word "maybe" becomes more important than a simple snap judgment of *good* or *bad*. Suddenly we see why wisdom traditions in every culture contain koans and paradoxical proverbs: wise people know that common sense brought us to this moment where we see no way forward, and we will need *uncommon* sense to make a way where there is no way.

Because of my background in traditional Christian ministry, I invested a lot of energy over several decades fortifying and spreading the familiar common-sense binaries that I inherited from my tradition: good/bad, orthodox/heretical, biblical/unbiblical, saved/damned, heaven/hell, and so many more. Then, I passed through a time of letting go and reached a field of letting be where "maybe" became a path of liberation and new insight. I look back on my inherited binaries: "Maybe they're good. Maybe they're not," I say.[4]

I see how much harm has been done by my tradition in upholding these binaries. They presented God as bipolar, prone to moods of extravagant blessing at one moment and extreme rage the next. As a result, crusaders, conquistadors, and colonizers of my tradition saw themselves as the exceptional beneficiaries of God's blessing mood, and they saw those they conquered, killed, enslaved, and oppressed as

---

4 It's important to note that the heaven/hell binary as a postmortem destination is found nowhere in classic Hebrew Scriptures. That binary enters Jewish thought late and stays only as a minority view, perhaps borrowed from Zoroastrianism by the Pharisee sect or from Plato by the Hellenist sect (or from both by both). Jesus interacts with the imagery of hell in complex ways, but later Christianity takes the binary to simplistic extremes that would be unimaginable to Jesus or his Jewish community. For more on this, see my books *The Last Word and the Word After That* and *A New Kind of Christianity,* Sharon Putt's *Razing Hell* (Westminster John Knox, 2010), and also Brian Zahnd's *A Farewell to Mars* and *Sinners in the Hands of a Loving God.*

the targets of God's damning mood. Our theological binary created good guys who were always "us," and bad guys who were always "them." So I have worked hard over the course of my life to undermine that binary, and I did so for good reasons. If you had told me, "God is loving!" I would have said, "That's a good belief!" And if you had told me, "God is wrathful!" I would have said, "That's a bad or dangerous belief!"

I had a point, but can you see what I was doing? I was reassigning my binary categories without deeply challenging the categories themselves.

In recent years, as I've sat in Rumi's field with my inner Chinese farmer at sunset, I've watched myself disembark from that train of thought and consider yet another possibility. Maybe the character named God in the stories of ancient culture was, in some cases at least, a personification of the natural world in which we humans "live and move and have our being."[5] Maybe when indigenous people told stories of a wrathful God, it was actually more of an ecological and sociological insight than a theological one. Maybe their God stories were (among other things) the cultural container for their highest and deepest indigenous wisdom about how the mysterious universe works.[6]

Maybe their stories were upholding this core ecological wisdom from generation to generation: "If we live within wise ecological limits, if we don't take more from the Earth than she can provide and if we don't pump out more waste than she can detoxify, we will experience nature as a loving and generous parent . . . showering us with bountiful sunshine, rain, and harvest. If we don't live within wise ecological limits, if we consume too much of the Earth's bounty and produce too much pollution, if we consider ourselves exceptions to the laws of nature, we will experience nature as an angry, punishing parent."

---

5 The phrase in quotes is from a fascinating public lecture given by the early Christian thinker/apostle Paul (Acts 17). Religious naturalist and eco-theologian Michael Dowd, who died as I was completing this book, brilliantly explored this idea of God as personified nature or reality in his writings and videos: https://postdoom.com/conversations/.
6 It's worth noting that scientists make a similar move when they use the term "laws of nature" to name the predictable cause-effect patterns in the universe. Laws are a human construct from human society that scientists project upon the universe. You'll notice that I use this metaphorical projection in the next paragraph.

And maybe their stories of God also preserved their highest socio-logical wisdom: "If we are people of integrity and mutual respect, if we are good to the poor, the alien, and the vulnerable, if we uphold wise and just laws, we will create a culture of justice and compassion that will lead to cooperation, solidarity, trust, and prosperity. Our na-tion will be like a loving and gracious family, and the corporate spirit of our culture will protect us like a caring parent who is both gener-ous and fair. But if we are dishonest, duplicitous, and careless toward the poor, the alien, and the vulnerable, if we don't uphold wise and just laws to assure mutual well-being, our deceitful and hard-hearted culture will lead to apathy and callousness toward our neighbors' suf-fering, which will lead to a lack of social cohesion. The result of our uncaring and corrupt culture will be division and that division will lead to civil war, or it will render us vulnerable to defeat when en-emy nations invade. And when we turn on each other, or when brutal nations invade us, our cities will be burned to ash, with no stone left upon another. Our crops and wealth will be plundered, leaving us either dead, enslaved, or barely surviving in a hellscape of misery. We will experience life as being part of a conflicted family with an angry, punishing, vengeful parent."

Do you see it? If so, you see how I'm coming to realize that, yes, I was right in undermining the way the old theological binaries were abused by my religion.

But I'm also coming to realize this: Although minimizing the idea of divine wrath may have sprung from good motives, it may have bad ecological consequences. So now I'm leaning toward a different strat-egy. First, I want to tell this fuller story of the important role bipolar gods with benevolent and wrathful moods played in ancient indige-nous cultures. I want to show how these stories were necessary and useful containers in which ancient people could preserve and pass on hard-won indigenous ecological and sociological wisdom. And then, second, I want to tell the story of the ways unsustainable civilizations like our own have twisted and distorted the old indigenous stories of bipolar gods to legitimize their colonization of the vulnerable and exploitation of the Earth.

In the ancient indigenous language of the Bible (and many other indigenous cultures), here's what I believe the experience of doom is helping us see: we can live reverently, gratefully, and humbly with the Earth as a bountiful garden, and we can experience it as a loving source and abiding parental presence (Father God and Mother Earth) . . . or we can turn that garden into a hellscape that we experience as a raging, angry parent or jilted lover that hates us and wants us gone.

Do you see the irony? I wanted to throw out something that my civilization was using to cause harm . . . and then I replaced it with something else civilization can use to cause harm, namely, the idea that God or the Universe or the Earth or the Economy can bless us with unlimited resources for unlimited economic growth with no limits and no negative consequences. If this God chooses you for blessing, you can kill and oppress everyone who gets in your way. You can exploit the Earth and drive as many of its creatures into extinction as you want. You can make yourself the apex predator and dominant herbivore of every ecosystem. You can ignore every scientific finding because of your faith that the Presence in which you live, move, and have your being will forgive all your foolishness and deliver dependable profits every quarter, as long as you keep defeating your enemies.

Few of us go from "I'm dead right!" to "I'm dead wrong!" in one simple step. Usually, our first step is into "maybe": "Maybe I'm not as good and right as I think I am. Maybe they're not as bad and wrong as I think they are. Maybe this situation isn't as simple as I thought it was."

The brilliant novelist Octavia Butler said, "Civilization is to groups what intelligence is to individuals. It is a means of combining the intelligence of many to achieve ongoing group adaptation."[7] Ideally, I think she's right. But if a civilization is speeding toward collapse, we would have to say that civilization can also express combined or collective ignorance. When that happens, as we said in chapter 5, we need to step away from the seductive stories it is telling, disentangle from its "common sense," and move out beyond its accounting of wrongdoing and rightdoing. This is not a flight from absolutist morality into a fog

---

7 From adrienne maree brown, "What Is Emergent Strategy?," in *All We Can Save* (One World, 2020).

of amorality, but rather, it is an exodus out of the shallows of simplistic moral binaries and into the depths of moral wisdom.

Sitting at sunset in Rumi's field with the old Chinese farmer, the words of the poet Wendell Berry may finally make sense to us:

> It may be that when we no longer know what to do,
> we have come to our real work
> and when we no longer know which way to go,
> we have begun our real journey.
>
> The mind that is not baffled is not employed.
> The impeded stream is the one that sings.

The instinct to judge everything good or bad, the urge to reduce all unknowns to simple certainties, the allure of echo chambers where our opinions are reinforced all day, every day . . . I know their appeal is strong. But if you're willing, we can venture out beyond that space, to a place of bafflement that looks a lot like wonder . . . a place of "maybe" that looks a lot like humility . . . a place of unknowing where something in us sings.

It sings even in the face of death, as we'll consider in the next chapter.

Dear Reader,

This chapter is an invitation to critical thinking, which is the careful, intentional, and self-aware process of acquiring and evaluating information with the goal of understanding accurately and living wisely. Critical thinking is important because nearly all of us think we're above-average thinkers, and we are prone at times to jump to conclusions that we later regret. For that reason, critical thinkers keep in mind that their reasoning is often flawed and their judgments premature, that they are prone to biases and errors, and that their personal perspective and experience give them both advantages and disadvantages in understanding what is real and true.

Critical thinking is hard work because it requires taking many factors into consideration, including evidence, context, assumptions, methods, bias, self-interest, conflicts of interest, intended and unintended consequences, conscious and unconscious criteria, logical fallacies, and virtue. Critical thinkers learn to separate their ego from their opinions, and they learn to live with uncertainty and ambiguity. They pursue understanding with patience, persistence, and humility, and they freely admit they may be wrong or their understanding may be partial or one-sided.

Critical thinking involves curiosity (a strong, sincere desire to know the truth, even if the truth is painful or costly), imagination and creativity (viewing a subject from multiple perspectives), the ability to both trust or give a fair hearing to others and to doubt or question others, along with the ability to think for oneself and question one's own current thinking. In our current situation, when so much is at stake, it makes sense for us to strengthen our critical thinking skills. "Maybe it's good; maybe it's not" is one important step in that direction.

In your journal or with your reading group, take the description of critical thinking above and evaluate yourself as honestly as you can. What elements are you weak in and strong in?

How might you strengthen your critical thinking skills?

In what way is critical thinking an individual sport—and a team sport?

You might even pause and consider how well you have been practicing critical thinking in reading the first ten chapters of this book. Maybe you will find some places where you think I need to think more critically as well. And maybe you will sense that there is a kind of thinking that goes beyond critical thinking: the thinking that comes naturally in Rumi's field.

Be prepared, because in the next chapter, we will venture into territory relatively few of us ever enter, at least not for very long.

11

I Am a Candle

Life is not about me. I am about life.

—Franciscan teacher Richard Rohr[1]

Poignancy . . . is the richest feeling humans experience, one that gives meaning to life—and it happens when you feel happy and sad at the same time. It's the state you enter when you cry tears of joy—which tend to come during precious moments suffused with their imminent ending. When we tear up at that beloved child splashing in a rain puddle . . . we aren't simply happy . . . we're also appreciating, even if it's not explicit, that this time of life will end; that good times pass as well as bad ones; that we're all going to die in the end. I think that being comfortable with this is adaptive. That's emotional development.

—Author Susan Cain[2]

The sense of my own irreplaceable life, then, is inseparable from my sense that it will end. When I return to the same landscape every summer, part of what makes it so poignant is that I may never see it again. More-over, I care for the preservation of the landscape because I am aware that even the duration of the natural environment is not guaranteed. . . . My time with family and friends is precious because we have to make the most of it. Our time together is illuminated by the sense that it will not last forever and we need to take care of one another because our lives are fragile.

—Swedish philosopher Martin Hägglund[3]

---

1 See https://cac.org/daily-meditations/lesson-three-your-life-is-not-about-you-2020 -04-01/.
2 See her book *Bittersweet: How Sorrow and Longing Make Us Whole* (Crown, 2022). This quote is from her TED Talk, "Why Bittersweet Emotions Underscore Life's Beauty," available here: https://www.youtube.com/watch?v=ZTg54BbjJfA/.
3 *This Life: Secular Faith and Spiritual Freedom* (Anchor, 2019).

A few years ago, my wife gave me a DNA test for Christmas. In free moments since then, I've been trying to build out my family tree. So far, I've traced ancestors back to around 1500, when fragments of the DNA that constitute me were scattered across nine European countries, from Denmark to Italy. Let me give you a quick snapshot of sixteen of my ancestors more recently, in 1825, about two hundred years ago. The McLarens, McCrindles, and Templetons lived in Scotland. The Lees and Hambleys were born in England and emigrated to Canada. The Smiths lived in New York and the O'Briens in Ireland, and the Meheusens were born in the Netherlands and later migrated to New York.

Today, not one of them is alive. The same is true of my eight ancestors in the next generation. And my four ancestors of the next generation. And my two ancestors of the following generation.

The same will be true of me in a few years.

It's pretty safe to say that one hundred years from now (whenever your "now" is), not one single person reading these words will be alive.

That was an easy sentence to read, but its meaning may not be so easy to take in. An impressive array of psychologists, anthropologists, and sociologists tell us that we are well fortified, individually and as groups, against thinking about our own mortality.

I have a primal memory of death terror from early in my childhood. I must have been four or five, maybe six. As I lay in bed, unable to sleep, I felt I was about to explode with horror. I was not afraid of dying myself. I was afraid of my parents dying. That possibility of being alive without them so terrified me that I remember having a conversation with myself that went something like this: "I'm just a kid. I can't handle thinking about this. Quick . . . think about something else! Popcorn, cotton candy, swimming, catching crayfish in the creek, visiting Grandpa Smith . . . anything!"

Over the years, thoughts of my parents' death were replaced with fears about my own death. Often, the terror was so great that I remember feeling I could not stand to think about the subject for one more second. During adolescence, I remember thinking: "I'm just a teenager. When I get older, I'll be more mature. Now, I just can't handle it. Someday I'll be able to think about death—the death of others, and my own death—without being so scared. But for now, quick, let's think about something else, anything else: soccer, summer camp, grades . . . girls!"

I was right. I'm old enough now to have had a few brushes with death and I don't feel the same terror I felt as a child. I can imagine my death without a rise in pulse or blood pressure. I can see my family and friends getting on just fine when I'm gone. I can imagine a time when I'm only a name on the family tree of a descendant who never knew me, wondering what it was like to live in those strange and dangerous times of ecological doom in the twenty-first century.

About fifteen years ago, I had an episode of extreme heart arrhythmia and drove myself to the emergency room. After a blood test, a hospital orderly suddenly rushed in and started pushing my gurney down the hall for an emergency heart scan. I asked what was going on. He replied, "Sir, your magnesium is so low, it's amazing your heart is still beating." I remember thinking, "Wow. That sounds serious. This could be it. If this is the end, all I can say is thank you. Thank you to God, to life, to my family, to all of the people and animals and plants and places and experiences that have made my life so full and meaningful."

It turned out that I had acquired two tick-borne diseases that were causing an array of potentially lethal symptoms. They were hard to diagnose but easy to treat. I hope when my real time comes, I feel that same deep peace and overwhelming gratitude.

I'm probably more death-aware than many people. After all, I spent most of my adult life as a pastor and conducted many, many funerals. I accompanied many parishioners in their final hours and moments of life. More recently, I did the same for my parents. One of my children is a cancer survivor, and all parents who have walked with their child through chemotherapy know what it means to "walk through the valley of the shadow of death." In addition, I come from a Christian tradition in which death was a point of focus, even if it was often minimized and marginalized by a strong belief in an afterlife.

It's not being dead that bothers me at this point in my life, closing in on seventy. It's what will bring me from here to there. Dementia runs in my family. Will that be my final chapter? Will it be civil war, or famine, or a storm, or a mass shooting, or a pandemic, or cancer, or a car crash, or . . . ?

In 1973, anthropologist Ernest Becker published the Pulitzer Prize–winning book *The Denial of Death*. The book explores how our species has a deep aversion to the brute fact of our mortality. Our death anxiety is so troubling to us that we devise elaborate strategies to distract ourselves and deny our mortality. On an individual level, we stay too busy or too entertained to think about the subject. We take drugs or seek pleasure through sex or sport to make us feel alive and invincible. We portray ourselves as transcendent heroes in the narrative of our lives. On a societal level, we launch massive immortality projects through business, politics, war, and religion. Becker came to see the whole of human civilization as a massive defense mechanism against the full realization of our impermanence. Our civilizational death-denial project builds a death-averse rationale that helps both us and civilization: "My individual life is meaningless because I will die. But if I tie my life to something that lives longer than me—like my religion, nation, party, or civilization—then my life will have meaning, and I will, in a sense, live on in that transcendent community."

You can see where this leads. As we feel a sense of doom about ecological overshoot and the possibility of civilizational collapse, we feel personally threatened, which is traumatic enough. But even more traumatic, we feel that our all-encompassing shared immortality project, namely, our civilization, is threatened too.

More recent researchers have buttressed Becker's theoretical work with empirical study.[4] Their findings suggest that when our minds are troubled by persistent thoughts of death, we become more rigid in our adherence to the norms of our social in-group and more hostile to outsiders. The more anxious we become about our own death, the more

---

4 See Sheldon Solomon, Jeff Greenberg, and Tom Pyszczynski, *The Worm at the Core: On the Role of Death in Life* (Random House, 2015). "Over the course of human history, the terror of death has guided the development of art, religion, language, economics, and science. It raised the pyramids in Egypt and razed the Twin Towers in New York," they say. Among their findings: When we are engaging in death-related "terror management," we often become more interested in our connection to our ancestors, which may shed light on my interest in my family tree, recounted at the beginning of this chapter.

we experience what researchers call "collective neuroticism," and the more likely we are to harm or even kill others. Perhaps you are beginning to see how simply being aware of the danger of civilizational collapse could send people into a spiral of anxiety leading to mutual hostility . . . which could in turn hasten the very thing we fear.

In this light, it's not surprising that a number of outspoken influencers are working hard to tamp down our fears. Some, no doubt, are themselves in denial about the seriousness of ecological overshoot and our other civilizational maladies, and they are trying to preserve their bubble of denial by creating a crowd that shares it. But others can foresee that the unleashing of human death terror may lead to consequences that are even more terrifying than death itself: namely, a desperate collapse process that degenerates into an Armageddon of all-against-all violence. People with this kind of foresight would privately acknowledge global overheating and overshoot, obscene economic inequality that leads to obscene political inequality, and our susceptibility to supremacist narratives and the authoritarian demagogues that profit by them. But publicly, they might try to minimize our fear in order to pull us all back from a death spiral of death terror.

If you "get" that last sentence, you'll probably feel as I do right now as I write: we live in between two impending dangers, both real, both potential threats to our existence. To our left, we face the frightening gradual accumulation of environmental and social consequences of ecological overshoot. To our right, we face the more sudden social consequences of having our terror management strategies fail, plunging us and our neighbors into our most reactive, most neurotic, and least rational behaviors right at a time when we need cool heads and a collaborative spirit.

As one of our coping strategies, I think those of us who have the internal fortitude to do so would be wise to stop sidestepping our fear of death and, instead, face it head-on. We could prepare ourselves by doing some inner death and dying work to come to a place where death terror has been replaced with a sense of serenity, peace, and reconciliation with our impermanence.

A few months ago I found a simple mantra to help in this inner work.

I help lead an annual conference on the Georgia coast called Southern Lights. At our last gathering, we created a ritual to end the conference in which participants would come forward and pick up a small candle. Then, they would approach one of several large bowls of sand, each with a large lit candle in its center. They would light their candle and place it in the sand, pausing to say a silent prayer or intention about the kind of light they would like to spread in the world when they returned home.

I was seated in the front row, so I watched as over six hundred people came forward. A surge of emotion took me by surprise. I watched a woman come forward who had confided to me that she had late-stage cancer. I realized this would probably be the last time she would participate in an event like this. I watched a young man light his candle and thought that he probably had many more years ahead of him, but his flame was no less fragile and his future not guaranteed. We hadn't planned the ritual to be a meditation on death and impermanence, but that's what it became for me.

We're all just wax and wick, I thought. On the day of our birth, our life flame begins to burn, and from that moment, each new moment of life brings us one moment closer to its inevitable end. I felt how little control we have: we choose neither the length of our candle nor the conditions in which our wick, wax, and flame come together.

In one sense, I'm sure this all seems terribly obvious, perhaps even clichéd. But as I watched the ritual unfold, I felt, in a way I hadn't before, life's fragile beauty, life's bittersweet wonder and impermanence, and death's inevitability, baked into life from the start, not as a flaw, but a feature.

The experience wasn't morbid. It was deeply touching. It made me feel that each life, each moment, each experience was unspeakably precious. *We're all candles,* I thought.

We're all candles. As I reflected on the ritual over the following days, a beloved poem/prayer by St. Francis of Assisi kept coming back to me. "Canticle of the Sun" begins with Francis praising God for all creatures, beginning with brother sun, sisters moon and stars, "brothers wind and air, and clouds and storms, and all weather." Praise continues for sister water, brother fire, mother Earth, and more. Finally,

Francis thanks God for "sister bodily death." She will embrace every living thing, Francis says.

For many of us, to be grateful for death sounds strange. We have been taught that death is an enemy intruder, never part of the original plan, and certainly an interruption to our plans as well. If death is a creation, it's the devil's work, not God's, we think. That understanding, though widespread, is hardly the best or only way to understand the Bible or Christian theology. It certainly makes no sense when you think of it logically: to create a planet and tell its creatures to "be fruitful and multiply" would guarantee an overcrowded world in short order . . . unless death had a part to play from the start.

Each religion is unique, but all religions seem to offer resources for terror management. In my own Christian tradition, death is often reduced to a consequence of sin, not as a feature of life. Then it is minimized as nothing significant, since the eternal life of the soul continues when this moral life ends. The weight of eternal life makes the few years of this mortal life seem short, and death, insignificant. That's one way of managing the fear of death: by denying that death is of any significance.

I think Francis offers us a better approach. To Francis, death is neither insignificant nor terrifying. She is our sister, one of God's creatures, part of the family tree of creation, like sun and moon, like clouds and storms, like water and fire, like our fellow living creatures. Just as we learn to live with day and night (both of them good and necessary) and sunny and rainy weather (both of them good and necessary), we can learn to live with a time to be born and a time to die (both of them good and necessary).

This isn't the place for a deep philosophical or theological engagement with death, but I would like to offer three brief conclusions of my own for you to consider. First, death adds value to life.[5] Death tells us that our lives matter because they are precious, long enough to be meaningful, but short enough that we can't take even a single day for granted.

---

5 For an in-depth examination of this proposal, see Martin Hägglund's *This Life: Secular Faith and Spiritual Freedom* (Anchor, 2020).

Second, learning to accept the reality of death is an essential dimension of maturity and wisdom. We come to see that life is not about you or me: we are about something bigger than ourselves. We are about life itself.

And third, in this light, we do not have to see death simply as defeat by an evil enemy.[6] Instead, we can see our death as a final act of generosity. In *natality* (or birth),[7] I am given a name and a niche to occupy. I am given the privilege of using a share of the Earth's resources for a time. In *mortality*, I recognize that this privilege is like a turn in a game; my turn will be over some day, and it will be time to give up my space and my share of resources for someone else. Life isn't about receiving only; it is also about giving away. Life isn't about grasping and enjoying only; it is also about letting go so that others may have their opportunity to enjoy. This is what every living thing must do. Yes, there's sadness in realizing that every living thing will pass. But if we stay with the sadness instead of marginalizing or minimizing or otherwise denying it, the sadness will be taken up in a greater beauty, which is the poetic bittersweetness we explored in chapter 4.

To live as part of this universe of beautiful impermanence, of generous self-giving, with some constantly departing and others constantly

---

6 Some of my conservative Christian friends may want to quote 1 Corinthians 15 to me, where Paul clearly refers to death as an enemy (15:25–26). Indeed he does. But in the following sentences, he masterfully inverts death as enemy, showing how it is actually an essential agent of creation's transformation, as necessary to God's creative project as it is necessary for a seed to be buried before it can germinate and grow into something new. His conclusion makes his ultimate point clear (15:54–58): When we put death in a larger, deeper context, death loses its sting. It doesn't make our lives meaningless; it helps create the context in which our labors are not in vain. If we follow Paul's larger arc, we realize that death was never the real enemy, but rather what Paul calls "sin." (15:56). And sin, for Paul, is associated with a grasping for power rather than a release of power in love (see Philippians 2:1–11, evoking and reversing imagery from Genesis 3 of grasping at the forbidden fruit). In this light, then, selfishly clinging to life at all costs is a refusal to accept the necessity of death and even the *goodness* of death. Paul does not provide a "terror management strategy" for denying death, but rather, he offers a way of accepting death without the sting of fear. (We see his non-anxious attitude toward his own death in Philippians 1:23–26.)
7 I am using "natality" in the rich sense used by Hannah Arendt, especially in *The Human Condition* (University of Chicago, 1998, originally 1958). She explores natality as "the arrival of others" who constantly bring newness to society. See Wolfhart Totschnig's article, "Arendt's Notion of Natality," available here: https://www.redalyc .org/journal/809/80955136014/html/.

arriving, is to be faced with the most profound and meaningful choice imaginable. On the one hand, we can refuse to accept that our turn will someday come to an end. We can refuse to face the limitations that come with being a part of this universe. We can fight to rise above creatureliness and grab life tight as our selfish eternal possession, refusing ever to release it. If that is our choice, we may not realize it, but we are grasping at divinity, demanding to live as gods, not creatures. (If that imagery makes you think of an old, old story about a snake and a fruit and a garden, you can go back and reread chapters 8 and 9.)

That story of grasping and not letting go, of hoarding and demanding more than is our share, of acting like selfish and immature gods rather than mature and humble humans . . . that, of course, is the story that has brought us to the place of doom to begin with. If the drive to deny death has gotten us here, maybe it's time for us to change our strategy. Maybe it's time to stop seeing our problem as death and instead to see our problem as the fear of death.

Just the other day, I was telling a friend about this book. When I shared some of the ideas in the "Hope Is Complicated" chapter, she told me, "I used to think that hope was the confidence that what I fear won't happen." Then she added, "Now I think that hope is the confidence that what I fear *will* happen, but that I don't have to be afraid."[8]

I can't stop thinking about that powerful shift in perspective.

What a surprise: here in the presence of doom, we find a portal into maturity and wisdom. Doom challenges us to face our greatest fear, and as we do, we discover that this fear played a big part in driving us toward doom in the first place.[9] We begin to see, to feel, to understand in our depths that we are candles, that we are lit and we are alive now, and that when our candle is gone, the flame will live on in others. We are overcome with a profound appreciation for ourselves, for our family and friends, for everyone everywhere, for all living creatures who have been, who are now, who shall be. And with that appreciation

---

8 Thanks to Heidi Franklin.
9 For more on coping with fear, including seeing it as a gift, see Gareth Higgins, *How Not to Be Afraid* (Broadleaf, 2021).

comes compassion. We say, "I am a candle. So are you. Just wax and wick of unknown length, carrying a fragile gift of flame for the time we are given."

There's an old biblical proverb that at first glance sounds terribly morbid, but in this light, seems deeply wise (Proverbs 7:2): "It is better to go to the house of mourning than to go to the house of feasting, for this is the end of everyone, and the living will lay it to heart."

When I began assembling my family tree, I didn't see it at first, but now it is clear. Sister Death has always been there on every branch, embracing each life. At first glance, mortality may seem to swallow natality: death appears to defeat every birth. But no: mortality and natality are interwoven, like day and night.

Sister Death is part of every branch of the whole tree of life: every kingdom, phylum, class, order, family, genus, and species. Eventually, she will embrace us all. When we "lay it to heart," this life we enjoy for a time doesn't become less meaningful, beautiful, or precious, but more.

The terror of death has haunted our species since we left our hand-prints in ochre on cave walls. Over the millennia, we have developed elaborate terror management strategies . . . religions, philosophies, economies, cultures, even civilization itself. Driven by fear, we tried to transcend our impermanence, to deny that we are candles, to grasp for rights and power without responsibilities and limits.

Here in the presence of doom, I see death as I never have seen it before. I see how our fear of death fuels our denial of death, and how our denial of death fuels our species' desperate obsessive neuroticism . . . to grow, conquer, colonize, control, dominate, steal, kill, and destroy.

If we are to get through this dangerous time, if the darkness of the tomb can also be the creative "darkness of the womb" (to use Valarie Kaur's apt phrase),[10] our denial of death is one thing that must die. Sooner or later—and preferably soon enough, we must come to the joyful, humble wisdom of St. Francis, and become not only tolerant but truly thankful for Sister Death. We will see, as another of humanity's greatest sages once said, "Unless a grain of wheat falls in the soil and

---

10 See her powerful book *See No Stranger* (One World, 2021).

dies, it remains alone. But if it dies, it brings forth much fruit." Or, "If you try to save your life you will lose it. But if you lose your life for my sake, you will find it." (I will comment on that phrase "for my sake" in chapter 13.)

Dear Sister Death . . . she is not a failure or flaw in the universe. She is a feature of it, part of the beauty that will live on as long as this universe itself.

In the coming decades we can expect to experience intensifying disruptions in our geosphere, biosphere, and social sphere. Those disruptions will shake our personal sphere too. As feelings of doom break through our personal and cultural terror management strategies, we can easily become more desperate and neurotic in our denial.

But we can also become more wise, letting denial, anger, bargaining, and depression pass through us like a storm. In the calm beyond the storm, we will see our remaining moments, days, and years for what they have always been: a precious gift, fleeting as morning mist, a fragile flame on a tiny wick in a bit of wax, gloriously impermanent and too magnificent to waste.

Yes, we are candles, just wax and wick. But now, at this moment, we are aflame!

So let us shine our little light while we can, doing all we can to leave our descendants with a habitable world and the skills and virtues to flourish in it. And when our wick and wax are gone, may we let go graciously and generously. Let us trust ourselves to the mystery, and quietly disappear into the embrace of Sister Death, joining our ancestors in peace, having done what was ours to do, whispering, "Thank you. Thank you. Thank you," to the Earth, to all life, to our family and friends, and to the sacred flame of life itself . . . what St. John of the Cross called the "living flame of love."

Dear Reader,

You may feel that I was lying when I told you that chapter 2 was the most emotionally challenging of the book, because you found this chapter to be more so. But however challenging, I hope you felt it was meaningful, important, needed.

Whether in a journal for your own reflection, or with others for shared conversation, I hope you'll begin by recounting (as I did at the beginning of this chapter) your own feelings about death since you first became aware of death as a child.

Do you feel your feelings about death changing as a result of your engagement with this chapter?

Why might overcoming our "denial of death" be especially necessary in a time of doom, when we face a number of existential threats, not just to our individual survival, but also to the survival of our species and major parts of the biosphere?

Some readers, knowing of my faith background, might be surprised when I reject the popular religious teaching that death is a punishment for human sin rather than a feature of the universe.[11] Can you reflect upon some of the scientific, theological, and ecological reasons I might take this approach?

Can you see any other way, besides learning to "face head on" our death terror and denial of death, to avoid "collective neuroticism" in a time of fear?

How does the mantra "I am a candle" work for you? If not, can you develop a better alternative?

---

11 The biblical text associated with this teaching is from Paul's Epistle to the Romans. There, he calls death a "wage" of sin . . . not a punishment, but a consequence. Ecologically speaking, as we will see in chapter 19, we could say that the more we grasp for power and domination and more than our fair share, the more quickly we will create the very ecological conditions that will kill us.

12

Start with Step One

What if the way we respond to the crisis is part of the crisis?
—Nigerian philosopher Bayo Akomolafe

We admitted we were powerless over alcohol—that our lives had become unmanageable.
—Step 1 of the Twelve Steps of Alcoholics Anonymous

The Twelve Steps aren't really talking about alcohol as the ultimate problem. The ultimate thing we cannot control is, well, life. The ultimate addiction is to our own capacity to control. . . . These three things—uncertainty, impermanence, and powerlessness—lie at the heart of this collective, global teachable moment. We cannot know (uncertainty) or control (powerlessness) our world, because it is inherently relational and in flux (impermanence). Each moment is pregnant with possibility and potential, fraught with danger and mystery. Paradoxically, it is when we can be at ease with uncertainty, when we can accept our own powerlessness, we become free.
—Educator/writer/philosopher Theodore Richards[1]

I became part of the Alcoholics Anonymous community in a rather unexpected way.

It wasn't through alcohol, but through friendship. And a stupid mistake.

I was on the faculty of a local college at the time, teaching English and also helping to start a new congregation on the side. I showed up at my building one Monday morning at about nine-thirty for a ten o'clock class. I was confused. The hallways were dark and empty. I made my

---

1 From "Impermanence, Uncertainty, Powerlessness," available here: https://reimagining magazine.com/project/three-skies/.

way to the main office, also dark and quiet. At the end of a hallway, I saw one light shining through a partially opened door. I entered and found a colleague sitting with his feet up on the program director's desk. "Ah," he said, "so I wasn't the only idiot who didn't get the memo that school was closed today."

He explained that there was work being done on the building's water supply and that the school would be open the next morning as usual. We exchanged some banter and I turned to leave. "Just a minute," he said, taking his feet off the desk. "You're religious, aren't you," he said, less a question and more of an accusation. I had often heard him express his disdain for religion.

"Spiritual," I said, "and I suppose religious, too, depending on how you define it. I'm helping form a little experimental church."

"This is really weird. Really weird. Can I trust you with something I haven't told anyone?" he asked, leaning forward.

I came back and sat down and his story poured out. "Nobody else knows this, not even my mother. I haven't gone a single day without drinking since I was twelve years old," he began, "until eleven days ago. I started going to AA and have been sober for ten days. When I showed up this morning and saw that classes were canceled, I realized I had a free day with nothing to do, and for the last"—he looked at his watch—"ninety-three minutes I've been sitting here feeling every cell in my body telling me to go get drunk and make up for lost time."

I nodded.

"If you know anything about the AA program, it's really big on having a higher power, but I'm an atheist and I don't really believe in any of that crap. So for the last ninety-three minutes I've been sitting here trying to keep my ass in this chair for one minute at a time, thinking today might be the end of the longest string of sober days in my whole adult life. They teach you this prayer in the program, which I've been saying even though I have a major problem with the whole higher power thing. So here I am, praying a prayer to a higher power I don't really believe in, and then who walks in but the only God guy on the whole faculty. Pretty weird, right?"

"Pretty weird," I replied.

"Is there any chance . . . I know this is asking a lot . . . the first AA meeting nearby is at noon. Is there any chance you'd hang out with me until the meeting? Just to make sure I don't take any detours?"

We went out for a long breakfast and then I walked him to his meeting in the basement of a Catholic church. He invited me to come in with him. "You can leave if you don't like it," he said.

That next hour had a huge impact on my life. Banged-up metal folding chairs in a circle, a coffee pot on a cheap card table with way-too-strong black brew, and about thirty people who had a capacity for cussing that was only surpassed by their capacity for honesty. . . . I'd never experienced anything like it. As a "God guy" who had a conflicted relationship with both Christianity and the conventional idea of church, I felt that I had stumbled into something life-changing.

To this day, I have never been drunk even once, but as I sat in my rickety folding chair and read a handout with the twelve steps, I felt I belonged in this circle. The twelve steps felt incredibly relevant to my life—and to the lives of everyone I knew. I accompanied my friend to a few more meetings in the coming months. Some time later, I shared my experience in a sermon. Soon after, several members of my congregation told me they were part of "the program" too. I started receiving invitations to accompany church members to a meeting where they would receive a chip for thirty days sober or a year sober or whatever. Members of the program began inviting others from their recovery program to our church. ("I found a church that welcomes people like us," they would say.) Soon I was regularly invited to speak at twelve-step retreats, helping people like my teaching colleague try to grapple with the "whole higher power thing" in a way that felt right and honest and true. When someone from a local twelve-step group would relapse and die of an overdose, I would often be asked to perform the funeral, and I performed quite a few weddings for people in the program as well.

Through the years there was a growing overlap between my congregation and local addiction recovery programs, and I always felt the relationship was mutually beneficial. During my twenty-four years as a pastor, one of the highest compliments our congregation ever received was, "Wow, this church has the feel of a twelve-step meeting."

The prayer my colleague learned in the program is called the Serenity Prayer, written by a twentieth-century pastor named Reinhold Niebuhr:

> God, grant me the serenity to accept the things I cannot change, the courage to change the things I can, and the wisdom to know the difference.[2]

As this book has been unfolding, this prayer has come to mind often because ... well, I might as well admit it: I've come to realize that my primary addiction is to fixing things, or, more accurately, to fixing everything. Saving everything. Healing everything. That's what attracted me to become an English teacher: I didn't simply want to help students get A's in grammar or literature; I wanted to help them edit their lives and get A's in humanity. That's also what drew me to ministry, and later, to write books. That might sound like a rather positive addiction, but when you find yourself lacking serenity because you keep trying to fix, save, or heal things that cannot be fixed, saved, or healed ... your life quickly becomes unmanageable.

Maybe you're wondering what I'm wondering—whether writing this book is an expression of my addiction? Perhaps it is. Or perhaps it's therapy. Or perhaps a little bit of both.

When I first learned about climate change back in the late 1990s, I set out to fix it with a beginner's innocence. We must save the Earth. We must heal the planet. We must liberate the poor. There's nobility in an aspiration like that. There's also just a sliver of naïveté and egotism, don't you think? Sure, these are big problems, I thought, but they have never had the benefit of the wholehearted attention and talent of someone like me! So I did what I knew how to do as a writer and preacher. I wrote a book and with the help of some amazing friends, I went on a speaking tour. (*Everything Must Change* is a great title for a

---

2 Niebuhr's original prayer included the following: "... living one day at a time; enjoying one moment at a time; taking this world as it is and not as I would have it; trusting that You will make all things right if I surrender to Your will; so that I may be reasonably happy in this life and supremely happy with You forever in the next. Amen."

book and tour until you take the Serenity Prayer seriously.) Our goal was to change everything, one tour stop at a time.

You can imagine a therapist asking, "How's that *changing everything* project working out for you these days?"

It's no wonder that many idealistic people like me eventually burn out and descend into cynicism and disillusionment. Our world resists fixing. Our vulnerability as activists is even greater because we grew up during the halcyon days of peak fossil-fueled capitalism. You might say that fossil fuels filled us with delusions of omnipotence because of the superhuman power they gave us.

A BBC television crew tried to demonstrate that power by recruiting one hundred volunteers to provide a typical British family's electricity for one day. The volunteers had to generate that electricity by pedaling bicycles next door. Just to heat the family's oven required twenty-four cyclists; to make two pieces of toast, eleven. After their day as "energy slaves," the volunteers were exhausted and famished, many barely able to walk. The experiment vividly demonstrated how powerful we have come to feel because of fossil fuels.[3] They have given us power over gravity (through airplanes), power over hunger (through fertilizers and genetic engineering), power over disease (through wealth to fund research), power over hard physical labor (through bulldozers and backhoes), power over everything . . . over every damned thing except our ability to stop burning them.

Consider this: to produce the same amount of energy stored in one barrel of oil, a single cyclist would have to work forty hours per week for between five and nine years. As I write, an employer could buy that much power for about $75. No wonder the average American would feel powerless if he were deprived of his usual 2.6 gallons of fossil fuels per day (five times the global average). No wonder the managers of the global economy deny reality rather than waking up and welcoming it: the amount of cheap labor they gain through fossil fuels each year is equivalent to about 500 *billion* full-time employees. That's the equivalent of over sixty servants doing hard labor to make each living

---

3 See https://thetyee.ca/Opinion/2011/05/05/EnergySlaves/.

person's life a little easier.[4] (Of course, those imaginary energy servants are distributed as inequitably as money.) To put it starkly, fossil fuels set us up like plantation owners in the antebellum American South.

The analogy to slavery in the American South is painful to consider. It raises the question of whether fossil fuel–dependent people today would go to war to keep our current energy arrangement going for one more generation.

Here's another analogy to consider: fossil fuels have become an addictive substance for our civilization. They are the fentanyl, heroin, or crack of energy sources. Just as American slaveowners were so dependent on the social and economic arrangement of slavery that they were willing to tear apart their nation, risk their own lives, and take others' lives to maintain it, addicts I've gotten to know over the years have told me how addicts often risk everything to keep their addiction going. They lose their job because of their addiction, but that isn't enough to make them admit how much trouble they're in. Then they lose their marriage. Still not enough. Then they lose the respect and trust of their children, siblings, and parents. Still not enough. Then they lose their health. Still not enough. By then their money is long gone, and their debt limits have been reached and exceeded. Still not enough. Crime often follows. Violence. Imprisonment. For many, it comes down to a choice between their addiction and their life. And for many, that still isn't enough.

That's why, in the rooms of Alcoholics Anonymous, I've heard people in recovery repeat that first of the Twelve Steps like a life-changing mantra: *We admitted we were powerless over our addiction and our lives had become unmanageable.*

I wonder how many of us who have been made to feel so powerful because of fossil fuels are willing to take that first step in regard to our current situation: *Our civilization is powerless over our cheap energy addiction; our civilization has become unmanageable and needs to be restored to sanity.* I know that kind of admission offends the optimists who tell us, "Hey, we can do this! It's not that hard! We have the new

---

4 See this interview with Nate Hagens, director of the Institute for the Study of Energy and Our Future, on the *Voicecraft* podcast: https://youtu.be/pREjkXuc_DU.

technology to fix it. And the power of capitalism will carry us through even if governments fail!" I know they speak this way because they're trying to encourage us so we don't feel overwhelmed and give up, and I respect that. But I'm worried about that kind of talk. I'm worried that in a well-meaning attempt to encourage us to keep trying, we will, recalling the words of Bayo Akomolafe, respond to our crisis in a way that perpetuates the crisis.

So far, all or nearly all of our fixes, all of our plans to heal the planet or save the Earth . . . use the same logic that got us into this mess. Renewable energy is a great example. Solar, wind, geothermal, tidal, and other energies are fantastic short-term solutions. But they're also a long-term problem, because renewable energy is only partly renewable. Yes, solar panels and wind turbines have amazing advantages over fossil fuels. Yes, electric cars and heat pumps are indeed breakthrough technologies. Yes, I am all for them in our current emergency. But if we are to decarbonize fast, to shift away from fossil fuels, we are going to need—and fast—massive amounts of copper, aluminum, cobalt, graphite, and manganese, along with rare earth metals, especially lithium. On top of that, we are going to need huge quantities of fossil fuels to mine, transport, and process these raw materials.

When you look on a map and ask where we should dig the mines to acquire these resources, you see that in many cases, they are on the lands of indigenous peoples, and you wonder how they will be treated by governments, corporations, and electorates desperate for what they possess. Past history suggests a sad answer. Other resources lie beneath forests and other delicate ecosystems; again, you wonder how many will be sacrificed for our climate emergency.

In our lust for carbon-power, we were happy to "externalize costs." Have we learned our lesson, or will we externalize even more costs in our more desperate need for lithium or copper or rare earth materials? And then, what happens when they run out, because eventually they will? Of course, you say, we'll find substitutes. But recalling Akomolafe, will our way of responding to the crisis merely prolong and perpetuate the crisis—the crisis that we need a radically new relationship to the Earth, to one another, and to life itself?

"But there are no alternatives," you say. "We have no choice."

And I think you're right. So let's play the story forward. What if we proceed . . . and succeed? What if we successfully decarbonize and create a new post-carbon economy?

What then? The next crisis will come, and we will solve it with the same logic, of course.

That prospect raises frightening questions, questions you don't want to ask even in secret, much less in public. Imagine that we successfully decarbonize and avoid collapse. In so doing, imagine that we buy human civilization in its current form 250 more years of resource consumption and waste production, and give, say, five more generations of humans (maybe fifty billion people total) the same chance to exploit the Earth for fun and profit that we have enjoyed. Imagine that each one of those fifty billion consumes more than they regenerate and leaves the Earth a little poorer when they pass away.

Imagine that for 250 years we continue to plunder wild places and reduce the biomass of all wild living creatures to make room for the billions of tons of chicken, cattle, pig, salmon, and tilapia flesh our carnivorous majority wants to eat.[5] Imagine that many of our religious communities continue to decline, leaving a moral and spiritual vacuum. And then imagine that other religious communities experience a fundamentalist resurgence, throwing their power behind violent authoritarian political leaders. And let's say that during this time, we continue to multiply the number and kill power of our weapons, a highly likely prospect based on our past and current performance. And then, let's say we begin to run out of lithium or its substitutes that we need for our so-called renewable economy.

And then, let's say between 2220 and 2280 or so, we really do manage to self-destruct, driving ourselves and most vertebrate life into extinction, leaving the Earth far more devasted than it is now. Can you see how "fixing" today's crisis in a superficial way could kick the time bomb down the road to create an even greater ultimate catastrophe? The Collapse Avoidance scenario of today could turn out to be the Collapse Delay and Intensification scenario of the future,

---

5 On the power of veganism to make a difference in our current situation, see the work of Climate Healers: https://climatehealers.org/.

leapfrogging over Collapse/Rebirth and Collapse/Survival and plunging our species, along with many others, into Collapse/Extinction.

When I face this possibility, I have to ask questions that I will want to delete as soon as I express them, but they are questions that must be asked: What if Earth's eight billion living humans might succeed in saving ourselves now, but in so doing, we would even more catastrophically destroy the biosphere in a century or two, eliminating the possibility of human life for all succeeding generations after that? Are we willing to discount the immeasurable value of uncountable future lives (humans, animals, plants, ecosystems) to squeeze out a few more decades of comfort for ourselves?[6] Might it be better for collapse to happen now?

That thought experiment supports a conclusion reached by many of my friends and other people I respect greatly, namely, that doom is one of the things from the Serenity Prayer that cannot be changed. Our baked-in, slow-release catastrophe of ecological overshoot combined with our habits of economic injustice, social hostility, and spiritual superficiality, will inevitably create a steep, bumpy downhill slide toward civilizational collapse and possibly near-term human extinction as well. "The wisdom to know the difference," they say, leads us to accept this inevitability. When we accept what we cannot change, we can at least live out our remaining days with a measure of serenity and we can prepare to exit as gracefully as we can as a species.

In short, they have concluded that there is no escaping scenario 4, Collapse/Extinction, and they are trying to model acceptance with serenity for the rest of us. I know there are some misanthropic kooks out there glibly saying these kinds of things. But the people I am referring to are not kooks. They are good-hearted, clear-minded, well-informed people. They show extraordinary courage in not turning away from the full crushing weight of disturbing evidence.[7]

---

6 For a window into how economists engage in discounting future human lives, read Lisa Heinzerling, "Discounting Life," *Yale Law Journal*, vol. 108, no. 7 (May 1999), p. 1911–1915. Available here: https://www.jstor.org/stable/797456. Also available here: https://core.ac.uk/download/pdf/215559161.pdf.

7 In 2019, Dharma teacher Catherine Ingram wrote a moving essay called "Facing Extinction" in which she candidly shares her thoughts and feelings about this acceptance. She reads the essay aloud here: https://www.youtube.com/watch?v=bN-O-01dXqE.

I do not know if they are premature in reaching this gravest of all possible conclusions. I worry that accepting the inevitability of scenario 4 becomes a self-fulfilling prophecy. In other words, if too many good people give up working for less catastrophic scenarios too soon, the people who are oblivious to our current situation could bring about even more catastrophic scenarios. Continuing the struggle, even without any hope that it will save humans, could perhaps still save parts of the biosphere that would otherwise be destroyed.

Do you see why I keep coming back to the Serenity Prayer? I do not know for certain whether our current doom trajectory can be changed with courage, or if it should be accepted with serenity. I do not yet have that wisdom. The only thing I know is that I want to set a moral course for myself, without judging others if they take another course. So then the question becomes personal: What is mine to do?

For me, the moral choice is to do what addicts do in recovery programs. In praying the Serenity Prayer, they admit their need for courage, their need for serenity, and their need for wisdom, just as they admit their powerlessness: "The way I'm living will kill me," they say. "So I'm going to band together with people who admit they are in the same mess I am. And we will seek together, one day at a time, to be restored to sanity."

That first step brings them to a second step: *Came to believe that a power greater than ourselves could restore us to sanity.*

Now you might think this is where I start talking about God swooping in to save us with a miracle. But that's not how I understand God or our current situation. For me, if the idea of hope is complicated, the idea of God is far more complicated, especially in situations like ours. If we say, "Hey, God will fix it, so we don't have to worry about anything. Hallelujah!", I think we are in the same boat as people who say, "I can't see a way forward, so let's all give up." I think that pious complacency brings us to the same place as both stubborn denial and premature resignation.

So let's not bring a skyhook God into the equation right now, at least not under that name. Let's stick with "a power greater than ourselves." I wonder how this might sit with you as our first step:

Humanity in its current form has been organized and shaped by a set of stories, beliefs, values, practices, and institutions that have produced a global civilization that billions depend on. But we have come to realize that this civilization is addictive, and it is killing the Earth, which will kill our species. Unfortunately, when we respond to this crisis, we do so having been shaped by the stories, beliefs, values, practices, and institutions that created the crisis. As a result, our solutions perpetuate the very crisis they are intended to solve. We are powerless. Left to ourselves, we are utterly doomed indeed.

And then imagine this as a second step:

To fulfill the possibility of long-term survival, or to face the trauma of near-term extinction, we will need new resources . . . new wisdom, courage, virtues, values, practices, new ways of thinking and seeing . . . in short, new power. Only something that comes from outside our civilization's current toolbox can help us become sane again, sane enough to shape a new way of life for survival or sane enough to face and accept our end with serenity. We aren't even sure what those new needed resources might be, so we have to trust that they're there, and trust that they will be sufficient to help us find sanity, for as long as we live.

Those two first steps may fail us, and if so, scenario 4 awaits us, leaving us to accept it with whatever serenity we can when the time comes. But if we take those first two steps, we may survive long enough to find a third step we cannot now see, and after that, a fourth and a fifth that we cannot now imagine. Those steps may lead to a scenario where some of our descendants may learn to live courageously, serenely, and wisely with Earth, with one another, with themselves, and with life itself. Or they may lead us to a scenario where we or our descendants must face the end of our story as a species.

More and more of us are saying, "Enough. We can't go on responding to our crisis in ways that perpetuate the crisis. Now is the time to admit that it might already be too late for us. Now is the time to go deep and face the deepest roots of our current situation, our sickness, our addiction." That admission might admit us to new possibilities that we do not or cannot now see. It might not. But none of our scenarios are good. So we make our admission of powerlessness in risk, in trust beyond knowledge.

My friend and colleague Jim Finley reflects on "the transformative power of admitting." He observes that in every recovery community, "if you admit, you're admitted. If you don't admit, you're not admitted."[8] The stakes are high, because "if you admit, you live; and if you don't admit, you might die."

Those who have concluded that our situation is terminal and beyond recovery, often derided as "doomers," are helping me more deeply face my powerlessness, our powerlessness. They are helping me see that the more confident we are in our ability to "fix" our situation, the less likely we may be to succeed, because our responses to the crisis will perpetuate the crisis. The paradoxical possibility then presents itself: to the degree we face our powerlessness, we may find a power greater than we currently possess. Perhaps that power will help some sliver of us survive, or perhaps it will help us accept an inescapable end with serenity.

I want to take us to a better place, truly. And I will. But first, I hope you will dare to sit with me in this place just a little longer. A place to which we are admitted when we descend to the bottom. Where we feel our powerlessness as a civilization. Where we admit our powerlessness as individuals. Where we know our current stinking thinking cannot fix the mess created by our stinking thinking. Where we don't simply substitute one new "fix" for an old one. Where we feel the insanity of our situation and want to be restored to sanity. Where we seek the serenity to accept what cannot be changed, the courage to change what can be changed, and the wisdom to know the difference.

---

8 Adapted from James Finley, *Mystical Sobriety* (Albuquerque, NM: Center for Action and Contemplation, 2022), online course.

Dear Reader,

Perhaps you now see why I grouped these chapters together under the heading "Letting Be." To be willing to open our eyes in new ways. To see indigenous people as holding wisdom that the "civilized" lack. To learn to face and to embrace our own mortality. To experience an intervention regarding our civilization's addiction. To feel our fossil-fueled power and our paradoxical powerlessness.

These considerations take time and space, being admitted to an inner sanctuary in which we're not obsessed with fixing and solving and doing, doing, doing. They require us to shift our focus, at least momentarily, from what we do, fix, solve, and know to who we are and desire to become. They require letting some dust settle and panic pass.

The word "admit" is important in this chapter. Reflect on that word.

The experience of *addiction* is also important in this chapter. Does the diagnosis of our civilization as addictive ring true with you?

I suggest that fossil fuels have given us delusions of omnipotence. Reflect on that idea. What other elements of our civilization may also make us delusional?

The Bayo Akomolafe quote that begins this chapter echoes through it. How does his question sit with you?

Do you feel you are ready to move from *Letting Be* to *Letting Come*? Or do you need to pause here a little longer?

PART 3

LETTING
COME

A Path of Resilience

13

We Are Not the First Ones Here

The world has been ending off and on for almost all of recorded human history. . . . Some people take comfort in the sheer number and historical variety of the prophecies of doom, supposing that if they've been wrong about it up to now (after all we're still here) then we can probably relax and assume we'll still be here tomorrow. But this attitude overlooks the frequency with which the end really has arrived. In fact, it always does arrive. Every great and small civilization before our own has ended one way or another and some of those endings were abrupt and terrifying. It would be simple-minded to assume that we're special.

—Mathemetician and collapsologist B. Sidney Smith,
"How to Enjoy the End of the World"[1]

Rome didn't fall in a day. It took centuries.

—Economist Umair Haque

A culture does not tend to train its young to endure its own breakdown.

—Philosopher and psychoanalyst Jonathan Lear

Back in chapter 7, I shared an insight that came when I was up to my knees in the cold water of a mountain stream. Fly-fishing, it turns out, is good for epiphanies.

Not long ago I was up to my knees in another stream, taking a break from the intensity of writing this book. I was peering through the amber-tinted current at the cobble beneath my feet. (A fellow fly-fisher once shared this advice: "Be where your feet are." Since then, I pause frequently and simply focus on the space between my feet.) Each rounded rock, I knew, had once been part of the snowcapped mountain ranges

---

1 https://www.youtube.com/watch?v=5WPB2u8EzL8.

behind me. It had broken off as a jagged boulder and been slowly, gradually smoothed by tumbling against other rocks for millennia of millennia. This rock by my right foot, white quartz. That rock by my left foot, gray schist flecked with mica. Between the two, zebra schist—banded with gray and white. Right in front of it, black gneiss dotted with pink quartz. Rocks in this stream, I had read, are over 1.8 billion years old, and over those vast expanses of time, these rocks from long-gone layers of surrounding mountains had tumbled into place between my feet.

As I gazed, I suddenly saw my own body of muscle, blood, and bone in a shimmering reflection on the water, as the current ran between me and these ancient cobbles. My entire life-span seemed, compared to each rock, utterly insignificant, a flicker, a flash. All of human history—the same. In that contemplative moment, I felt the immensity of time, awesome and dizzying in its vastness. The vastness felt familiar, recalling the immensity of space that I have often felt beneath a clear night sky or standing on the rim of a vast chasm. I felt a strange sense of respect for these stones . . . so old, so durable compared to fragile, fleeting, fleshy me.

Lines from the indigenous poetry of the Bible came to me . . . a lasting effect of my years as a pastor and preacher:

When I consider the heavens, the work of Your fingers, what are we humans that you are mindful of us? (Psalm 8:4)

All flesh is like grass and all its glory like the flower of grass. (Isaiah 40:6)

Lord, let me know my end, and what is the measure of my days; let me know how fleeting my life is. (Psalm 39:4)

We are foreigners and strangers in your sight, as were all our ancestors. Our days on Earth are like a shadow, without hope. (1 Chronicles 29:15)

For we are but of yesterday, and we know nothing, for our days on Earth are but a shadow. (Job 8:9)

Fleeting, fleeting, all is fleeting! (Ecclesiastes 1:2)[2]

---

2 Traditional translations render this verse, "Vanity of vanities, all is vanity!" or "Meaningless, meaningless, all is meaningless!" The Hebrew word means "mist,"

For the briefest moment, aided by those ancient rounded rocks and those ancient biblical texts, I felt deeply what my mind understands but struggles to fully accept: of course, our civilization will pass like a surge of water flowing between my feet, like fleeting shadow or a wave rolling across a field of grass. Of course, just like my individual life, our civilization will reach an expiration date. Of course. I knew this, but hadn't felt it as intensely as I did in that instant, gazing simultaneously at my reflection, the rushing water, and the stones underneath.

People who study civilizations note that every civilization has passed through a similar cycle. The stages of this cycle parallel a pattern we see across nature—in forest succession, for example, or in the life cycle of a star. Ecologists call it the adaptive cycle. First comes what ecologists call the exploitation or growth phase. In this phase, there is an abundance of easily accessible energy and other resources that can be exploited in some new arrangement. For example, there may be an abundance of space dust that can congeal into a star, or an abundance of rich soil, rainfall, and sunlight that creates the conditions for a forest to grow.

Then comes what ecologists call a conservation phase, when the new arrangement conserves or consolidates its shape or form for as long as it can, in a state of balance, or homeostasis. This is the stage of a stable climax forest or a mature star. Then, after a period of relative stability, conditions change and a release phase begins, a period of destabilization and decline leading to collapse or death. We see this phase when a forest burns suddenly or dies gradually due to climate change or a parasitic infestation. As the trees fall, they release their monopoly on sunlight, and as they decay, they release all the chemical and mineral wealth they had stored up in their tall trunks and branches.

We also see the release phase when a star begins to exhaust its fuel. In a smaller star, the outer layers expand and its core contracts, and eventually, the core doesn't have enough gravity to hold the outer layers. They are released into space as interstellar stardust, spreading new atoms and altering the chemistry of their galaxy. Larger stars release their matter and energy more dramatically, exploding out into

---

"vapor," or "breath." I think "fleeting" or "transitory" would be a better rendering in English.

a supernova, also spreading new elements and changing the chemistry of their galaxy.

Next comes what ecologists call a reorganization phase, when the new post-collapse conditions create the possibility of rebirth for some new arrangement of matter and energy. From the ashes of the climax forest, a new ecosystem takes shape, or from the dispersed dust and gas of the old star, a new star system begins to form. We humans wouldn't be here now if countless old systems hadn't exploited available energy, conserved their arrangement as long as they could, and then released and reorganized multiple times.[3]

Growth/exploitation, stability/conservation, release/collapse, and reorganization: we can trace this pattern through virtually every civilization of the past about which we have sufficient information. In Mesopotamia, the Sumerians, Akkadians, Assyrians, Babylonians, and others rose and fell by this pattern. In the Mediterranean, the Minoan, Mycenaean, and Greco-Romans did as well. In India, it was the Mauryan and Gupta Empires; in Southeast Asia, the Khmer Empire; in China, the Zhou, Han, Tang, and Song Empires. In the New World and the Pacific Islands, there were the Maya, the Mississippian, the Pueblo and Hohokam, the Tiwanaku, the Easter Islanders, and many more. Many factors, external and internal, can tip a civilization from stability toward collapse. It might be an enemy invasion or a volcanic eruption. It might be climate change or soil degradation, economic inequality or mass migration, civil war or a plague. Though the triggers differ, the pattern remains remarkably similar.[4]

In my faith tradition, we often call this the paschal mystery: birth and growth, suffering and death, followed by rebirth.

You could say that our current global civilization began its growth phase about five hundred years ago, as European nations conquered and colonized discrete regional civilizations around the world and

---

3 The best illustrations of this four-stage iterative process don't present it as a straight line, but as an infinity loop, a sideways figure eight. You'll find a good example here: https://www.resalliance.org/adaptive-cycle/.
4 See Safa Motesharrei et al., "Human and Nature Dynamics," available here: https://www.sciencedirect.com/science/article/pii/S0921800914000615. See also work by other collapsologists, including Joseph Tainter, Jared Diamond, Yves Cochet, Agnes Sinai, Jem Bendell, David Wallace-Wells, and B. Sidney Smith.

consolidated them into their own imperial economies.[5] This growth phase was, as the ecological name suggests, heavily exploitive. The most valuable external resource for the emerging global civilization, fossil fuels, came along just in time to propel the civilization forward to levels of size and sophistication never achieved by any previous civilization. Regional civilizations around the world joined (or were assimilated by) this increasingly complex political, economic, and cultural super-civilization. Relative homeostasis was conserved during this conservation stage through uneasy, constantly evolving institutions, treaties, alliances, supply chains, social movements, technologies, and armed forces with weapons of increasing kill power.

And now, we find ourselves in the late days of the conservation stage or (more likely) the early days of the release stage, as our current global system finds both growth and homeostasis harder and harder to sustain. It's a paradox, both ironic and tragic: if we keep fueling our civilization with fossil fuels, we destroy the ecological balance on which our civilization depends. But we cannot easily stop fueling our civilization with fossil fuels because both the elites and the masses are too comfortable with the status quo and want to keep it going . . . just a little longer.

Less than three hundred years after naming ourselves Homo sapiens, we have had to face the fact that the term is aspirational, not actual.[6]

In my writing this book and in your reading it, we are learning what our ancient ancestors knew: that all human civilizations, like all individual human lives, are fleeting like grass, blooming for a day then withering like a flower, extending themselves like an afternoon shadow until they disappear. We dreamed that we would be like gods, exceptions to the adaptive pattern, but our bubble of exceptionalism has burst for many of us, and it will eventually burst for everyone else.

---

5 This global colonial expansion was made possible by many factors, including a new transportation technology (oceanic sailing ships, and later, the sextant), new weapons technology (guns and cannons), new communications technology (the printing press), new financial technology (as colonialism brought unprecedented wealth to capital markets and banks created new ways to leverage that wealth), religious justification (through the Doctrine of Discovery), and eventually, of course, a new energy breakthrough (fossil fuels).
6 The term was first used by Carl Linnaeus in 1758.

We thought we could hold on to the exploitation and conservation phases forever, and forever keep release and reorganization at bay. Now, many of us are beginning to see that is not possible.

It's a sad moment for us. Even terrifying.

But being humbled in this way is also strangely comforting. It brings a sense of relief. Like a couple who goes through a divorce after a long, hard, bitter marriage, we realize that the arrangement for which we fought so hard for so long to save wasn't really that great. We faced our great, unspoken fear . . . that without this marriage, each of us would be nothing . . . and we found out that after the collapse, we each survived and had the chance for a new beginning. We face the opportunity hidden in the tragedy: to begin again, to reorganize our lives. We may even be a little closer to our aspiration of being both *Homo* and *sapiens*.

I'm still standing in the stream, staring down, and a sentence forms in my mind: *We're not the first ones here.*

Other civilizations have collapsed, and some people survived it. Now it's our turn.

After returning home from my fishing trip, I came across this story from retired Episcopal bishop and Choctaw elder Steven Charleston:

> I was asked to write a brief commentary about the Christian theology of the apocalypse: the final, terrible vision of the end of the world. I said my Native American culture was in a unique position to speak of this kind of vision, because we were among the few cultures that have already experienced it. In historic memory, we have seen our reality come crashing down as invaders destroyed our homeland. We have lived through genocide, concentration camps, religious persecution, and every human rights abuse imaginable. Yet we are still here. No darkness—not even the end of the world as we knew it—had the power to overcome us. So our message is powerful not because it is only for us, but because it speaks to and for every human heart that longs for light over darkness.[7]

7 *Ladder to the Light* (Broadleaf, 2021). See also *We Survived the End of the World* (Broadleaf, 2023).

Charleston makes it clear that he is not claiming that his ancestors were superior to other people. Instead, their suffering was a window into our shared human condition during times of release and reorganization: "In their suffering, [my ancestors] embodied the finite and vulnerable condition of all humanity." They modeled both that the suffering is great, and that the end of the world can be survived. Not without unimaginable pain. Not without unimaginable social and psychological disruption. Not without heartbreaking tragedy and loss. But it can be done.

Back in the stream, my thoughts are rushing faster than the water between my feet. I feel the tiniest fragment of what a Wampanoag, Powhatan, or Taino mother must have felt, standing on the shore of what we now call Massachusetts, Virginia, or Hispaniola, watching ships arrive, heavy with cannons, carrying armed men who will destroy in a matter of years everything a hundred generations of her ancestors had built. This is what Lakota or Cheyenne fathers must have felt, watching wagon trains of armed settlers snake across the prairie, shooting bison by the millions, each bullet killing their economy, their way of life, their civilization, their children's future.[8]

"We have been here before." I recall these words from my friend and colleague the Rev. Otis Moss III. He reminds us that his Black ancestors, too, have survived the end of the world. I imagine what a West African grandmother must have felt, watching a British or Dutch slave ship carrying away her kidnapped sons and daughters and grandchildren, and within them, all her future descendants, never to be seen again. She cries. She wails. She falls to her knees and rocks herself back and forth, inconsolable. Her world is ending. Her tears join those of thousands of other mothers and fathers around

---

8 In 1800, about sixty million bison roamed North America, from Florida to Alaska. By 1900, they were on the verge of extinction, with only three hundred remaining. General Sherman had advocated their total annihilation, and the US Secretary of the Interior explained why in the early 1870s: "Kill every buffalo you can! Every buffalo dead is an Indian gone." In short, the extinction of the bison was a tactic to achieve indigenous genocide. For more, see J. Weston Phippen, "Kill Every Buffalo You Can! Every Buffalo Dead Is an Indian Gone," *The Atlantic* (https://www.theatlantic.com /national/archive/2016/05/the-buffalo-killers/482349/), and this article from the Ozark Valley Bison Farm: http://www.ozarkbisons.com/aboutbison.php.

the world who have experienced this disruption, the ending of their world, long before us.[9]

So here I stand, bent over in the stream, my hands on my knees now. The last five hundred years of our civilization's exploitation and conservation pass by me as a river of tears. If there is any atom of truth at all to the biblical words that pride goes before a fall and that individuals and groups reap what they sow, then collapse of an unrepentant civilization like this one is inevitable. My prayer is that release will come before even more horrific damage is done, while there is still enough environmental health left so that human, animal, and plant survivors can keep surviving long enough to reorganize, to begin again, to be born again after the worst happens.

It has only been a few seconds, maybe twenty, maybe sixty, and all these thoughts and feelings have swept through me too fast for words as I watch the amber water flow between my feet over the ancient stones. I feel surprised to realize that I am no longer interested in saving this civilization, at least, not as it is. I am interested instead in something else. I'm not sure yet how to describe it.

I look up and make my way across the stream. I think of those fathers, mothers, grandparents . . . those who have been here at this point of civilizational collapse before. Those survivors must become our teachers. They must be our inspiration. They knew how to survive the end of their world.

I climb up the bank and sit on the grass. We are not the first ones here, I think.

We have been here before. We are not the first ones here.

Will we be the last?

Our individual survival is not the point, nor is the current arrangement of matter and energy we call civilization. The point is those who will begin anew.

A biblical passage (Matthew 16:25) that I referred to in a previous chapter comes to mind once again as I look across the valley: "If you

---

9 See Otis Moss III, *Dancing in the Dark* (Simon & Schuster, 2023), and this interview on the *Prophetic Resistance* podcast with Michael-Ray Mathews: https://faithinaction.org/podcast/episode-69-rev-dr-otis-moss-iii/.

try to save your life, you will lose it. If you lose your life for my sake, you will find it." The words "for my sake" can make Jesus sound like another typical egocentric demagogue, happy for other people to die as part of his narcissistic pursuits. But that doesn't match with everything else we see of Jesus. Here's what I suspect he meant: "You have a life as a member of this civilization, this age, this economy. Your life means something within it. If you think that is the only way your life can have meaning, you will hold on to that life. And when this arrangement collapses, so will your life. But look at how I am living. I am pouring out my life for a bigger framework of meaning, for a story that is so much bigger than this little civilization that will soon run its course. If you join me in letting go and letting be, you will find what your life has really been about all along."

If we let go of exploitation and conservation . . . if we release, for the sake of others, for the sake of future generations, for the sake of our fellow creatures . . . we can pour our energy into what can live on beyond us. What that might be, we cannot know. We can only dream.

Dear Reader,

At the beginning of this chapter, I share an experience of *the vastness of time*. Have you ever had an experience like that?

In that vastness of time, I am able to consider the fact that we are not the first ones here. How does that realization help me? Does it help you, and how?

Review the four phases of the adaptive cycle and explain each in terms of a forest, an individual human life, or our civilization: exploitation, conservation, release, reorganization.

How do you respond to the idea that our job, during release, is to stop trying to return to conservation and instead turn our focus to reorganization? What would reorganization mean in our four scenarios: Collapse Avoidance, Collapse/Rebirth, Collapse/Survival, Collapse/Extinction?

14

Imagine Safe Landings and
New Beginnings

The oppressors maintain their position and evade their responsibility for their own actions. There is a constant drain of energy which might be better used in redefining ourselves and devising realistic scenarios for altering the present and constructing the future.

—Womanist author Audre Lorde[1]

When asking people to enlist in a grand societal undertaking, we have to make a commitment to them that the society that will emerge from the other end of that effort will be more just and fair than the one they are leaving behind.

—Climate Emergency Unit[2]

"All organizing is science fiction," writes Walidah Imarisha. I suppose the inverse is true—our disorganizing, our entrenchment, and the intractability of our brokenness are a failure of imagination, a failure to believe in the possibility of new worlds. . . . Writers imagine ways out.

—Melissa Florer-Bixler[3]

By "poet" I mean the broadest sense of creative maker of meaningful space. The possibility for such a poet is precisely the possibility for the creation of a new field of possibilities. No one is in a position to rule out that possibility . . . to clear the ground for a rebirth.

—Philosopher and psychoanalyst Jonathan Lear

---

1 From *Sister Outsider: Essays and Speeches* (Penguin Classics, 2020).
2 See https://www.climateemergencyunit.ca/emergencymarkersframework.
3 From her article "Science fiction writers imagine the way out," *The Christian Century,* available here: https://www.christiancentury.org/article/voices/science-fiction -writers-imagine-way-out/.

I'll tell you something I've never shared in public before.

The day after Donald Trump was elected in 2016, I opened a new file on my computer and started writing a novel. I wasn't sure why I was doing it. I just knew I had to. For my sanity. To engage my imagination in something constructive. To keep my imagination from being sucked into a vortex of doom.

My genre was science fiction. But I was not writing yet another novel about the end of the world.

Instead, the novel explored release and reorganization (recalling the adaptive cycle in the previous chapter), the end of one world and the beginning of another. It was a novel about life after doom. The novel eventually grew into a trilogy, and when the three novels are published, they will be a good companion to this book.

Apocalyptic novels and movies—works that imagine the end of the world—are important. From *Planet of the Apes* to *The Road* to *Don't Look Up*, works of apocalyptic fiction wake up complacent people. But once complacent people are awake, once doom is staring back at them each morning when they brush their teeth, they need a different kind of imagination. They need to imagine life after doom. They need to *imagine safe landings* after a turbulent passage.

I first encountered "safe landings" language from the World Climate Research Programme (WCRP). The WCRP partners with the United Nations and the Intergovernmental Panel on Climate Change (IPCC) to bring solid scientific research to bear on our current global predicament.[4] One of their projects focuses on safe landings, exploring "the routes to 'safe landing' spaces for human and natural systems." You'll notice the plural: they are searching for *multiple routes* to multiple *safe landing spaces*. They are not looking for one perfect route, one magic solution, one silver bullet.

My wise friend and joyful colleague Cameron Trimble is an entrepreneur, pastor, consultant, and avid pilot. She has a saying that I love that points to the same need for plural routes, for flexibility and agility: You can always have your way if you have enough ways. She explains:

---

4 See https://www.wcrp-climate.org/safe-landing-climates.

Our world today is nothing if not swirling, turbulent wind tossing us around.... [W]e have experienced economic meltdown, climate countdown, racial throwdown, political breakdown, technology showdown, and religious letdown. We are living through the breakdown and breaking open of much that has defined modern life.[5]

She recalls what her flight instructor told her about flying through turbulence: "We are going to hit some turbulence ahead and you will learn something about your airplane.... If you tighten your grip on the yoke, you reduce the aerodynamics of your aircraft. You, as the pilot, actually make the flight less safe, steady, and stable. So, remember: When the going gets rough, fly loose...." Rather than tightly grasping at single solutions to help us regain a feeling of control, we need to loosen up our imagination, so we can imagine multiple ways through the turbulence, multiple routes to multiple safe landings.[6]

Cameron's saying explains one of the reasons I shaped the book you are presently reading around the four scenarios of Collapse Avoidance, Collapse/Rebirth, Collapse/Survival, and Collapse/Extinction.

First, I wanted us to imagine more than the one option, that option being white-knuckling the yoke of the status quo, maintaining our current assumptions and power arrangements in homeostasis a little longer, at all costs.

Not only that, I wanted us to imagine more than two options, a utopia and a dystopia.

I even wanted us to imagine more than three options, a good one, a bad one, and one in between.

The four scenarios we have explored in these pages are like four cairns of stacked words spread across the horizon. They're constructs that invite us to look up from our feet, to draw our attention beyond one, two, or three possible futures. The number four is a choice I made, and in that sense, it is artificial: complex enough to confound

---

5 From her article "In Times of Turbulence, Fly Loose," in the Center for Action and Contemplation's journal *Oneing* (Spring 2023), p. 35.
6 From her article "In Times of Turbulence, Fly Loose," *Oneing* (Spring 2023), pps. 32, 35–36, 37. See also her book for clergy, *Piloting Church* (CBP Press, 2019).

oversimplification, and simple enough to distinguish one from another in a way that helps us (I hope) see what is at stake. You and I both know that there are infinite gradations among the four, and beyond each, many different futures might unfold.

The four cairns mark four possible landings, none of them safe, but some safer than others.

Back in chapter 1, I explained how I first got a glimpse of the possibility of ecological and civilizational collapse when I wrote *Everything Must Change*. My first reaction was to intensify my activism: to alert everyone I could to our situation, so we could do all we can to turn our lives and societies away from collapse and toward sustainability. Over these years, I have urged people to seek wisdom, justice, compassion, character, honesty, and mutual respect while we can, in hopes that these values can catch on and sufficiently transform enough of our civilization that it doesn't go over the cliff. I think that my first response was sensible and typical. It was a path through the turbulence of scenario 1 to a safe landing: our civilization radically redesigned so it can avoid collapse.

But what if the Collapse Avoidance scenario becomes untenable? Do we curl in a fetal position of defeat and despair? If we understand the idea of multiple routes to multiple safe landings, we shift our imagination toward new ways forward: sowing the seeds for a better way of life that can arise from the compost of our current arrangement. We shift our imaginative energies from averting collapse to building life rafts and arks of sanity, resilience, and morality. Then we can make it through a turbulent passage in the company of people who share humane values and creative vision. If we survive, then we can become midwives of new ways of life on the other side, budding ecological communities, piloting multiple ways for humanity to live as part of Team Earth rather than writing a cliched script for a rerun of overshoot.

But what if the Collapse/Rebirth scenario becomes impossible? Then we shift our imaginative energies toward multiple ways of surviving in a different world . . . a post-industrial, post-democratic, post-capitalist, post-technological world. That world may have more in common with the world of our distant ancestors than with our current world. If that's the case, inspired by the examples of our ancestors, we can find or make multiple ways forward, ways we can choose under circumstances we did not choose.

But what if human ignorance, arrogance, and folly prove incapable of even that Collapse/Survival scenario? Then we will have to choose multiple ways in which we want our story to end. If we are alive during the last days of our species, do we want to replicate the selfish, hoarding, violent version of humanity that got us in the mess we're in? Do we want, in our final chapter, to be cartoonish Gollums still clinging to our last precious can of baked beans or our last precious plastic bucket of freeze-dried nutrition powder, ready to go out with our teeth bared and our guns blazing? Or do we want to go out with a beautiful demonstration of generous, gracious, kind human magnificence . . . embodying our deepest ideals, holding one another's hands, and rejoicing for the trees and fish and birds and salamanders and lichen that will have the chance to survive the Anthropocene murder-suicide event?[7]

You can always have your way if you have enough ways. That's why it makes sense to imagine good ways of living in multiple undesirable scenarios.

I know it's not pleasant to imagine these undesirable scenarios. But I learned why it's worth doing during my years as a pastor in a multistaff church. For most of my years in ministry, whenever I hired new staff, both I and the new staff member would be filled with idealism. I would be thinking, "This is going to be the best staff member I've ever hired! She will solve all of the problems the last staff member left us with!" At that very moment, the new recruit would be thinking, "This is going to be the best job, the best church, and the best boss I've ever had! This pastor will have none of the faults of that last narcissist I worked for!" You might think these high hopes would set us up for

---

7 Randy and Edith Woodley offer an alternative to the term "Anthropocene": "Many scientists say we are living in the Anthropocene. . . . But let's not lay the responsibility of climate change on all humans, since all humans have not influenced nature negatively. That's like making the whole class stay in from recess and calling them 'delinquents' because two kids have been acting up. . . . We choose to call our era the Europatricene: a geological era dominated and determined by white European-based men." From their upcoming book *Journey to Eloheh*. (Broadleaf, 2024).

success, but the opposite was the case. Our high expectations were disappointments and resentments waiting to happen. So after a lot of unhappy endings, I changed my approach. (Apologies to my former staff! I wish I had been a faster learner.)

A humbler version of me would meet with each potential staff member, and I would say something like this: "Listen, before you sign the agreement and make this official, let's imagine how this is going to end. You may work here until retirement, and we will throw you a party. Or you may die suddenly on the job, and we will conduct your funeral." For some reason, this would often make the new recruit laugh. "More likely, though, either you will grow less happy here with me and this congregation, or I or a future successor will grow less happy with your performance. For your employment to end, things will probably get pretty bad for one or both of us."

The new staff member would usually look a little surprised at this point. Then I would ask, "Let's talk now about how we want to handle tough situations when they develop, because we both know that I will eventually disappoint you, and you will eventually disappoint me. Let's think from the beginning of how we want to handle inevitable problems. And let's talk now about how we want our working relationship to end when the time comes. Let's try to set ourselves up for a good ending, right from the beginning. Does that make sense?"[8]

The irony was, the more we prepared for a painful situation, the less painful it was when it happened.

You and I have tried to do something difficult in these chapters. We have imagined a lot of super-undesirable, painful situations we never would choose, situations of great turbulence at the intersection of environmental overshoot and civilizational collapse:

Melting polar ice caps leading to weather disruption, sea level rise, and coastal flooding.

Rapid climate disruption leading to extinctions, crop failures, and far-reaching economic impacts.

---

8 I learned this idea of thinking of the end from the beginning from Stephen R. Covey's *The 7 Habits of Highly Effective People* (Free Press, 1989).

Flooding, wildfires, extreme weather leading to mass migrations.

White supremacist and nativist attacks on immigrants and minorities, with conspiratorial falsehoods and stupidities spread by demagogues seeking power.

Volatile stock markets, runs on banks, credit and bank defaults, currency failures.

Cascading failures of political leaders, leading to cascading failures of public institutions.

Mass and social media spreading mass deception leading to mass delusion leading to mass hysteria.

Authoritarian regimes preying on fear and resentment, eventually replacing or compromising democracies.

Food shortages. Water shortages. Supply chain disruptions.

Decline in both health and health care, and increases in violence.

Electric grids and internet crashes due to weather events or terrorist action.

This imaginative work has, unfortunately, been easier than we might have expected, because we see many signs of this turbulence already in motion. You may have felt a sense of relief to get these issues on the table, but even so, I know this process has been emotionally challenging. Frankly, if we stop here, I don't know if we're better off. Imagining undesirable scenarios can leave us in a pretty scary place. It is only half of our imaginative challenge. Now we have the more creative part: to imagine piloting our planes or life rafts through these terribly turbulent times. Now it's time to imagine safe landings on the other side.

John Michael Greer, one of the leading thinkers about civilizational collapse, reminds us that although some collapses are rapid and dramatic, many are not. Many happen in a gradual, stair-step fashion. When the civilization is at a peak of complexity and "progress," most people don't realize it's the peak. They just assume the problems they face are like problems they have always faced: somebody will solve them.

But little by little, as their civilization's level of complexity is too costly or impossible to preserve, their civilization can't solve its problems. It takes a step down; it regresses. Quality of life declines a little bit. Then it stabilizes at that level for a while until some new disruption occurs and it drops another step down. It's possible to imagine people two or three generations into the decline of the Roman Empire who didn't even realize it was in decline. "The Empire is fine," they would say, "it's just those damned Huns and Visigoths who keep invading," or "We just had a bad run of emperors," or "It's harder to find good soldiers than it used to be."

Just as progress can be normalized for generations, decline can be normalized. People slowly lower their expectations through a series of losses, defeats, failures, and other humiliations. Eventually, fatal blows are dealt and the civilization is too weak to recover. For Rome, the first fatal blow came when Alaric led his army into Rome and sacked it in 410 CE. Then, Odoacer staged a revolt in Rome in 476 CE. He dethroned the emperor, the Senate fled for their lives, and the story was over.

One prominent Christian leader at the time of Alaric's invasion, Jerome, was devastated. He wrote, "I was wavering between hope and despair. . . . When the Roman Empire was decapitated . . . the whole world perished in one city. . . . If Rome can perish, what can be safe?" In contrast, another Christian leader, Augustine, preached to his congregation, "Do not lose heart, brethren. There will be an end to every earthly kingdom."

Studying the past can help us imagine ways of living through and beyond the period of decline. For example, during and after the long, slow collapse of the Roman Empire, monastic communities sprang up from the deserts of North Africa to the green hills of Ireland. They created islands of learning in a time when libraries were being burned. They created islands of nonviolence in a time of rampant violence. Monastic women created islands of empowerment and dignity where they could lead and live, even though a culture of crass patriarchy ruled outside. That's one way to make it through the growing turbulence.

Just as we learn from the monastics, we can also learn from the enslaved and colonized. How did they survive their centuries of brutal oppression? They couldn't exactly retreat to spiritual communes. We can learn from the phenomenon of the brush arbor or hush harbor, secret gatherings in the middle of the night where enslaved people met to speak freely (albeit quietly), to sing, to moan, to pray. My friend and colleague Dr. Barbara Holmes calls what they practiced "crisis contemplation."[9] That's another way to make it through the growing turbulence.

We can also learn to strengthen communal spirit in turbulent times from the history of mass noninstitutional gatherings, from the spontaneous outbreaks of festive dancing and jubilation that occurred in the Middle Ages to contemporary festivals like Burning Man, Greenbelt, and the Wild Goose Festival.[10] To these historic ways we can add new ways, ways that involve social media and the internet (while we have it—that may not always be the case), ways that are only now emerging in embryonic forms, ways that have not yet been imagined.

I think we will see at least three overlapping phases of imaginative work going forward. First, in the early stages of decline, in the time after peak complexity when our systems are stairstepping down, we will imagine ways to resist decline, ways to fix broken systems, ways to recover lost ground, even if temporarily. That is important work. Then, when broken systems collapse beyond repair, people will imagine ways to cope with loss and grief, ways to self-organize to support one another, ways to fill gaps and share resources. And third, as it becomes clear there is no going back to a lost status quo, increasing numbers will imagine something new, something beyond fixing broken systems and surviving turbulent times. They will imagine new worlds.[11]

---

9 See her book *Crisis Contemplation* (CAC, 2021). In *Joy Unspeakable* (Fortress, 2017), she explains how the Black church tradition in America is another community that retains indigenous wisdom, recalling chapters 8 and 9.

10 See *Dancing in the Streets: A History of Collective Joy,* by Barbara Ehrenreich (Holt, 2007).

11 Cameron Trimble puts it similar terms: "We are not attempting to fix 'broken systems' but are, instead, summoning entirely new worlds." From "In Times of Turbulence, Fly Loose," *Oneing* (Spring 2023).

Imagine if you could be transported in a time machine back into the Middle Ages somewhere in Europe, say, in 1325 CE. People meet you and ask, "Where are you from? What is it like there?" Imagine saying, "Where I am from, there are buildings where people go to have their diseases healed. They receive new hearts and kidneys taken from the bodies of people who die. Where I am from, people fly in giant winged carts across the oceans, or in carriages that need no horse or oxen, and they travel faster than any hawk or deer. Where I am from, people move their finger or say a word and their homes light up at night, without any candle or flame. Where I am from, we cook without log, fire, or smoke. Where I am from, there are no kings or queens, because people choose their own leaders, and women have the same rights as men. Where I am from, all children can go to school for at least twelve years, and everyone can read and write. Where I am from, we carry a little box in our pockets that allows us to listen to a million songs and read a million pages, and, using that box, we can talk to people on the other side of the world as if we are in the same room. Where I am from, people travel to the moon and back."

Your words would seem like a fantasy. People would laugh at you. They would think you are crazy, maybe even dangerous to suggest such things. Some might even start gathering wood because you sound like a witch or sorcerer.

But imagine that a few people are interested, and they meet with you privately. They ask where you are from. You tell them it is right here, under their feet, but in the future. Imagine they ask what happens to make that future world possible. Does it involve angels, or miracles, or magic? Imagine how you would answer: "Your political system will need to crumble. There will be many wars and terrible bloodshed. Eventually, there will be no such thing as kings or queens or lords or serfs or nobles or . . ." Imagine their shock.

You continue, "The church will no longer have the power and wealth it currently has. In fact, in place of one church with one hierarchy, there will be thousands of churches that do not recognize the pope and cardinals. Many people will not even go to church, and in many places, people of different religions will live together in peace. But again, to get to that place, there will be many wars and terrible bloodshed."

On and on your conversation continues, and the more you tell them, the more anxious they become. What at first sounded magical and appealing, too good to be true, begins to sound strange and terrifying, too horrible to even think about. They cannot imagine being happy in a world so different from their own. "Your world is not our world," they tell you. "We are content with things as they are. You must never speak of such things again."

Now imagine someone coming to us from seven hundred years in the future, on the other side of many wars and much bloodshed and loss. Imagine them telling us of a world without money. Or a world without war. Or a world without nations. Or a world without racism. Or a world without poverty. Or a world without guns and bombs. Or a world without fossil fuels and ecological overshoot. How would we respond? Could we even imagine such a world?

If they told us that collapse would be required to get there, what would we say? "No thanks. The only way forward that is of interest to me is to keep everything exactly the same, except to make it a little better."

It can be a terrifying thing to live at the end of one world and the beginning of another. If you hold too tight to the steering wheel, if you insist there is only one future you will accept, you'll panic. But if you have imagination, you can use it to imagine new ways to resist, new ways to adapt, and new worlds waiting to be born. You can imagine safe landings.

I've noticed something about imaginative people. The people who imagine how to repair or improve current systems, the people who imagine how to adapt as systems collapse, and the people who imagine new worlds are often frustrated with each other. Each group feels that their work is so urgent, so utterly important that the others should drop everything they're doing and join them. They wonder why the others are not pitching in. Their disappointment and angst are understandable.

But we need good people exercising fresh imagination in all three arenas—repair, adaptation, and imagination. If any remotely safe landing is possible, it will take all three groups, working with mutual respect, doing a billion different creative things in a billion different places.

As we move from letting go (a path of descent), to letting be (a place of insight), to letting come (a place of resilience), we cannot guarantee that the world ahead will be more just, more peaceful, and more humane than our world today. We cannot even guarantee that we will survive.

But we can commit to work for justice, peace, and compassion wherever we are in this world, as long as we live. Our first act in fulfilling our commitment is to imagine such a world, or better, to imagine many such worlds and many ways to get there.

Dear Reader,

In your journal or with a reading group, I invite you to reflect on and respond to four selections from this chapter:

"You can always have your way if you have enough ways."

"The more we prepared for a painful situation, the less painful it was when it happened."

"We will imagine ways to resist decline, ways to fix broken systems, ways to recover lost ground, even if temporarily. . . . [We] will imagine ways to cope with loss and grief, ways to self-organize to support one another, ways to fill gaps and share resources. . . . [We] will imagine new worlds."

"Our first act in fulfilling our commitment is to imagine such a world, or better, to imagine many such worlds and many ways to get there."

15

It Only Takes Two or Three

We're all just walking each other home.

—Ram Dass

The secret that our poets and philosophers have been trying to tell us for centuries is that our longing is the great gateway to belonging. . . . If we could honor sadness a little more, maybe we could see it. . . . Sadness, of all things!—has the power to create the "union between souls" that we so desperately lack.

—Susan Cain,
Bittersweet: How Sorrow and Longing Make Us Whole

It is certain, in any case, that ignorance, allied with power, is the most ferocious enemy justice can have.

—James Baldwin

I had just settled in seat 3A, a window seat on one of those small commuter planes that flies to smaller airports in out-of-the-way places.

A young fellow in his early twenties made his way down the aisle and plopped down next to me. He nervously made brief eye contact and asked for help getting his seat belt fastened, and then added in a quivering voice, "Sir, are you nervous?" I sensed that he was a person with disabilities, and asked if this was his first flight. He nodded and said, "I always take the bus because this flying thing *really* scares me, especially on these small planes." I was so touched by his honesty, his vulnerability, in reaching out to me. I smiled and told him he sat next to the right guy, because I flew all the time and could tell him what to expect.

I tried to visualize what he was about to experience and forecast what might scare him. I told him what the taxi and takeoff would feel like. I prepared him for the jolt when the landing gear would retract. I told him about turbulence that might come, and tried to make it sound fun. I explained that the flight attendants would offer him a drink and a snack, and asked what his selections might be. I previewed what the landing would be like, and told him that was my favorite part.

He grabbed my forearm during the takeoff and let go only after the landing gear thudded into place. Throughout the flight, he reviewed with me what to expect next. As we taxied to the terminal, he smiled at me and said, "That wasn't so bad. I'll never take the bus again!" We high-fived when we descended the stairs to the tarmac. He said, "I will never forget you, sir," and I said the same, and as you can see, that promise has been kept.

I've forgotten his name, but not his face, voice, or smile. He has come to mind often in recent months. Normally, I sit in isolation as I travel, immersed in a book (reading or writing), often with earphones in. But he brought me out of my isolation. His unguarded honesty about being afraid invited me into connection, and in that connection we shared comfort and strength. Transparency, sadness, unknowing, insecurity, fear, need . . . something happens when we encounter one another in vulnerability rather than strength.

When we are vulnerable about our fears, honest about our sufferings or sadness, and open about our need for help . . . we create a model that others can mirror. We might say that these qualities are contagious. Encouragement and mutual concern are also contagious, and that's important to know in dangerous times. One person shares their friendliness or insight or virtue or emotional health, and their example invites another and another to do the same. The little spontaneous community might then experience a depth of insight or virtue or well-being greater than the sum of individual contributions. Each would have the benefits of collective intelligence, collective virtue, and what sociologists call collective effervescence, or group joy.

Unfortunately, there is also such a thing as collective stupidity, when people come together in a race to the bottom, mirroring one another's resentment, bigotry, or vengeance. We see it in the feeding frenzy, in scapegoating, in rivalry, in racism, in the angry mob.

We live in a time of stunning and contagious collective stupidity.

Anti-Nazi German theologian Dietrich Bonhoeffer wrote in *Letters and Papers from Prison*:

> Against stupidity we are defenseless. Neither protests nor the use of force accomplish anything here; reasons fall on deaf ears; facts that contradict one's prejudgment simply need not be believed. . . . In all this the stupid person, in contrast to the malicious one, is utterly self-satisfied and, being easily irritated, becomes dangerous by going on the attack. For that reason, greater caution is called for when dealing with a stupid person than with a malicious one. Never again will we try to persuade the stupid person with reasons, for it is senseless and dangerous.

Dr. Martin Luther King, Jr., similarly observed, "Nothing is more dangerous than sincere stupidity and conscientious ignorance." When you begin paying attention to our current predicament, you get a daily baptism in stupidity, especially among the cynical media personalities and ideologues who are part of the climate denial community. They have the power to make mountains of scientific evidence disappear in a magician's *poof*. (When Jesus said that "faith moves mountains," I'm sure this is *not* what he was talking about.)

Climate denial and skepticism are losing ground, as dissenters fall back from one position to defend another and then another, eventually capitulating to some or all of the scientific consensus. But many still refuse to take our situation seriously.[1]

As Bonhoeffer observed, arguments and counterarguments based on scientific evidence have little or no effect on most deniers and skeptics. Over recent months, I have felt the responsibility to expose myself to their writings and lectures as a necessary part of this research. I've encountered nine basic arguments against the scientific consensus. Like

---

1 See https://climate.nasa.gov/faq/17/do-scientists-agree-on-climate-change/. For an example of someone who acknowledges but still minimizes climate change, see this book review about Bjorn Lomborg: Joseph E. Stiglitz, "Are We Overreacting on Climate Change?," *The New York Times*, available here: https://www.nytimes.com/2020/07/16/books/review/bjorn-lomborg-false-alarm-joseph-stiglitz.html.

the sweetest of stupidities, each argument appeals because it contains a spoonful of truth:

1. *You're scaring the children!* Some knowledgeable people point to the recent rise in adolescent depression, anxiety, and suicidal ideations, and they blame those of us who take the environmental crisis seriously for causing this mental health crisis. They tend not to mention that young people have been subjected to several other stressors in recent years, notably a pandemic, the ubiquity of social media and life on screens, facing an inhospitable job and housing market, and (here in the US) the proliferation of mass shootings—many in schools, combined with the shocking failure of politicians to do anything about it beyond sending "thoughts and prayers." But in spite of these lapses in logic, the dissenting voices are right about the negative impact that overshoot awareness can have upon mental health. As far as I know, nobody has figured out a way to inform children about the environmental challenges they will face without causing mental distress. In fact, mental distress would be the only rational response to a genuine understanding of our current situation. (I'll offer a brief script for talking to children about climate change in appendix 5.)

2. *The media are exaggerating everything!* "The media," of course, are an easy target, especially since billions of us have a social media account on Facebook, Twitter, Instagram, TikTok, and the like, which makes us part of "the media." Sensationalism and appeals to fear are great at attracting page views and other media hits—on all sides, so we can expect that many will use media to exaggerate scientific findings in a variety of ways. We can also expect other people using media to exaggerate those exaggerations, or to present them unfairly. Unreliable sources frequently compare "our best to their worst." In other words, they ignore both the inaccurate reporting of their allies and the accurate reporting of their opponents. Then they focus upon the worst inaccuracies of their least respectable opponents.

3. *Climate alarmists are only motivated by money!* Climate scientists and ecologists, they claim, are rolling in money; they are craven, greedy liars willing to lie for cash from vested interests. The fact that most climate scientists and ecologists work for moderate or low wages doesn't seem to bother skeptics; nor does the fact that many climate deniers and skeptics are themselves funded generously by vested interests. (It's the old familiar authoritarian tactic of accusing others of exactly what they themselves are doing.) Even so, because more and more of us are becoming climate and collapse aware, there is a growing market for climate and collapse information, which creates the conditions for distortion . . . by everyone who communicates anything.

4. *Past scenarios and predictions were wrong!* Scientists in the past created scenarios and predictions based on their best available knowledge. As knowledge increases, some scenarios are validated and others are discredited and adjusted. That's how science works. Past scientific inaccuracies—corrected by further scientific research—shouldn't undermine our confidence in science itself, but the opposite. Skeptics don't seem to understand this, nor do they acknowledge the shocking accuracy of even the earliest climate forecasts.[2]

5. *Environmentalism has become a religion!* I've seen both religious and nonreligious dissenters use this critique. The former seem to be saying, "We have the true and legitimate religion, and environmentalism is our competitor." The latter are saying, "All religion is false, and to the degree that environmentalism resembles a religion, it must be false too." Both environmentalists and

---

2 A brief review of modern climate science might begin in 1824 with Joseph Fourier, who accurately predicted the existence of a greenhouse effect. Then, in 1856, Eunice Foote correctly identified carbon dioxide and water vapor as critical elements in retaining heat. John Tyndall issued a first warning about the greenhouse effect in the 1860s, followed by Svante Arrhenius in 1896. Scientists built on these foundational studies in the twentieth century, beginning with Guy Callendar, Milutin Milankovic, and Gilbert Plass. Understanding and accurately predicting climate change is one of the most impressive scientific breakthroughs in history. See https://climate.nasa.gov /evidence.

anti-environmentalists are working from a set of values, and those values often have religious roots. That fact doesn't make them right—or wrong. But it does make self-righteous dogmatism a temptation on all sides.

6. *You'll destroy the economy!* With this response, dissenters reveal the degree to which the global economic system is more real and significant to them than the ecological systems in which the economic system exists. Telling them that their economy is destroying our ecology doesn't seem to register with the same degree of intensity. But even so, in the short run, eight billion people do depend on the economy in its current form to one degree or another for their survival, and if it is severely disrupted, billions will suffer. (And if it is not severely disrupted, billions will also suffer.)

7. *You can't exclude the poor from the fossil-fuel bonanza!* This line of thinking often has an "own the libs" tone to it, as if to say, "You liberals are supposed to care about the poor. Do you want to exclude the world's poor, especially in Africa, Asia, and Latin America, from sharing in the economic development that comes from fossil fuels? Aren't you being classist and racist if you tell them they can't have the luxury you enjoy in Europe or North America?" This argument conveniently ignores the billions that are being excluded from fossil-fueled prosperity right now. It often prepares the way for a population argument: the best way to slow human population growth is to help the poor gain greater affluence, and the quickest way to affluence is through fossil-fuel wealth. Better to wait until populations are stable or declining to try to shift away from fossil fuels, they say. So for now, drill, baby, drill, and deal with the consequences later. The shortsightedness and insincerity of this argument do not negate its spoonful of moral truth: that we do need to show great care for the poorest during this turbulent time. Meanwhile, we must remember that global overheating is already devastating the world's poor, and their suffering will multiply if we stay on our current path.

8. *Innovation has always saved us in the past!* It's quite common among climate dissenters to disparage the dire warnings of Thomas Robert Malthus in 1798 or Paul and Anne Ehrlich in 1968. Climate dissenters then commonly point to how technological innovations defanged those warnings. For example, fossil-fuel based fertilizers and pesticides produced an agricultural revolution that reduced hunger and increased population. They fail to point out the degree to which these population-enhancing innovations have also created new threats, even as they reduced some old threats. As we go forward, technological innovations are going to do the same: they will provide solutions, and those solutions are going to create new problems too. By the way, regarding Malthus, it's good to remember the wry insight of economist Herman Daly: "Malthus has been buried many times, and Malthusian scarcity with him. But . . . anyone who has to be reburied so often cannot be entirely dead."[3]

9. *We can adapt!* A number of dissenters argue, "It will cost more money to avoid climate change than it will to adapt to it, so let's save the trouble and expense now and just adapt later." Their assertion is demonstrably false, but like many popular falsehoods, it has staying power.[4] Its advocates point to how humans have adapted to remarkable changes in the past, and they label those who take climate change seriously as "alarmists" who don't have enough faith in human ingenuity. They're right about one thing: adaptation will be part of any survival strategy, but to take an either/or approach to a both/and predicament is . . . not smart.

Again, each of these nine lines of dissent has at least a small teaspoon of truth. We must be careful about how we induct our children into the reality of our civilization's overshoot. We must guard against media exaggeration and sensationalism . . . whoever does the

---

3 From *Steady-State Economics* (Island Press, 1991), p. 43.
4 See https://www.npr.org/2022/04/07/1091258821/the-future-cost-of-climate-inaction
-2-trillion-a-year-says-the-government.

sensationalizing. We must expect that some of our current understandings will be validated by further research, and some will be corrected by further research, and that is how science is supposed to work. We should be suspicious about the corrupting role of money . . . whoever is being corrupted. We have to face the consequences of destabilizing the economy at the wrong time and in the wrong way, because doing so could cause unintended and unnecessary suffering, which could then cause a strong backlash against further climate-related action. We have to face how easy it is to unintentionally harm the world's most vulnerable people even in our sincere attempts to protect them from future harm. We can't underestimate the importance of technological innovation at this critical moment, nor can we afford to misspend billions of dollars or euros or yen on unworkable solutions, especially when that money is needed for more constructive investments.

I think dissenters to the scientific consensus are, at their best, saying something we all need to hear: yes, climate alarmism and reactionary climate activism can be dangerous. But we must remind ourselves that we face an even greater threat from climate denial and insufficient climate action. In between the two extremes, there is a lot of work for good people to do, as wisely and carefully as we can.

I have to admit that my skin crawled as I read and listened to many of the climate skeptics. For example, a popular skeptic's argument went like this: "It's a scientific fact: plants love carbon dioxide. We should too! We humans aren't villains as the climate alarmists say! We are heroes for releasing so much carbon dioxide to benefit plants. We are the ones who are greening the planet! But those evil climate alarmists are painting us as villains!" That kind of talk can easily be exposed as dangerously misleading.[5] But as recent political developments around the world have shown, an appealing lie often has more power and allure than an inconvenient truth.

I must also admit: I felt the allure. "How could anyone resist this

5 See, for example, Jean-Marie Questiaux's "REPLY To: Should We Celebrate Carbon Dioxide? By Dr. Patrick Moore," available here: https://www.linkedin.com/pulse /reply-should-we-celebrate-carbon-dioxide-dr-patrick-moore-questiaux. See also Cristobal Spielmann's piece on fact-checking, available here: https://climate360news .lmu.edu/how-to-tell-if-theres-climate-misinformation-on-your-feed/.

kind of propaganda?" I wondered. "Reality is tough to swallow, and this climate skepticism is as sweet and fatty as a jelly donut."

Immersing myself in the climate-skeptic literature plunged me into a new depth of doom. When skeptics exaggerate and mislead in one direction, won't climate realists be tempted to up the heat of their rhetoric in an equal and opposite way? Won't this overheated rhetoric play into our preexisting condition of political hostility, where people retreat into opposing echo chambers, where they hear what they already think, again and again and again, further hardening the categories of our polarized, hyper-tense populace? Won't our overheating planetary climate and our overheating social climate click into their own feedback loop, driving us ever deeper into collective reactivity and stupidity? Writer and philosopher Roy Scranton captured the paradox:

> Alerting people to the problem and educating broad audiences has proven ineffective against deliberately sown confusion, deep scientific ignorance, widespread apathy, and outright hostility. . . . Warning people of the danger we face only seems to sow anxiety and fear . . . and to provoke not restraint, but scapegoating and aggression.[6]

In this context, Scranton captured my sense of powerlessness (remember that word?) in a nine-word question: "What can mere words do for a doomed civilization?" Tough *words* for a writer—or reader—to read.

If you sat next to me in seat 3B on this flight through ecological and social turbulence, and if you told me that facing the future *really* scares you, here's what I'd say:

I'm scared too.

It's going to be a bumpy ride to an unknown ultimate destination. We can't expect it to be smooth. We're all going to have to face dimensions of reality we don't want to face, namely, that we humans aren't as rational as we think we are, and even at our best, our rationality is limited.

---

6 From *We're Doomed. Now What?* (Soho, 2018).

People around us are going to panic. Some are going to shout at the flight attendants for suspending in-flight service, as if the turbulence is a hoax. Some are going to start shouting to hang the captain, as if she's piloting us into turbulence for spite. Some of us are going to lapse into panic and start screaming, "We're all going to die!" as if that will help the situation. Some preacher is going to start yelling: "This turbulence is God's punishment on the people in exit rows! Join my religion now, or perish!"

Count on it: any stupid thing that can be said will be said.

Every conspiracy theory and lie that can be uttered will be uttered. And repeated.

Every inane political distraction and deflection that can be foisted on a public rendered gullible by stress will be foisted. Don't be too surprised or shocked; that will just waste your precious emotional energy.

Some people will show their worst selves in this turbulence. Don't react to them. They're like toddlers in a temper tantrum or drunks in a bar fight. They're out of control. If you start yelling back, you'll mirror their frenzy or fury, and there will be one more person mirroring the worst of our humanity.

It's going to be a bumpy flight. There will be no peace in this cabin until we land. We may not make it, but we may. The landing may be the scariest part of all.

Between here and there, our only choice, here in seats 3A and 3B, is how we respond. Will we get sucked into the panic and collective stupidity, or will we find a way to maintain some semblance of balance, maturity, and sanity? There are two things beyond our control: the external turbulence outside this aircraft and the internal turbulence among our fellow passengers. But here are two things we have some power over: our own individual behavior and how we support one another through this flight. We can choose to huddle together, here and now, to create an island of sanity and mutual support, even as all around us, stupidity levels rise like the oceans and temperatures.

So let's focus on what we can control to at least some degree. You and I, in 3A and 3B, can try to help each other get through this, one day, one moment at a time. Whatever the pilot, copilot, flight attendants, and other passengers do, here in 3A and 3B, we can try to let our best selves shine. It only takes two or three of us to create a little island of composure in a climate of chaos.

During times of doom, people become what they never before imagined. Many are sucked into a black hole of shared, mutually confirming stupidity. Some become blamers, shamers, thieves, thugs, criminals, vigilantes, terrorists, traitors, escapists, hoarders, panic-stricken crybabies, cultic conspiracy theorists, scammers, or craven cowards. Others become heroes, saints, resisters, martyrs, organizers, problem solvers, protectors, community builders, non-anxious presences, leaders, healers, and old-fashioned good neighbors. There may be times when we have to make our way alone, but finding or forming a little huddle of just two or three or five or fifty can make all the difference.

We could be that for each other, like strangers sitting in seats 3A and 3B. *It only takes two or three to build an island of sanity in a world falling apart.* And it only takes one to reach out as my seatmate did that day, risking vulnerability, asking for help, asking for connection. Somebody has to say the first word.

If you are reading this book with others, you have already taken an important step in this process, and it's not too late to pull some people together for a shared reading and learning experience. The *All We Can Save* anthology (a book I highly recommend) has led to over a thousand "leaderful" reading communities in over forty countries, some in-person and some online, and they and other organizations offer a wide array of helpful resources.[7]

In addition to creating reading circles for mutual learning and support, now is the time for us to build deeper connections with our geographical neighbors. We can do what my neighbor in 3B did: tell our neighbors we're nervous about what is coming, and if they share our concern, we can establish connection and trust now, so we know we aren't alone when troubles intensify. If we take neighborhood walks and get in the habit of meeting and sharing contact information with neighbors, if we throw neighborhood picnics and parties, and if we

---

7 See https://www.allwecansave.earth/circles and https://www.climatepsychology alliance.org/index.php/find-support.

join or form existing neighborhood organizations, we can invite others into these conversations.

We can bring our growing awareness to all the local groups we belong to: our companies, our gyms, our churches, synagogues, or mosques, our libraries, our nonprofits, our PTAs. If we have a functioning local government, we can get to know our elected and appointed leaders, asking them if they have begun to develop plans to deal with an uncertain future. We can volunteer to help.

All of us who hold leadership positions can bring our concerns to the organizations we serve. As a former pastor, I would make a special plea to faith leaders in this regard.[8] We can create spaces for imagining and talking about what to do now, and what to do when the flight gets bumpier and we're all tempted to panic. Canadian policy expert Seth Klein suggests six markers of leaders and groups that are treating our situation with the urgency it deserves: 1) they spend what they need to spend, 2) they create new institutions or structures to get the job done, 3) they shift from incentive-based and voluntary policies to mandatory measures, 4) they tell the truth about the severity of the crisis and communicate a sense of urgency, 5) they leave no one behind, and 6) they understand that indigenous rights and leadership are essential.[9] We can't assume somebody else at a higher pay grade will do this work for us. We must assume it's up to each of us, at whatever level we have influence. Then, we can start sharing what we are learning about creating spaces of mutual support with others.

That's the preparedness we need in these times: not people storing up "50 Day Survival Food" buckets they bought from a guy on cable TV, and then amassing enough guns and ammunition to kill their desperate neighbors who want to steal their stash of dried food buckets.[10] If that's the kind of hostile future they prepare for, it's probably the

---

8 As for first steps I would recommend, here are two: first, have your congregational leaders read Jim Antal's *Climate Church, Climate World* (Rowman & Littlefield, 2018), and second, make your building available for climate support groups such as these: https://www.allwecansave.earth/starting-with-circles and https://www.climatepsychologyalliance.org/.

9 See https://www.climateemergencyunit.ca/emergencymarkersframework/.

10 See https://www.npr.org/sections/thesalt/2015/12/03/456677535/apocalypse-chow-we-tried-televangelist-jim-bakkers-survival-food.

future they'll get. If the only people who survive are people like this, frankly, it won't be much of a world to live in. Those hostile survivalist values—build a wall around me and my circle, and to hell with everyone and everything outside—will guarantee a repeat performance of our current overshoot trajectory.

That's why we need people reaching out and building huddles of sanity and mutual kindness, preparing to share and support each other when turbulence comes and we're all tempted to be sucked into collective stupidity.

When flight attendants give their safety spiel, they always advise putting on your own oxygen mask first, and then helping others. Self-preparation is not to the *exclusion of* helping others: it is *for the purpose of* group cooperation. It's the same when they talk about "the unlikely event of a water landing." They tell you where to locate your individual personal flotation device and then where to locate and deploy the life rafts. The goal in an emergency is not every person for himself. The goal is to get through it together. *It only takes two or three* to get started.

Dear Reader,

In this chapter, I contrasted collective intelligence and collective stupidity, realizing that in times of doom, we will be pulled toward the latter unless we choose consciously to seek the former.

The chapter begins with a story about a young man who had the honesty to admit he was afraid, and whose vulnerability created connection. Can you think of a similar experience, where people were brought together by one person's vulnerability?

How did you feel about my choice of strong words like "stupidity" and "ignorance"?

I did my best to show that even bad ideas have allure, and part of their allure is a spoonful of truth. Which of the nine examples interested you the most, and why?

Respond to this statement: "It only takes two or three to build an island of sanity in a world falling apart."

The end of the chapter includes a number of concrete suggestions for building islands of sanity now, before things get a lot worse (which could happen faster than we think). Which of them do you feel motivated to put into practice?

In this chapter I wrote, "During times of doom, people become what they never before imagined. Many are sucked into a black hole of shared, mutually confirming stupidity." The first epigraph for the next chapter provides a chilling example.

16

When Life Gets Tough, We Get Tougher

I'm starting to think about having to eat my neighbors. You think I like sizing up my neighbor, how I'm going to haul him up by a chain and chop his ass up? I'll do it. . . . I'm ready to hang them up and gut them and skin them and chop them up. . . . I will eat your leftist ass like corn on the cob, I'm ready. I'll barbecue your ass flat. I will eat you. I'll drink your blood. You understand that? . . . Let me tell you something right now. I swear to God, if it's the last thing I do I'm going to get my hands around your throat.

—Popular far-right radio host Alex Jones[1]

I REALLY DON'T CARE. DO U?
—Former first lady Melania Trump's jacket[2]

The other day, someone asked me, "Should I prepare? Should I stockpile? Should I get a gun or whatever?" I said, "I was a sharpshooter in the military. I'm a skilled marksman. I can use lots of different weapons. But I don't have a weapon. I would rather die with my neighbors than protect my stuff from my neighbors, thank you very much."

—Eco-theologian Reverend Michael Dowd[3]

It may be hard for an egg to turn into a bird: it would be a jolly sight harder for a bird to learn to fly while remaining an egg. We are like eggs at present. And you cannot go on indefinitely being just an ordinary, decent egg. We must be hatched or go bad.

—British writer and professor C. S. Lewis

---

1 See https://kutv.com/news/nation-world/video-alex-jones-in-detail-describes-killing -neighbors-to-feed-to-his-kids/, and https://www.youtube.com/watch?v=rfZcKCIcug8/.
2 See https://www.cnn.com/2018/10/13/politics/melania-trump-jacket-i-really-dont -care-do-u/index.html/.
3 See https://www.youtube.com/watch?v=yafao_FWJ8A/.

One of my granddaughters was crying. She was scared because her parents were going out for a date, and I was the babysitter. She loved me and trusted me, but look, I wasn't her mom or dad.

Back when I was a dad of small children, I probably would have told her to stop crying and be brave. I'm ashamed to admit it, but I might have tried to shame her by saying, "Come on! Don't be a baby!" But I had learned through a book written by some friends (yes, way later than I should have) that telling children (or anyone) not to feel what they feel doesn't generally work out well. Telling stressed children to stop feeling what they feel puts impossible pressure on them when they're already past an emotional breaking point.[4]

I felt in her tears an expression of a fundamental human need, the need for security and attachment. So I offered connection and reassurance: "Oh, sweetheart, this is a really tough situation, I know. I remember how I felt when my parents went out when I was your age. So I feel terrible that you miss them and I'm here with you. I won't leave you. I'll do my best to help us have a really good time together until your parents come home later tonight."

I added: "It's really tough being a kid sometimes, isn't it?" She nodded and wiped her eyes. "It really, *really* is," she replied. A new flood of tears flowed, but I think they were different this time: I think they were tears of relief. Now she felt downright understood, which made her feel a little bit safer and a little less alone, which made the absence of her parents feel a little less acute.

"There's only one thing to do when life is tough like this," I said. Her eyes got big, like she was about to be let in on one of the deep secrets of the universe. "When life gets tough, *we get tougher,*" I said. And to my surprise, I noticed a tiny crack of a smile form on the edges of her lips. Then I added, "And we eat ice cream."

A few times over the course of the evening, I would say, "When life gets tough . . . ," and she would complete the sentence.

---

4 See *The Six Needs of Every Child*, by Amy and Jeffrey Olrick (Zondervan 2020). Also see their podcast, *Growing Connected*, available here: https://www.growingconnected .com/the-6-needs/.

Frankly, I think we're all a lot like my granddaughter these days, and I expect we'll feel this way even more so in the years ahead. We will need repeated encouragement as we cope with situations that push us to and beyond a breaking point. Whichever of the four scenarios plays out, tough times are ahead, and we will either break down under pressure, or we will break through. We will either get tougher or get destroyed.

When I say "tougher," I mean "capable of meeting deteriorating conditions with increasing capacities."

Sadly, many adults think that personal growth is only for kids. They assume that they arrive at the peak of their capacities in late adolescence or early adulthood, and then spend the rest of their lives either coasting at that level or (truth be told) slowly deteriorating. At their eighteenth, twenty-first, or thirtieth birthday, it's as if they're given an invisible certificate of entitlement on which is written, "From this moment forward, reality owes the bearer of this certificate a guaranteed lifetime of normalcy that demands no more strength, intelligence, or virtue than is presently possessed." The "waking up" we considered in chapter 1 was, among other things, awakening to the reality that life offers no such guarantees, especially for people like us who have been born, through no choice or fault of our own, at the beginning of the end of civilization as we have known it. Instead of a certificate of entitlement, we need a student ID card that says, "This individual is enrolled full-time in the school of life, in the adulthood program." Along with it, we would receive a big poster to hang on our wall, on which is written this aphorism: "As the child is to the adult, so is the adult to the sage."[5] In other words, if you think you're done growing up, you have another think coming. In fact, if you don't keep maturing in wisdom, you will not remain at your current level of awesome. Like an egg that doesn't hatch, your awesome level will—I'm sad to say this—decline along with civilization.

This openness, this receptivity to lifelong learning and growth, is what Zen Buddhists mean when they speak of *shoshin*, the beginner's

---

5 See John Vervaeke's lecture "What Is Wisdom?" available here: https://youtu.be /WpVVcVRkLok/.

mind. It's what Jesus meant when he said, "Unless you become like little children, you shall not enter the kingdom of heaven." He wasn't urging adults to regress toward childish ignorance or uncritical trust: only a demagogue would want that. He was inviting arrogant, complacent, or misguided adults who think they have arrived to humbly realize that they are only beginners in adulthood, and they have a lifetime of adult growth ahead of them. His language of being "born again" offered the same invitation: to become beginners again, with the insatiable curiosity of children who know that there's a lot they don't know, and aren't ashamed to admit it.[6] Bob Dylan brought a similar message in 1964: You'll either learn to swim or "sink like a stone," he said, "for the times they are a-changin'."

So let's briefly consider seven deteriorating conditions that we can expect to swim in (or sink in) for the foreseeable future, whatever our age, as the drama of overshoot continues to play out.

First, we have entered a gilded age of misinformation, when liars are going to lie, cheaters are going to cheat, propagandists are going to distort, ideologues are going to suppress, bigots are going to inflict cruelty, scammers are going to scam, and click counters are going to sensationalize. In times like these, we need to become *tough-minded* as never before. If we have lazy, flimsy, foolish minds, we will be sitting ducks for deception. We will need to train our minds for wisdom as athletes train their bodies for the Olympics.

To become wiser, you don't just learn: you learn to keep learning in deeper and broader ways. You don't just expand your knowledge: you expand your capacity to think. You strengthen the teamwork and collective intelligence of the internal board of directors of You, Incorporated, as we considered in chapter 3. You become savvy about how logical fallacies and cognitive biases can lead you and others into folly. (See appendix 6.) You become savvy about how thinking is a social

---

6 In the lone Gospel passage (John 3) where Jesus uses the term "born again," he is in a conversation with an adult who approaches him "man to man," not with a humble question, but with a confident statement that begins with "We know." The "we" suggests he is part of an adult in-group who have arrived. Jesus replies with his enigmatic statement about being born again, which so confuses the man that he is suddenly operating out of a beginner's mind, full of questions. In fact, in the brief conversation that follows, he never utters a statement again, only questions.

act, which leaves everyone susceptible to groupthink . . . not only *their* kind of groupthink, but also *our* kind. You develop the skills of contemplation, where you learn to observe your own observation, climb out of your own mental ruts, detach from your habitual reactions, understand the limitations of your perspective, and widen the aperture of your awareness.

Just as children need wise adults to lead them toward adulthood, adults need wiser adults, sages, people who can lead them on the path of wisdom. This, by the way, is the right use of religion: healthy religion exposes us to the deep wisdom of sages, past and present, so we can learn to imitate their way of life—so we can live in our time with the same creative insight they modeled in their time. Unhealthy religion does the opposite. It draws us into a constricted chamber of rigid elites who endlessly echo conventional interpretations of dead sagely founders. Too often, religious leaders sincerely believe they are being faithful to those founders, but in fact their attitude and behavior betray the creative and groundbreaking example the founders set. Instead of continuing their bold, living legacy, they build and manage their founders' institutional tombs. In the years ahead I expect we will see uglier expressions of religion than we've seen in a long time, and that ugliness will wake up others to embody more beautiful expressions too.

Second, our current situation is a petri dish for fear and mean-spiritedness. It takes moral courage to stand against scapegoating, to risk violence by standing with those who are being scapegoated. We often call this kind of moral toughness *kindness* or *compassion*. Interestingly, there was only one time in the Gospels where Jesus used the phrase "Go and learn what this means": when he quoted Hosea's words that God does not desire religious bloodshed, but rather, God desires the opposite: compassion.

Third, just as vultures gather wherever there is the smell of death, during times of decline and struggle, demagogues, authoritarians, scammers, and other deceivers smell fear and resentment; they see an opportunity to gain wealth and power by exploiting those emotions. If we don't want to join that race to the bottom, we will have to pursue *strength of character*. When others tolerate deceit, we become even more dedicated to honesty and authenticity. When others are so desperate to win that they brazenly cheat, we become even more dedicated to justice and integrity, even in small things. When others stoop to theft, we become more generous. When others stoke fear and resentment, we radiate courage and grace.

Fourth, we are entering a time of increasing fragmentation where everyone will be tempted to turn on everyone. So, in addition to developing tough minds, kind hearts, and strength of character, we will need to develop the skills of *interdependence*. Some will fall prey to dependence; they will find security in dictators, autocrats, and cult leaders. Some will flee into independence, building survival shelters surrounded by high walls and razor wire, behind which they wait with their AR-15s, dreaming about which of their neighbors they will kill and eat when their own buckets of nutritional survival powder are empty. "I really don't care, do you?" will be their narcissistic motto. Others will follow a strategy of counter-dependence, always finding an enemy to oppose, battling to the end against some enemy, real or concocted.

Interdependence is a tougher path, tougher but better. It integrates the previous three strengths of wisdom, kindness, and character so that old barriers of race, class, religion, and politics can be transcended, and so that diverse, resilient, and collaborative communities can be built. Those who aim for interdependence know that the only way through tough times is *together*.

Fifth, the tough times ahead will constantly suck us down toward despair. To face and endure that despair with wisdom, kindness, character, and interdependence, we will need courage, especially *the courage to differ graciously*. When we are intimidated into silence, afraid to speak our truth, we lose heart. That's why my sagely friend David Dark says we have to claim "the right to not remain silent." So we learn to stand up and speak up, self-reporting our unfolding experience of waking up, welcoming reality, grieving, and all the rest. In my experience, people who speak up with courage and grace are non-attacking, non-defensive, non-judgmental, non-shaming, and non-directive. They speak what they feel and say what they see, recalling Edgar's last words in Shakespeare's most relevant play for these times,

King Lear. That integration of courage and grace is what I have aimed for (imperfectly, I'm sure) in these pages. Each of us can find ways in our daily lives to show the courage to not remain silent, the courage to differ graciously, the courage to stand for what we believe is right . . . regardless of the outcome. (See appendix 3 for some conversation prompts.) If you set a courageous and gracious example, others will be inspired to follow.

Sixth, in the tough period after peak civilization, we're going to need the toughness of *agility*. We're going to have to accept that constant change is here to stay. Millions of us are going to have to relocate. Millions of us are going to have to change jobs, or change the way we do our jobs, or change our very idea of what a job is. Millions of us are going to change our diet, our recreation, our hobbies, our celebrations. Some changes will feel like losses; others will bring surprising gains.

Finally, to grow stronger in wisdom, kindness, character, interdependence, courage, and agility, we'll have to discover new depths of the human spirit. Call it religion, call it spirituality, call it contemplation or *centeredness* . . . whatever we call it, we're going to need it. As the unsustainable and flimsy trappings of religion fall away, more and more of us will have the chance to discover the deep core, the strong spine and vigorous heart of our spiritual traditions. In my experience, the more we migrate toward that deep heart of spirituality at the core of our traditions, the more we'll find resonance with people of other traditions who are experiencing the same inward migration.

So much to learn, so little time. But as both Joni Mitchell and Marvin Gaye sang, life is for learning.

When my granddaughter's parents got home late that night, they were pleased to find her sleeping soundly. She discovered that she could manage her fear. She discovered that she was capable of more than she thought. She grew up a little through her struggle. And so did I.

I believe the same can be true for all of us, whatever our age. When life gets tough, we get tougher. (And a little ice cream helps.)

Dear Reader,

In this chapter, I offer seven specific ways in which we will need to grow tougher in turbulent times. Review them, and pick one or two that ring true most strongly with you these days. Explain why.

Respond to this saying: "As the child is to the adult, so is the adult to the sage."

Think of the beloved children in your life. Imagine if one of them came to you crying and said, "I'm really scared about what's happening to the Earth, and especially climate change, and all the people saying mean and hateful things, and I wonder if I'm going to be safe." What might you say to demonstrate empathy, assure them of your supportive presence, and give them the confidence that if life gets tough, you and they together can get tougher?

PART 4

SETTING
FREE

A Path of Agile Engagement

17

Beauty Abounds

To reclaim the awe of our child selves, to allow ourselves to be taken by the beauty of a thing, allows goodness to take up the space it's often denied in our interior worlds. . . .

—Black liturgist and author Cole Arthur Riley[1]

FRODO: I can't do this, Sam.

SAM: I know. It's all wrong. By rights we shouldn't even be here. But we are. It's like in the great stories, Mr. Frodo. The ones that really mattered. Full of darkness, and danger, they were. And sometimes you didn't want to know the end, because how could the end be happy? How could the world go back to the way it was when so much bad had happened? But in the end, it's only a passing thing, this shadow. Even darkness must pass. A new day will come. And when the sun shines, it'll shine out the clearer. Those were the stories that stayed with you. That meant something. Even if you were too small to understand why. But I think, Mr. Frodo, I do understand. I know now. Folk in those stories had lots of chances of turning back, only they didn't. They kept going. Because they were holding on to something.

FRODO: What are we holding on to, Sam?

SAM: That there's some good in this world, Mr. Frodo . . . and it's worth fighting for.

—*The Lord of the Rings: The Two Towers*[2]

We will need the bravest of writers. . . . They will need to see beauty despite the destruction, experience deep sorrow, and find that incorruptible truth amid the growing dust storms. . . . Their stories will tell of all life

---

1 *This Here Flesh: Spirituality, Liberation, and the Stories That Make Us* (Convergent, 2022).
2 This version is from Peter Jackson's 2002 film adaptation of J. R. R. Tolkien's classic book.

being of equal value, how the light shines not just on ourselves (and our own personal address) but on the whole.

—Waanyi aboriginal writer Alexis Wright[3]

I didn't become a news junkie all at once. I got sucked in gradually with good reasons. As a writer/activist, I needed to keep track of the latest injustices so I could activate people to oppose them. I needed to keep track of the latest political or ecological outrage so I could post about it on social media, or show up somewhere to protest, and somehow use my platform as a writer to help sway public opinion.

I still believe in all those things. I still do them. I still watch and read the news, too, but less than before, and differently than before.

I guess I'm no longer a news junkie. It's one of the things from which I've been set free by the experience of doom.

I've accepted the fact that there are two primary news stories that matter in our current situation. Only two. First is the ongoing story of humanity's bumpy descent toward collapse, an inevitability—sooner or later—for a civilization in overshoot. This story is not just about atmospheric gases. It's about our toxic political atmosphere and hot air from the pundit-sphere. It's not just about rising global temperatures and extreme storms; it's about our lukewarm spiritual climate and overheated religious extremism. It's not just about rising sea levels; it's about rising levels of economic inequality and racial injustice. It's not just about melting ice; it's about bonds of connection dissolving among us. It's a sad story, full of lies and deceit.

This story dominates the daily news with a million headlines about craven politicians, crazed shooters, greedy corporate titans, record profits and record temperatures, failing institutions, religious scandal, exploitation of the poor, celebrity distractions, and destruction of the Earth. Over recent years, I've come to realize that this kind of *news* isn't new at all. It's the same old decadence and denial, day after day; different headlines, but same old ugly story. When I'm immersed in

---

3 From "The Inward Migration in Apocalyptic Times," *Emergence Magazine* (October 26, 2022), available here: https://emergencemagazine.org/essay/the-inward-migration-in-apocalyptic-times/.

the ugly news of collapse, I come away feeling the same every time: *ugliness is everywhere.*

The second story is different. In one sense, it's older; in another sense, it's always new. It's the ongoing story of beauty unfolding in the world. It seldom appears on the *news,* but amazing stories of beautiful news appear every day if we know where to look.

For example, not long ago, I was visiting a relative, and I was working on this book from her guest room. I sat at a little desk beside a window, and outside the window was a white pine tree. Among its branches an American robin built her nest over the course of three days. From an intimate vantage point less than a meter away, I watched her weave grass and mud into a durable home, an act of love for her future babies. I watched her shape the rounded cup that would hold her precious blue eggs using the roundness of her rust-red breast.

I imagined all the different kinds of nests birds build: weaver birds and orioles dangling intricate globes from trees in Africa and North America; burrowing owls and kingfishers digging deep burrows where they lay eggs on a simple mat of moss or grass; Canada geese creating downy mounds beside a river; bluebirds and woodpeckers finding or making a hollow in a tree for their progeny; cliff swallows constructing a neighborhood of mud condominiums under a rock overhang. Millions of birds build millions of nests every spring, and each one is unique, amazing, a story of love, skill, and goodness in the world. Many humans are up to a world of mischief, I think, but the birds are still being awesome. Each bird I see—really see—is an evangelist of the beautiful news. I see a bird and know in my bones: *beauty abounds.* Suddenly I start seeing beauty popping up everywhere.

I took my morning walk a few hours ago, and the same two words accompanied me. Some days I focus on sight . . . bold flowers, subtle patterns of light and shadow, shades of tree bark, change and consistency. *Beauty abounds.* Some days I focus on hearing . . . a cooing dove, a dog barking from inside a house, wind whispering in pine trees, a neighbor talking to her toddler. *Beauty abounds.* Today I focused on scent . . . smoke from a distant wildfire (essential to our local Everglades ecosystem), the smell of bacon from someone's breakfast, a frangipani in full, fragrant bloom just upwind from me. *Beauty abounds.*

I see it when I look at people . . . a husband hugging his wife good-bye at the airport, a mom feeding crackers to her toddler in a park, an elderly lesbian couple holding hands at a music festival, a jewelry maker displaying her art at a county fair, a roomful of people busting some impressive moves to "Uptown Funk" at a party. *Beauty abounds.*

During my years as a news junkie, I found myself getting a strange high from the latest ugliness report. Each time I indulged, I fanned the flames of something unhealthy . . . my moral superiority, or resentment, or fear, or despair, or desolation, or us-versus-them hostilities. I recently read an article by a group of scholars that suggested what may have been going on. Ugly news caused stress which likely reduced my levels of the hormone serotonin, leading to less happiness and more depression. At the same time, by inducing fear and anger and by driving me for solidarity in an in-group and against an out-group, ugly news increased my dependence on other mood-altering hormones like dopamine, endorphins, oxytocin, and adrenaline, creating a vicious cycle. The less happiness I felt, the more I needed likes on my social media as rewards for posting outrage about an outrage, or the more I needed to feel a deep belonging to an outraged in-group, or the more I needed to fight with somebody about something. I felt I was being sucked into a vortex where all other stories became insignificant: I was drawn irresistibly to ugliness. I saw it everywhere. I was becoming a connoisseur of the ugly, and maybe even an ugliness junkie.[4]

As I've been sensitized to this process in myself, I see it everywhere. When I walk into a home, office, or restaurant, I see cable news stations delivering a constant injection of outrage. When I get in the car of a friend, a radio talk show tells him whom to fear, whom to hate,

---

4 From *Deep Adaptation* (Polity Press, 2021), edited by Jem Bendell and Rupert Read, p. 171. The authors of chapter 6, "Unconscious Addictions," make it clear that they are using the language of neurobiology loosely, somewhat metaphorically, knowing that emotions are more complex than can be explained by any single neurotransmitter or hormone. The process they describe illustrates an ancient Hebrew proverb: "The one who is full loathes honey from the comb, but to the hungry, even what is bitter tastes sweet" (Proverbs 27:7).

whom to blame, creating an in-group of moral superiority and an out-group of moral bankruptcy. In an airport, I see nearly everyone checking their favorite sites and apps on their cell phones. I wonder how many are keeping up to date on the latest ugliness. I wonder how many of them turn off critical thinking whenever they turn on their preferred media device. I wonder how many, in the absence of happiness, are satisfying their need for intensity of emotion by seeking outrage, resentment, superiority, and conflict.

I think you'll agree: the internal realities we construct in our minds actually exist in our minds, ugly or beautiful, false or true. They shape our internal values which influence our external behavior. We tend to make the world around us resemble the world within us. Based on our focus, *ugliness is everywhere* or *beauty abounds*.

Alexis Wright is an aboriginal writer from Australia. As an indigenous person, she understands that the end of the world has been happening for centuries for indigenous people. She understands that both colonizers and colonized need to be liberated from the mindset of colonization. The first step toward freedom, she says, is to decolonize or de-capitalize the mind, so you can "develop strengths that will not be defined by how others believe you should think." She calls this liberation "sovereignty of mind":

> When you move into the realm of your own sovereignty of mind by shielding yourself from the kinds of interferences that rob you of the ability to think straight, that sap your spirit, or block you from seeing and making your own judgment, then you are able to govern your own spirit and imagination.

The journey to sovereignty of mind requires an *inward migration*, where we in a sense become refugees from our external nation, culture, economy, and civilization, even though we still live within its borders. We withdraw inwardly. We cross an internal border. We withdraw our consent from what is going on around us based on a story and set of values we no longer love. And while our neighbors carry on buying and selling, burning and profiting, extracting and exploiting, celebrating record-high profits and trying to ignore record-high temperatures, we create what Seamus Heaney called "a country of the mind."

When I heard Alexis Wright speak of this inward migration, I felt I gained new insight into Jesus and his oft-quoted but rarely understood term "kingdom of God." "The kingdom of God is within you," he said (Luke 17:21). He described the innermost room of your consciousness (Matthew 6:6), where you go to think differently, to sort out your desires and hopes authentically. When you learn how to make that inward migration, that spiritual migration, you find yourself looking for others who have also gone there, who have discovered a freedom and sovereignty of mind. No doubt, when Jesus traveled from town to town and spoke, everyone who had made the internal migration felt that Jesus was a kindred spirit. "Yes, he gets it! I thought I was the only one!" they would say to themselves. They would feel magnetically drawn to him, as if he were the fellow citizen of an invisible country where people spoke the same inner language.

Then they would hear him say, "Wherever two or three of you gather in my name, there I am," and they might understand him to say, "Listen, I understand that you are outnumbered. I understand that so many people around you have been sucked into the story of ugliness. I understand that you are learning to live by a different story where beauty abounds. You don't need me physically present to tell the beautiful story. You can tell it yourselves. Even just two or three of you can gather together, embodying my way of being in the world. You can be cells of resistance, outposts of transformation, seedbeds of beauty."[5]

That is the best future I can imagine for organized religion in these dangerous times. Instead of helping nostalgic people inhabit bubbles of the past, religious communities can help people go forward on this inward migration toward sovereignty of mind, where in defiance of a

---

5 Thanks to Ash Barker for the seedbed image. See his new book *No Wastelands: How to Grow Seedbeds of Shalom in Your Neighborhood*. For more information, check out https://seedbeds.org/.

rising level of ugliness, people cultivate beauty . . . seeing it, creating it, savoring it.[6] Savoring beauty within will lead to beautiful outward action.

I think of my friends Michael Dowd and Connie Barlow. They see and understand the ugliness as well as anyone, but they aren't just complaining about it: they are doing something beautiful in response. Because they appreciate the abounding beauty of trees, they are helping trees "walk" north so they can escape overheating habitats and survive in cooler habitats.[7] Others focus on preserving birds, or butterflies, or sea turtles, or elephants, or frogs . . . and the prairies, forests, bogs, wetlands, watersheds, or jungles that support them. All around the world, small groups of people are becoming modern-day Noahs, preserving in their backyards and basements pockets of Eden so species that would surely go extinct otherwise will survive another day. They're adding to the beauty of the world by preserving the beauty of the world, beauty that will outlast them as individuals and that may outlast us as a civilization, or even us as a species.

While some focus on a species or an ecosystem, others focus on their communities and neighborhoods. I think of my friend Todd Wynward who with a small group of friends is seeking to model in their little corner of New Mexico what he (and I) hope people will do everywhere: defect from the ugly story of overshoot to the beautiful story of ecological, social, and spiritual harmony.[8]

I think of people working to save democracy from authoritarianism, kleptocracy, and oligarchy, like my friends Doug Pagitt and Sr. Simone Campbell. They're writing books, leading movements, creating podcasts, running for office, launching bus tours, putting up yard signs, posting on social media, throwing concerts and picnics, doing what they can. Others are working for equality for their neighbors where people are being scapegoated, vilified, excluded, and erased, even though doing so risks being targeted for the same treatment. Others, like my friends Shane and Katie Jo Claiborne, are literally turning guns

---

6 I explored this quest in my book *The Great Spiritual Migration* (Convergent, 2016).
7 For more on assisted tree migraton, see https://thegreatstory.org/climate-trees-legacy .html.
8 For more, see https://www.taostilt.org/.

into garden tools and building movements to transform violence.[9] Some gather in person to celebrate beautiful things, some gather online, and some do both, like my friend Gareth Higgins with the Porch community or my friend Diana Butler Bass with the Cottage community.[10] So many beautiful people doing so many beautiful things!

I'm not going to tell you their stories in detail here; thankfully, there are too many to tell, with more new stories emerging every minute, every day. Even so, I don't want to give you the wrong kind of uncomplicated hope that turns encouraging stories into permission slips for complacency. I don't want you to feel or think, "Good. Others are fixing things. I can return to my previously scheduled complacency."

Instead of asking you to imagine other people's beautiful stories born of their inward migration, I want to ask you to consider your own beautiful stories born of your own inward migration. I want you to imagine losing interest in the daily deluge of ugliness, in part because it's boring, in part because it's discouraging and overwhelming, in part because one of the best ways to strengthen it is to pay attention to it, and in part because one of the best ways to weaken it is to withdraw attention from it. That doesn't mean denying the ugliness, pretending it's not real, popular, powerful, and deadly. It just means that every time ugliness presents itself, after noticing it, grieving it, and feeling furious about it, you commit yourself to fighting the ugly with the practice of the beautiful and joyful, celebrating and adding to the beauty that abounds, the goodness in the world that is worth fighting for.

A few months ago, I was helping lead a retreat in the mountains of North Carolina. On our last night together, we did something I haven't done in way too long. We had a campfire. We roasted marshmallows and passed around popcorn. And around the campfire, people shared beauty.

One recited a Wendell Berry poem he had memorized. Another recited a Mary Oliver poem. A professional musician shared some songs

---

9 See, for example, https://sojo.net/media/watch-ar-15-taken-apart-and-turned-garden -tool.

10 See https://www.theporchcommunity.net/ and https://dianabutlerbass.com/the -cottage/.

(no amplification, just his voice and guitar over the crackling camp-fire), and then he handed his guitar to some amateur musicians. Several shared stories, some very touching, some very funny, some both. A few shared some jokes. Apart from the carbon released from a few oak logs, no fossil fuels were burned and no electricity was needed. We entertained each other for an evening. For free. It was delightful, beautiful, one of the happiest nights I can remember.

Beauty abounds, I thought.

If the coming decades are anywhere near as challenging as I expect them to be, there will be a flood of ugly news to report every day. That news can dominate your life. It can drain your life. And it can create a self-fulfilling prophecy.

That night around the campfire, I could imagine people gathering in small circles of beauty everywhere . . . on front porches, in living rooms, in forest clearings, around kitchen tables, even in churches and synagogues and mosques. They wouldn't require anything: no screens or earbuds, no pipe organs and stained glass windows, no smoke machines and amplifiers, no shouting preachers or fancy lighting or excellent graphics or even electricity.

Even if their governments collapsed and electric grids failed, even if the internet was monitored by authoritarian goons, even if public schools were commandeered to teach Orwellian propaganda . . . even then, they would gather and give one another life, in twos and threes and tens and twenties. They would speak truth. They would celebrate goodness. They would honor beauty, to see it as the real story, the aboriginal story, the eternal beautiful story. They would sing songs, recite poetry, tell stories, tell jokes . . . they would laugh and cry and dance and sit in silence, watching the sparks rise upward. And life would be beautiful in that circle. There would be joy unspeakable in that circle.[11] No matter what happened outside it.

---

11 This paragraph is an improvisation on words from the Hebrew prophet Habakkuk (3:17–19). For more on the cultivation of joy in a world falling apart, see Dr. Barbara Holmes's *Joy Unspeakable* (Fortress, 2017), and listen to the song of the same name by Voices of Fire, with Pharrell Williams, available here: https://www.youtube.com/watch?v=pWxDU0y5Awk.

I recall the words of Robin Wall Kimmerer, Potawatomi botanist and one of my favorite authors ever. As we saw in chapter 4, love and grief are inseparably connected, but "it is not enough to weep for our lost landscapes," she writes: "Even a wounded world is feeding us. Even a wounded world holds us, giving us moments of wonder and joy. I choose joy over despair. Not because I have my head in the sand, but because joy is what the earth gives me daily and I must return the gift."[12]

There is so much goodness in the world, goodness worth saving, my friends, abounding beauty worth living for today. Whatever happened yesterday, and whatever may happen tomorrow, or next year, or in the next century, today, right now, beauty abounds for those who learn to see it.

Dear Reader,

I mention getting a "strange high" from ugly news. Have you ever felt this high, or seen it in others? What is so alluring and addictive about ugly news?

Think of a beautiful place that you love. Try to put into words what you love about it. Try to visit it soon.

Think of "beautiful people doing beautiful things"—people you know about or have heard about. Share their stories. If possible, send them a note or message of encouragement and appreciation.

Near the end of this chapter, I share a story of sitting around a campfire with a group of people. If you were to plan such a gathering, where people come together with beauty to share, whom would you invite and why?

Experiment with using this "beauty abounds" mantra (or your own version of it) each day for at least a week or two. Notice what happens when you remember, with Tolkien's Frodo and Sam, that "there's some good in this world, Mr. Frodo . . . and it's worth fighting for."

---

12 From *Braiding Sweetgrass* (Milkweed, 2014).

18

What a Time to Be Alive

"I wish it need not have happened in my time," said Frodo.
"So do I," said Gandalf, "and so do all who live to see such times. But that is not for them to decide. All we have to decide is what to do with the time that is given us."
—*The Lord of the Rings: The Fellowship of the Ring*

Even in a world that's being shipwrecked, remain brave and strong.
—Twelfth-century polymath mystic Hildegard of Bingen

You have the biggest opportunity in all of human history to live an incredibly meaningful life. The actions that you take because of the accident of the time of your birth are of an order of magnitude in importance compared to most people who've lived before, because you are going to affect the future of life on Earth in fifty, five hundred, and five hundred thousand years by what you do in the next couple of decades. So no one is asking for an easy life. Really deep down we're asking for a meaningful life.
—Podcaster and political strategist Tom Rivett-Carnac, on what he tells his children about our current situation[1]

I was raised to avoid using "naughty words." In our family, "darn" and "gosh" were in the yellow zone of acceptability. In fact, I don't think I heard the *F*-word until I was in high school. (I probably never said it until I was in college.) Even now, I feel that the overuse of vulgar words can lead to a kind of devaluation and desecration, intensifying disgust and hatred, violence and despair. That's why, as a writer, I'm stingy with vulgarity; I don't want to add to a downward spiral.

---

1 From episode 211 of the *Outrage and Optimism* podcast, available here: https://www.outrageandoptimism.org/.

But sometimes, strong and shocking words are the only words that meet the urgency and danger of the moment. Strong language (used with discretion) was invented for times like these.

You might remember that back in chapter 2 and again in chapter 6, I quoted activist Derrick Jensen, who said, "The most common words I hear spoken by any environmentalists anywhere are, 'We're f*cked.'" I can easily imagine how young people today would find those two words supremely fitting as they look around at the tangled hot mess of catastrophes left to them by previous generations. "We're f*cked. *What a time to be alive*," they could well say with a groan, and I couldn't blame them for feeling this way.

But there's another way to say, "What a time to be alive," also related to an apt use of the *F*-word. In the first verse of a popular song from 2019, Michael Franti laments "the situation goin' on / Up inside my head today." He's frustrated with politicians who try to divide people "with fear and hate." Then comes the chorus: "This world is so f*cked up / But I ain't never givin' up on it."[2]

As I listen again and again to Michael Franti singing this song, I realize the real lyrical obscenity is not the *F*-word. It's the possibility of "giving up on it."

I'll bet you've felt the allure of giving up multiple times along our journey, especially if you've thought deeply about each chapter. The temptation seems to grow the more you know and the stronger and longer you care. As I noted in chapter 12, many of my friends, some of the hardest workers in the struggle for our future, have become casualties of the struggle. They poured out all they could for as long as they could, but for all their effort, they felt utterly defeated.

Like soldiers who have been injured on the front lines, they deserve honor and appreciation for all they've done, and they deserve all the rest they need. Perhaps someday, after they've had ample time to grieve their losses and their disappointments, perhaps after they've experienced some healing from the PTSD of this intense struggle for our future, perhaps if they're given the option of action that is motivated by love rather than by outcomes, perhaps then they will feel

---

2 Thanks to Cliff Berrien and Tom Eberle for introducing me to this song.

re-energized and re-enter the struggle, especially if they see more of us getting engaged. Or perhaps they'll cheer us on from the sidelines. Or not. Whatever they do or don't do going forward, I am deeply grateful to and for all these heroes.

You already know from reading the previous seventeen chapters that I am not optimistic about getting through the tough time ahead without some very significant loss and grief en route. You already know that I think all four scenarios we considered in chapter 2 are possible. You already know that I feel the emotional body slam that comes from facing these scenarios. You've probably sensed, accurately, that I assess Collapse Avoidance to be a less likely outcome every day, and I believe that achieving short-term Collapse Avoidance could intensify long-term harm. You already know that I sense a certain grim momentum that is propelling us toward the deeper end of the collapse pool.

You already know that I am not one to glibly tell you to have hope, because hope is complicated.

But I also want you to know that even though I understand why people *give up hope*, I am not *giving up*. Even if I give up hope on *our current civilization*, I am not giving up on *you*, I am not giving up on *humanity*, and I'm not giving up on *this beautiful world*. There is a difference between *giving up hope* and *giving up*. J. R. R. Tolkien, the twentieth century's novelist of doom, captured the difference in this passage:

> "So that was the job I felt I had to do when I started," thought Sam: "to help Mr. Frodo to the last step and then die with him? Well, if that is the job then I must do it." [. . .] But even as hope died in Sam, or seemed to die, it was turned to a new strength. Sam's plain Hobbit-face grew stern, almost grim, as the will hardened in him, and he felt through all his limbs a thrill, as if he was turning into some creature of stone and steel that neither despair nor weariness nor endless barren miles could subdue. With a new sense of responsibility, he brought his eyes back to the ground near at hand, studying the next move.[3]

---

3 J. R. R. Tolkien, *The Return of the King*, chapter 11, "Mount Doom."

With or without hope in all its complexities, I want to stand with Derrick Jensen and Michael Franti, with Frodo and Sam, with dear and spunky Hildegard of Bingen. I want to be brave, strong, a "creature of stone and steel that neither despair nor weariness" can subdue. Whatever the outcome, *never giving up* is my commitment. Nearing seventy, I don't know how much time I will have left to stay in the struggle. With whatever time I am given, I will seek to discern what is mine to do . . . and do it with all my heart. I will discern what is salvageable . . . and do my part to save it. And I hope you will do the same, if you are able. I hope you will pace yourself and care for yourself in the process, and I hope you will appreciate rather than attack your allies; otherwise, you will respond to the crisis with habits that perpetuate the crisis.

For all the agony of our current situation, I think Ayana Elizabeth Johnson and Katharine K. Wilkinson speak the truth when they say: "It is a magnificent thing to be alive in a moment that matters so much."[4]

"Magnificent"—it's the polar opposite of a vulgar word, carrying all the shocking power of an obscenity, but shocking with a positive rather than negative charge. It recalls wisdom from historian/activist Howard Zinn back in chapter 6. He reminded us that it is easy to be totally demoralized by the ugliness of our species: the ignorant, the stupid, the craven, the cowardly, the greedy, the egotistical, the nasty, violent side of all of us that seems to predominate in too many of us. But, he warned, we must be careful not to empower our worst human traits by acting as if they are our only human traits. We must not let the worst of us eclipse the best of us, because "human history is a history not only of cruelty, but also of compassion, sacrifice, courage, kindness," and often, "people have behaved *magnificently*."

Just as Michael Franti and Derrick Jensen resonate with a highly appropriate vulgarity, that powerful word "magnificent" echoes back and forth among Ayana Elizabeth Johnson, Katharine K. Wilkinson, and Howard Zinn: "It is a *magnificent* thing to be alive in a moment

---

4 From their last chapter in the collection they edited, *All That We Can Save* (One World, 2020).

that matters so much . . . remember those times and places—and there are so many—where people have behaved *magnificently*."

Michael Franti joins the echo in the last verse of his song, using "billion" to evoke the same magnificence: he sings of "a billion different people" doing "a billion different things" to make "a billion places better today."

Living magnificently, a billion people doing a billion different things . . . saving all that we can save: this, Zinn says, would be "a marvelous victory."

This "marvelous victory" is not measured by the outcome, as we saw in chapter 6. Rather, it is measured by the way we live, by a billion people living as people should live "in defiance of all that is bad around us." It is certainly not a guarantee that we will achieve the Collapse Avoidance scenario with minimal disruption. It is a victory detached from any guaranteed outcome. In this way, Zinn's "marvelous victory" is a realistic hope, a complicated hope that requires no guarantees about outcomes. It doesn't point to a "grand utopian future." But it does point to a future worth fighting for.

Nearing the end of this project, I am no more certain of which scenario awaits us than I was in chapter 2 when I introduced the four scenarios of Collapse Avoidance, Collapse/Rebirth, Collapse/Survival, and Collapse/Extinction. Here is what has become clear to me: yes, we are f*cked. We have set our world and our civilization on fire in a number of scary ways, and none of our trusted social institutions are inspiring confidence that they can put the fire out. That is because those social institutions were framed within social narratives or framing stories that are also failing us . . . fantasies of unlimited growth, wish-dreams about guaranteed happy endings, delusions of power, fables about inevitable progress.

But, I remind myself, our humanity cannot be reduced to our current narratives and institutions. As they fail, we can disentangle and step away from them. We can tell better, more honest, more healing stories, and we can build better, wiser, more durable, representative, and ethical institutions, starting small, and, if necessary, rebuilding from the ruins or replanting in the ashes.

The failure of our inherited stories can be devastating to us, whether those stories are religious, political, or economic. But the failure of our old stories can also be liberating.

When our old stories die, or when we divorce ourselves from them, we are free of them.[5] So imagine it: imagine being set free from the ugly stories of consumption and accumulation that taught us to consume the Earth and accumulate wealth. Imagine being divorced from the ugly stories of domination and retaliation that taught us to control others and hurt them back if they hurt us. Imagine being set free from the disempowering stories of isolation and victimization that taught us to run away and hide from our problems or curl up in a ball and let our oppressors define our future. Imagine that freedom![6]

Then, as you imagine that freedom, ask yourself this: What new story would we tell after the fire of collapse burns the other stories to the ground? Could we discover, tell, and live a new story, a love story of renaissance, resilience, even resurrection?

What wisdom could we learn from the fall of the house of *Homo colossus, Homo theocapitus, Homo arrogans, Homo myopius*—the old humanity in its cultic theocapitalist greed, epic arrogance, and tragic shortsightedness? Could we tell a new story of *Homo humilis* (humbled humanity) so that eventually we might become *Homo novus* and perhaps eventually, after a long apprenticeship in a new way of seeing, *Homo sapiens*?

Do you feel it? A new, humbled, wiser humanity can only be born as the old, arrogant, foolish human civilization is collapsing. Like new life rising from the ashes of a burned forest, a new humanity can only arise when the old humanity is falling apart. Even if that new humanity is short-lived, even if it doesn't succeed in turning things around, at least it will have flowered in us.

Dear friends, we have no choice as to when we're born. If we happen

---

5 This line of reasoning is used by the early Christian thinker/apostle Paul in Romans 7:1–6.

6 Freedom from harmful stories is the theme of two books I cowrote with Gareth Higgins, one for adults (*Us, Them, and the End of Violence*) and one for children (*Cory and the Seventh Story*). You'll find information here: https://sites.prh.com/cory-and-the-seventh-story/.

to be born within a certain civilization, we have no choice as to which stage of its adaptive cycle we will experience. We might be born into its exploitation/growth stage, its conservation/consolidation stage, its release/collapse stage, or its reorganization stage. As Tolkien's Gandalf says, our only choice is what we do with the time that is given us. Whatever convulsions our current civilization goes through in the years ahead, including both the possibility that it dodges the current barrage of bullets coming its way and the possibility that it ends in a mushroom cloud of extinction, we can choose to accept lives we have been given with the neighbors we have been given in the place we have been given in the time we have been given, and give ourselves to them with magnificent love.

In times like these, many things become too late. For example, it is already too late to keep CO_2 levels below 350 parts per million. If it is not too late already, it will very soon be too late to keep Earth's temperatures below the 1.5 degrees Celsius limit proposed by scientists in Paris in 2015. It will be too late to save this coastline or that ecosystem, this city or that species, this democracy or that economy. But it is not too late to love, and it never will be. Love will count, no matter what. Even on the last day of the world.

In fact, as I imagine a last day for the world, it strikes me that love shown on that day matters no less than love shown on any other day. It may even matter more. Love to a frightened child. Love to a whimpering stray puppy. Love to a withering plant or a wounded bird. Love to the terrified parts of oneself.

What I'm about to say could be easily misinterpreted, but I want to say it anyway, trusting you will understand. Having gone on this journey through these eighteen chapters, I am glad to be alive now, seeing what I now see. I can't think of another time I would rather have been born.

If I had been born two hundred years earlier, I would have been alive during the exploitation phase of my civilization. I would have lived during the horrific era of slavery and colonization, during the genocidal campaigns against indigenous peoples, in a time when women were dominated and LGBTQ people were closeted. I might have been completely oblivious to the ugliness of what was happening. I might have been "a man of the times," giddy about the Enlightenment and intoxicated by industrialism.

If I had been born fifty years earlier, I would have lived during the conservation phase of my civilization, when competing wings of the civilization fought two world wars over control of the world's remaining resources. I would have understood my life in terms of those two wars. I would have framed my world view within the parameters of fighting to gain and conserve wealth and power. I never would have asked the questions that have helped me see what I am beginning to see now, so late in life.

As it was, I was born during the peak of the conservation stage, so full of paradox, just as our emerging global civilization tipped toward the release phase. I lived during the Cold War, when nations multiplied nuclear weapons, and when movements for nonviolence took to the streets. I lived during the Civil Rights era, and then watched the dream of equality and liberation spread to include women, people of diverse abilities, to LGBTQ persons. I also lived in the NRA era, when white people with guns fantasized about making my country white supremacist, patriarchal, ableist, and homophobic again. I lived during the time scientists came to understand the urgency of climate change rooted in ecological overshoot, even though for decades, nobody would pay attention or believe them. I lived during the time of the internet, when a college student directed me to a website where I first saw that graphic about melting ice caps that sent me on a journey that brought me here, to write this sentence. I lived to see the desperation of one set of angry people in New York on September 11, 2001, and the very similar desperation of other sets of angry people in Charlottesville on August 11, 2017, and in Washington, DC, on January 6, 2021. I lived to see organized religion recede like Matthew Arnold's tide at Dover Beach. Recalling the iconic movie *The Truman Show,* I lived to see the dome of our current civilization pierced, so that I could get a glimpse of something bigger, deeper, better, and wiser beyond.

I think of my five grandchildren, born in this century, born in a time when so much is at stake. I am so glad that my timeline gets to overlap with theirs.

And I'm so glad my timeline overlaps with yours as well.

In this time, in this moment, we get to participate in mutual liberation. We get to imagine new stories and new ways forward together in these turbulent, f*cked-up times.

True, this isn't a great time for an easy life, but if you want a meaningful life, you showed up right on time.

You can give up if you need to or want to, or you can deny or minimize the gravity of our current situation. You are free. But if you have the vision and strength, even if the world is shipwrecked, why not choose instead to live with wisdom and courage, as we think humans should live, magnificently, saving all that we can save, "in defiance of all that is bad around us"?

Dear Reader,

I wonder how you responded to my use of the *F*-word in this chapter.

Even more, I wonder how you respond to the difference between giving up hope and giving up.

I wonder how you responded to the words "magnificent" and "magnificently" in the two passages I quoted.

I wonder how you responded to me sharing why I'm glad I get to be alive now, and I wonder if you feel the same way. (It's OK if you don't. I might be asking too soon.)

Whether alone or with your reading group, I encourage you to play Michael Franti's song at full volume and maybe even throw a dance party.

19

Tell Them About the Dream

How is it that our imprint is now so deep and dangerous that we are not only the ark but the flood?

—Theologian and ethicist Larry Rasmussen[1]

Sometimes it seems like you never will succeed. And everything you've gathered—there's so little that you need.

—Singer/songwriter Fran McKendree, "Let Your Light Shine"[2]

As warriors, our job is to actively and consciously survive . . . for as long as possible, remembering that in order to win, the aggressor must conquer, but the resisters need only survive. Our battle is to define survival in ways that are acceptable and nourishing to us, meaning with substance and style. Substance. Our work. Style. True to ourselves.

—Poet and activist Audre Lorde[3]

In the previous chapter, we used the past participle of the *F*-word as a synonym for "doomed." It strikes me that this is a good time, now, as we near the end of this book, to look more deeply at the actual word "doom." I should warn you that the old preacher in me is going to come out a bit in this chapter. In fact, this chapter is a sermon of sorts, but maybe not the kind you expect.

The English noun "doom" means "inevitable downfall" of some

---

1 From *The Planet You Inherit: Letters to My Grandchildren When Uncertainty's a Sure Thing* (Broadleaf, 2022).
2 You can hear the song here: https://youtu.be/s1DznzeTr6I. You can see my brief tribute to Fran's life and art here: https://brianmclaren.net/celebrating-a-life-of-wonder-goodness-and-creativity/.
3 From *A Burst of Light and Other Essays* (Ixia Press, 2019, originally published 1988). She is writing about surviving cancer, but the insight applies to a wide variety of battles for survival.

kind: imprisonment, loss, death, punishment. To have *a sense (or feeling) of doom* means that even though the full effects of the downfall are not yet here, they are near enough and certain enough that they bleach our lives of color even now.

The word derives from the Middle English "doome" and Old English "dom," which meant a law or decree issued to bring justice. The word "kingdom," in this sense, means the region in which a king's laws, decrees, and justice prevail. A book of laws from the time was a *dombec* or doom book. You can see how, for example, a judge or king might issue a prison sentence or death sentence upon a wrongdoer, and from that moment on, the wrongdoer would be *doomed* . . . judged and sentenced, even though not yet imprisoned or executed. By the 1300s, doom meant "fate" or "ruin," and by the 1600s, doom referred to the Final Judgment, when God would decree people's eternal fate. Doomsday was judgment day, the day in which a power greater than humans assesses human behavior and issues a sentence as a decree of justice. This sentence is not necessarily a punishment; it can be the natural and inevitable effect of which civilized human behavior was the cause, recalling the words from the New Testament (Galatians 6:7): "Do not be deceived; God is not mocked, for whatever you sow you reap."

The Earth—the planet's geosphere and biosphere, a judge and jury consisting of the whole web of life—is issuing a sentence upon our current civilization, even while its crimes are still being committed. We have taken more than our due. We have traded the long-term health of the Earth for the short-term wealth of a few, according to the script of an economic ideology. We did this in ignorance for a long time. But now, with eyes wide open, our civilization is accelerating harm, shutting our ears and hearts to the cries of the poor and oppressed, drilling and burning carbon and overheating the climate, draining wetlands, impoverishing topsoil, depleting fisheries, polluting air and raping land and poisoning waters, shrinking populations of our fellow creatures and driving many to extinction, and leaving an ecological inheritance for our children that is a tiny fraction of the inheritance that our ancestors left us.

Our clever, successful, convenient civilization, which we thought was Noah's ark carrying us to safety, turns out to be the flood. It is the return of Chicxulub, the massive asteroid that ravaged the biosphere sixty-six million years ago.

The Earth's sentence upon our civilization is based on laws: not laws made by kings, congresses, parliaments, or courts, but deep laws written into the fabric of the cosmos, set in motion at the dawn of time . . . the laws of physics, the laws of complex systems, the laws of living systems, the laws of cause and effect. The Earth's judgment will be expressed not in decrees, but in degrees of rising temperature, in numbers and intensity of storms, famines, droughts, and fires. The charges against us will add up until our behavior changes. Of course, our behavior will not change until our hearts and minds change. A first step in that change is becoming humble enough to acknowledge that if we are to survive, we must fit in with this planet. We must adapt to her will and ways, instead of always demanding that she submit to our will and ways. We must live within limits, for we are accountable to a power greater than ourselves.

We thought we were the wise ones, masters of our fate, gods with dominion over the Earth. But the Earth is now judging the leaders of our civilization to be a confederacy of fools—arrogant, ignorant fools—and her judgment is just, and her judgment is here.

That word "fools" brings to mind one of Jesus' least popular parables (Luke 12:15–21). The story is worth considering in depth, beginning with its context:

> Someone in the crowd said to [Jesus], "Teacher, tell my brother to divide the family inheritance with me." But he said to him, "Friend, who set me to be a judge or arbitrator over you?" And he said to them, "Take care! Be on your guard against all kinds of greed, for one's life does not consist in the abundance of possessions."

The context is familiar: accumulated wealth creates conflict among siblings, recalling the primal sibling rivalry between Cain and Abel in the Genesis story. The brothers who approach Jesus are in conflict not because of earned wealth, but because of inherited privilege (a literal inheritance, probably of money and land), and the conflict centers on the equitable distribution of that wealth, a perpetual problem in civilizations past and present. As he always does, Jesus refuses to be drawn into a badly framed argument. As a teacher, he isn't interested in judging; he's interested in teaching. So he takes them deeper to the root problem: greed . . . and deeper still: a failure to understand what life is really about. Then comes the parable. It is a story about rapid economic growth and the problems it creates. (As you read, you'll notice that Jesus doesn't say this rich man produced this wealth. *The land* did. The rich man simply extracted profits from what the land produced.)

> The land of a rich man produced abundantly. And he thought to himself, "What should I do, for I have no place to store my crops?" Then he said, "I will do this: I will pull down my barns and build larger ones, and there I will store all my grain and my goods. And I will say to my soul, Soul, you have ample goods laid up for many years; relax, eat, drink, be merry."

This man epitomizes the confidence and narcissism of a civilization in its exploitation and conservation phases. He talks to himself about himself, and neither listens to nor thinks of anyone else. Even grammatically, the first-person singular pronoun dominates: *I, me, my.* (Even his second-person pronoun refers to himself!) He asks himself what to do to maintain stability, to keep the system going, to keep the growth in GDP flowing, so he can take it easy, party, and chill. He tells himself the answer (wealth is the ultimate echo chamber): *Grow! Build bigger barns to hoard more stuff.* Then comes the surprise that interrupts his dream of unlimited, unaccountable economic growth. The voice of ultimate reality speaks and asks a question about what he considers ultimate reality, namely, his possessions:

> But God said to him, " You fool! This very night your life is being demanded of you. And the things you have prepared, whose will they be?" So it is with those who store up treasures for themselves but are not rich toward God.

A collapse in the rich man's health interrupts his schemes for wealth. The profits he hoarded and refused to share will now be forcefully redistributed. He was rich, yes, filthy rich in a certain selfish sense. But rich toward God? Rich in wisdom to remember that he is a candle, that life is a gift, and that his flame will someday go out? Rich in caring about others, especially the poor and vulnerable, so beloved of God? He proves utterly bankrupt in all these departments. He is forever known as the rich fool. In contemporary terms, we might call him the idiot billionaire. He is the celebrity, the ultimate capitalist many of our neighbors work themselves to death to become.

Jesus was speaking to people in the early fourth decade, CE. For the next few decades, the local Palestinian society would be increasingly divided. The rich Sadducees, Herodians, and Temple elite were (according to the Gospels, at least) loyal to the corrupt, inept, but powerful local officials of the Roman Empire. It was religion and politics in a mutually profitable scam. Their opponents, the Zealots, the Sicarii, and later the Pharisees, galvanized the poor for rebellion against those who exploited them. Between 66 and 70 CE, their rebel alliance actually expelled the Romans. It was like David defeating Goliath, except that Goliath didn't die.

In 70 CE, the Roman army returned and crushed them brutally. Contemporary historian Josephus estimated that over a million Jews died, and thousands of the survivors were sold as slaves. In fact, the Roman Coliseum was built by seventy thousand of these Jewish slaves.[4] As they constructed this massive structure to entertain decadent Romans, they would weep to remember how the Romans had desecrated and destroyed their beloved Temple in Jerusalem, symbol of their religion and culture.

It was collapse. It was the end of the world as they had known it.

With that historical context in mind, let's go back to Jesus' story of the rich fool. After telling the parable, Jesus turns to his disciples. Notice how he echoes his earlier theme about life not consisting in "the abundance of possessions" when he speaks of life being more than

---

4 For more, see "The Great Jewish Revolt of 66 CE," available here: https://www .worldhistory.org/article/823/the-great-jewish-revolt-of-66-ce/.

food and the body more than clothing, and notice the reference to another rich man:

> Therefore I tell you, do not worry about your life, what you will eat, or about your body, what you will wear. For life is more than food and the body more than clothing. Consider the ravens: they neither sow nor reap, they have neither storehouse nor barn, and yet God feeds them. Of how much more value are you than the birds! And which of you by worrying can add a single hour to your span of life? If then you are not able to do so small a thing as that, why do you worry about the rest? Consider the lilies, how they grow: they neither toil nor spin, yet I tell you, even Solomon in all his glory was not clothed like one of these. But if God so clothes the grass of the field, which is alive today and tomorrow is thrown into the oven, how much more will he clothe you, you of little faith! And do not keep seeking what you are to eat and what you are to drink, and do not keep worrying. For it is the nations of the world that seek all these things, and your Father knows that you need them. Instead, seek God's kingdom, and these things will be given to you as well.

It's quite shocking: Solomon—Israel's billionaire king, renowned for his wealth and wisdom, who used slaves to build a temple—lacked the simple dignity of a wildflower, according to Jesus. He seems to be putting rich Solomon in the same category as the rich fool in his parable. Like the civilizations (or nations) of the world, they sought for things that don't really matter and missed what really matters: life lived simply, in harmony with neighbor, self, the Earth, and God. It's time to withdraw emotional attachment from the collapsing human system, Jesus implies. It's time to transfer attachment to the ecosystem of God, the sacred web of life that ravens and wildflowers thrive within, free of barns and bank accounts, free of worry and stress.

Every system of self-centered civilization with its barns and banks for hoarding will inevitably collapse, the story of the rich fool reminds us. Meanwhile, the divine economy . . . the divine ecosystem of interdependence and sharing, the holy and harmonious arrangement of life in which wildflowers and ravens live and thrive . . . it goes on. That's where to put your heart. That's where to invest your inner energies:

> Do not be afraid, little flock, for it is your Father's good pleasure to give you the kingdom. Sell your possessions and give alms. Make purses for yourselves that do not wear out, an unfailing treasure in heaven, where no thief comes near and no moth destroys. For where your treasure is, there your heart will be also.

What Jesus calls the kingdom of God or the kingdom of Heaven, in this light, is not a destination after death: it is the higher, bigger, vaster, deeper way of life here and now—that includes plants (lilies of the field), animals (birds of the air), and humans.[5] This higher ecosystem is oblivious to the latest polls and economic forecasts. It will go on when human systems crumble.

So, Jesus says, liquidate your capitol in the fragile, failing human system. Reinvest your energies in the larger-than-human system of life. That's why loving your neighbors, especially your poor neighbors, is so important. Better to have less stored in your bank account and more given to those in need. Better to be poor in money and rich in generous relationships.[6] That's also why loving God is so important: God is the love that loves every person (no exceptions) and loves every creature in every habitat in every ecosystem in the biosphere. If you love God and neighbor, you love what matters . . . unlike the rich fool, who loved only himself and his money.

People often link the word "doom" with the word "gloom." I can see why. If your heart is fully invested in the rich fools' economy, the

---

5 Jesus used "kingdom of God" as counter to "empire of Caesar," and "kingdom of heaven" as counter to "empire of Rome." Both terms refer to the same reality. Also, the English words "kingdom" and "empire" translate the same Greek word, *basilea*.
6 My Burundian friend Claude Nikondeha helped me understand why giving alms was so important in Jesus' day. In Burundi, one of the poorest countries in the world, banks have traditionally been unstable and untrustworthy. Much like our global stock markets today (ironically called "securities markets"), they were prone to bubbles and crashes. It is far better to invest your money in kindness to friends and those in need, because friends can be there for you when economies collapse. Jesus makes this very point in another of his least popular parables: see Luke 16, especially verse 9.

judgment that is passed upon that system is passed upon you. If the system in which your life has meaning is doomed, then your life feels meaningless. But if you withdraw your consent from the rich man's human system of wealth, if you transfer your trust to the larger system, if you seek first and foremost the divine ecosystem, you will end up with everything you need. You won't have to worry. You won't have to be afraid. Your life has meaning because of its place in the divine ecosystem.

That's true now, whatever happens tomorrow.

On August 28, 1963, a quarter million people gathered in Washington, DC. As a public speaker, I wouldn't have envied Dr. Martin Luther King, Jr., that day. He was the sixteenth speaker, and the people had been sitting or standing for a long time in the hot sun, listening to a lot of people, in a temperature of about 86 degrees Fahrenheit (30 degrees Celsius).

Shortly into the speech, at least one of his supporters, the great gospel singer Mahalia Jackson, didn't seem to think it was a home run in the making. As parishioners in Black churches often do, she decided to give the preacher some encouragement. She had worked with him many times, and she recalled hearing him speak in the past with more passion and fire than he was now demonstrating. So she called out to him six words: "Tell them about the dream, Martin."[7]

Dr. King glanced toward her and they briefly made eye contact. He gently slid his prepared notes to the side of the podium and decided to go off script and improvise. He faced the vast audience and began, "I have a dream." People who were there say that in that moment, the energy shifted. The echoes of the 461 improvised words that followed can still be heard today.

We need to talk about doom. We need to grapple with doom. We need to face the scenarios of doom and do all we can to avoid the worst of the bad scenarios. But in the end, doom isn't the point. The dream is. After doom runs its course, life will go on . . . perhaps without us

---

7 Thanks to my colleague and friend Dr. Barbara Holmes for reminding me of this story about Mahalia Jackson and Dr. King. For more on this story, see Clarence B. Jones share his memories of that day in this *Wall Street Journal Live* interview: https://youtu.be/KxlOlynG6FY/.

humans, but I hope with us, a humbled and wiser version of us. So as we grapple with doom, please don't let doom have the last word. Focus on life, and remember the dream. Tell them about the dream.

Dear Reader,

How do you respond to the parable of the rich fool (or idiot billionaire)?

In all likelihood, Luke's gospel was written ten to twenty years after the crushing of the Jewish revolt and the destruction of Jerusalem in 70 CE, so it's very possible that the author wove this story together as commentary on that fact. Imagine how a story like this would affect survivors of the collapse of Israeli society.

In this chapter, I'm recommending that we begin disentangling our identities, withdrawing our consent, and detaching our ambitions from our current civilization. That doesn't mean we hate our civilization. No, it has much of value along with its fatal flaws, so we must love it and salvage from it what has great value. We must fulfill our daily responsibilities, love our neighbors, and strive for justice and peace as participants in this civilization. And we also must acknowledge that our civilization is in overshoot, and a civilization in overshoot has much in common with the rich man congratulating himself on his plans for bigger barns. What would it look like and feel like for you to engage in this kind of disentanglement, withdrawal, and detachment? What would it mean to shift the terms of your struggle . . . from "making it" in the current system to imagining and embodying a better way of life that could arise from the ashes when it burns down?

Can you see how it takes a degree of detachment to understand that even if our civilization in its current form is doomed, it doesn't mean humanity is doomed? And can you see how it takes a degree of detachment to understand that doom will run its course, and life will go on?

How do you respond to the story of Mahalia Jackson and Dr. King? What does it mean to you to hear these words: "Tell them about the dream, [insert your name here]"?

20

Find Your Light and Shine It

We are heading into dark times, and you need to be your own light. Do not accept brutality and cruelty as normal even if it is sanctioned. Protect the vulnerable and encourage the afraid. If you are brave, stand up for others. If you cannot be brave—and it is often hard to be brave—be kind.

—Anthropologist and author Sarah Kendzior

You are the light of the world.

—Indigenous prophet and contemplative activist Jesus

The more we persist in misunderstanding the phenomena of life, the more we analyze them out into strange finalities and complex purposes of our own, the more we involve ourselves in sadness, absurdity, and despair. But it does not matter much, because no despair of ours can alter the reality of things; or stain the joy of the cosmic dance which is always there. Indeed, we are in the midst of it, and it is in the midst of us, for it beats in our very blood, whether we want it to or not.

—Thomas Merton, *New Seeds of Contemplation*

O come now, somehow, it's been done before . . . open up the door and let your light shine.

—Singer/songwriter Fran McKendree,
"Let Your Light Shine"[1]

I ended the previous chapter with the word "dream." In this chapter, I would like to share the dream I cherish in the face of doom. But first, I would like to share an epiphany I had along the way in this writing

---

1 You can hear the song here: https://youtu.be/s1DznzeTr6I. You can see my brief tribute to Fran's life and art here: https://brianmclaren.net/celebrating-a-life-of-wonder-goodness-and-creativity/.

process. It was revelatory for me, almost mystical in a science-nerd kind of way. It may seem utterly obvious and familiar to you already, but it was like a baptism into a new reality for me: I realized that *everything is energy. The universe is a cosmic dance of energy.*

I mean this, on one level, very literally: that matter is (metaphorically speaking) frozen energy, that every material thing is a container of potential energy. I realized on a deep level what I learned back in high school science class: that energy, in its frozen and unfrozen forms, can never be created or destroyed. It flows, changes, transforms, takes a thousand shapes, even into the shapes of the words I am now writing and you are now reading.

On this planet in this solar system on the rim of this spinning galaxy, life evolves to direct energy toward novelty and diversity, toward interdependence and community; we might even say toward beauty, consciousness, and love. We humans evolved as part of this energy evolution.

Everything we humans do is about energy. When we eat, we consume matter to extract its energy. When we drink, we take in this liquid mineral called water because it helps us to release energy from our food and it flushes out the waste products from our energy production. When we work, we expend energy so that we can get more energy. When we exercise our bodies or learn new mental and emotional skills, we spend energy now to build potential energy for the future. When we fall in love and make love, we merge our energy with another's energy. Sometimes, our intermingled energy creates a child who will continue the energy adventure when we're gone.

The energy we take in through food was originally solar energy. It was captured by plants, and through photosynthesis, it was turned into a chemical form that animals like us could convert into energy. When plants and animals die, their remains also release energy which will energize other plants and animals. As for the sun itself, its energy is derived from the energy that bloomed from the original singularity, the Big Bang, the "Let there be light!" that we read in the profound poetry of Genesis 1. If written today, the Creator might say, "Let there be energy!"

Music and art creatively organize energy. Speaking and writing are energy. So are listening and reading. At this moment, you and I are engaged in an amazing exchange of energy. These collaborative acts of creativity and communication energize us, and they can spark new creativity in others, even generations from now, long after we are long gone.

What we call power—political power—that's energy too. So is religious or spiritual power. So is the power of love.

In humans, love is like light passing through a prism, expressing itself in many colors: love for ourselves, for our mate, for that one best friend from childhood . . . love for the stranger we notice on a bus, love for our opponents or enemies when we realize they are just people like us, competing with us for some sort of energy . . . love for a beloved old golden retriever or for an apple tree planted by our grandfather . . . love for this old house, that turn in the river, this kind of rock, the horizon at that beach, the game of golf, the sound of a cello . . . love for the loving, creative energy we experience through all these loves . . . these are all forms of energy, no less real than light or gravity or electromagnetism.

Our attraction to energy has driven our history forward. Prehistoric ancestors who discovered the power of fire were pioneers of energy engineering. Ancient farmers who grew, stored, transported, and traded the first grains were working with concentrated solar energy in a form that could be preserved through a cold, dark winter. The first people who raised a sail or dried fruit in the sun or burned a lump of coal or baked bread or experimented with uranium—they were working with energy.

Why do we travel? Why do we build schools and read books and attend TED Talks and podcasts and live, in-person lectures and sermons? Because knowledge itself is a form of energy. Why do we play? Because the free, unforced flow of energy brings its own reward. Why do we sleep? So our bodies can renew themselves for more energy adventures tomorrow morning.

In the middle of this slow-motion epiphany, I realized that what got us into our current situation was not simply malice, stupidity, or greed, although each certainly played a part. We were lured into the mess we're in by our desire for energy. That desire for energy is not evil. It is part of life—as natural as the exploitation, conservation, release, and reorganization pattern we see everywhere in nature. Life is, we could say, a creative use of energy, and evolution is an ongoing trial and error experiment in energy discovery and sustainable use. This realization helped me release some of the blame and shame I've been feeling—blame of our species and shame as a member of our species. As I contemplate this insight, I am fascinated to feel a new surge of energy flowing in to fill the space that had been filled with blame and shame energy before: mercy energy, grace energy, compassion energy. To return to chapters 1 and 2, I realize I am still waking up, still welcoming reality.

This energy epiphany has felt like a baptism into a new perspective. Perhaps you can see it too: that our current situation . . . being part of a civilization torn between growth and decline, expansion and collapse . . . is all about energy: feeling unable to cut back on it, using too much of it too fast, running out of one source of it and struggling to find another. Our current situation is an energy drama, a significant moment in the evolution of life on Earth.

The epiphany encompasses this present moment: the energy you are investing to understand this book, the energy I am investing to write it . . . we could see this as an expression of love energy. I have tried in this book, as in all my books, to be guided by love for my readers in both what I've written and how I've written it. You are motivated to read it because you love learning, which is a product of thinking, which is also an investment of energy, in hopes of a good energy return on the investment. On a deeper level, I am writing and you are reading this book on *life after doom* because we love life. We love uncountable expressions of abounding beauty and vital goodness that are under threat. We want to align our creative energies to save people and things we love so they can thrive. That's what love does. So here we are, right now, doing what we are doing because of love energy. Perhaps in us, the tendrils of evolution are exploring new possibilities, some way forward in our predicament.

In dangerous times when familiar worlds fall apart, the things you've always depended on to provide you energy might fail you. The gas stations might fail. The electrical grid might go out. The grocery stores might be empty. The schools might contract and weaken. Our political systems—which we entrust with power to manage our shared social energy—might dissolve or grow more corrupt, draining energy rather than equitably administering it. Our religious systems might follow a similar path.

And that's why, as soon as possible, each of us must, if we can, *find our light and shine it*. In the spirit of the Serenity Prayer we considered in chapter 12, each of us has the opportunity to change what we can, beginning with the kind of energy we "run" on in the deepest parts of ourselves. You might say we need a personal energy conversion, from dirty energy—arrogance, rivalry, fear, hate, greed, lust, domination, revenge—to clean energy: love, joy, peace, patience, kindness, goodness, gentleness, faithfulness, self-control.[2] While scientists and engineers do important work on new energy technologies, and while activists and political players do important work on shifting the balance of social and political energy from personal and corporate wealth to ecological health, you and I can do important personal and spiritual work, engaging in an internal clean energy revolution.

Sarah Kendzior is an anthropologist who studies authoritarianism. She knows that in turbulent times, people grow afraid, and their fear is a kind of psychological energy. Just as musicians master the mechanical energy of sound and doctors master the biological energy of healing, authoritarians are masters at manipulating the energy of fear and resentment. During collapse, as fear and resentment intensify, we should expect authoritarians to line up and become more and more popular and powerful, feeding on our fear and being fueled by our resentment.[3] If we don't learn how to control the psychological energy of our own fear and resentment, we can be sure others will exploit our emotional energy for their own selfish and destructive projects. That's why, when Kendzior saw the authoritarianism she studied abroad growing in power in her own country, she promised to resist, and to help others resist. She wrote:

---

2 Some readers will recognize this list as "the fruit of the Spirit," found in the New Testament (Galatians 5:22–23).

3 For more on authoritarianism in its current forms, see this interview with Ruth Ben-Ghiat: https://the.ink/p/is-the-trump-indictment-a-sign-of/.

Authoritarianism is not merely a matter of state control, it is something that eats away at who you are. It makes you afraid, and fear can make you cruel. It compels you to conform and to comply and accept things that you would never accept, to do things you never thought you would do.

You do it because everyone else is doing it, because the institutions you trust are doing it and telling you to do it, because you are afraid of what will happen if you do not do it, and because the voice in your head crying out that something is wrong grows fainter and fainter until it dies.

That voice is your conscience, your morals, your individuality. No one can take that from you unless you let them. They can take everything from you in material terms—your house, your job, your ability to speak and move freely. They cannot take away who you truly are. They can never truly know you, and that is your power.

But to protect and wield this power, you need to know yourself— right now, before their methods permeate, before you accept the obscene and unthinkable as normal.[4]

In that context, she wrote, "You need to be your own light." For this old preacher, her words echoed words from Jesus, who lived in another dangerous time when worlds were falling apart. He said, "You are the light of the world." When you find that light within you and let it shine, it not only helps you remember who you are, why you're here, and what you love. It also helps others. People around you see your light, your love energy, and they remember that there is a light in the universe . . . call it Spirit, call it God, whatever . . . that can shine in and through them as well. The darker the night, the brighter the stars shine.[5]

---

4 From "We are heading into dark times. This is how to be your own light in the Age of Trump," available here: https://thecorrespondent.com/5696/were-heading-into -dark-times-this-is-how-to-be-your-own-light-in-the-age-of-trump/1611114266432 -e23ea1a6. See also her podcast with Andrea Chalupa: https://gaslitnation.libsyn.com/. 5 These words from Fyodor Dostoyevsky's *Crime and Punishment* continue, "The deeper the grief, the closer is God!"

John Michael Greer, one of the clearest voices on the subject of civilizational collapse, says, "Collapse now and avoid the rush!"[6] What he means, I think, is this: understand now that what we call normalcy, what we consider stable and solid and dependable, may be shaken sooner than we think. Instead of going along with the crowd until collapse comes and then finding yourself part of a panicking, unprepared, easily manipulated majority, do your inner work now. Reading this book, I trust, is helping you in this inner work.

First, you start waking up. You welcome reality. You learn to more intentionally and skilfully mind your mind. You let the poets and artists help you grieve. When a story is dead, you step away. You accept that hope is complicated. This inner work will help you let go of our current situation, our current form of civilization, our current energy arrangement that is passing away.

Then, as you come to the place of accepting what you cannot control, you open yourself to insight. You learn to see and to cherish indigenous wisdom. You stop reading the Bible and other sacred texts in the same old way, and you begin to discover the deep ecological wisdom our sacred texts offer. You find yourself increasingly able to hold back from judging everything in simple binaries of good and bad. You begin to see your life as a candle, temporary but blessed with the flame of life, and you see Sister Death not as somebody to be afraid of, but rather as a trustworthy companion to all life. That will help you to start with step one, which is admitting your powerlessness, for that is the only way to find new power, new energy.

That will bring you to a path forward, a path of creative resilience . . . not a nostalgic path backward to the "good old days" when life seemed easier. You realize that we are not the first ones to walk this path; we can be inspired by the courage and resilience of our biological and spiritual ancestors. When your energy isn't being drained by fear, you can imagine safe landings and new beginnings for yourself and future generations. You see the power of gathering with two or three as seedbeds of love energy, and you share an experience

---

6 This is the title of his 2015 book (Founders House).

of deep belonging, perhaps deeper than you've ever known. You see the need, when times are tough, to grow tougher in character, which always includes kindness of heart, and you share this understanding with others, especially the young and the afraid.

Perhaps unexpectedly, through this sometimes terrifying engagement with doom, you feel yourself being set free . . . free of constraints and assumptions that were imposed upon you by an unsustainable, energy-addicted civilization. Your creative energy is unleashed as you notice and celebrate the abounding beauty that remains . . . because beauty always abounds and remains. Suddenly you feel, not unlucky to be alive in hard times like these, but privileged—privileged to be alive "in a time that matters so much." You realize that in the end, either overshoot will end or our civilization will end, and either way, life will go on. And perhaps, in this process, you have your own epiphany . . . and you begin to understand a sliver of what the contemplative activist Thomas Merton meant when he said:

> The more we persist in misunderstanding the phenomena of life, the more we analyze them out into strange finalities and complex purposes of our own, the more we involve ourselves in sadness, absurdity, and despair.

It starts to be clear: the doom we face in our current civilization is a result of our misunderstanding . . . our misunderstanding of energy, of overshoot, of what matters more (ecological and social health) and what matters less (monetary wealth). We realize that our civilization has become addicted to these misunderstandings because it has defined life as the rapid consumption and hoarding of energy rather than as the wise sharing of energy. We see our civilization collapsing into sadness, absurdity, and despair . . . and we feel the need to be set free to discover a new agility, resilience, and simplicity as humans. What Merton says next seems shocking at first: "But it does not matter much."

What? What could matter more than the continuation of our civilization, the perpetuation of our economy, the triumph of our technologies, the proof of our wisdom as Homo sapiens? Merton continues:

But it does not matter much, because no despair of ours can alter the reality of things; or stain the joy of the cosmic dance which is always there. Indeed, we are in the midst of it, and it is in the midst of us, for it beats in our very blood, whether we want it to or not. . . . [W]e are invited to forget ourselves on purpose, cast our awful solemnity to the winds and join in the general dance.

And there the epiphany begins to sparkle. Our civilization is not the point. Our species is not the point. If we are to exist, we must exist not for ourselves, but for the health of the whole, for the joy of the cosmic dance, the dance of energy, light, love.

The dinosaurs and ancient forests did not exist to die, be fossilized, and power our civilization. Their lives mattered for their moment and their presence in the cosmic dance! The oceans, the atmosphere, soil, the billions of living creatures on this planet today . . . they do not exist to sustain our civilization. They are vital participants in the cosmic dance. Our job is not to dominate and exploit them, but to share in the dance with them!

If we want to survive long-term and if we want to keep our sanity short-term, we will have to disentangle ourselves from our persistent "misunderstanding of the phenomena of life," a misunderstanding on which our current civilization functions. The term used by contemplatives for this disentanglement, from the Buddha to Meister Eckhart, is "detachment."[7] You will realize that our journey through these chapters has been leading us deeper into detachment, even when it was not named. But detachment is not intended to leave us separated. No, the very opposite! Detachment means disentangling from all delusions of separateness, so we can stop being wallflowers and join the dance of energy exchange that we call the universe. Detachment from our delusions of separateness is the portal to coming together with wisdom and courage when worlds fall apart.

That brings me back to the dream I have been trying to articulate through this book.

---

7 If you're interested in reading Eckhart on the subject, here is one of his essays: https: //german.yale.edu/sites/default/files/meister_eckhart_on_detachment.pdf.

This is my dream, and perhaps it is your dream, and our dream, together: that in this time of turbulence when worlds are falling apart, all of us with willing hearts can come together . . . together with one another, poor and rich, whatever our race or gender, wherever we live, whatever our religion or education. I dream that some of us, maybe even enough of us, will come together not only in a circle of shared humanity, but in a sphere as big as the whole Earth, to rediscover ourselves as Earth's multi-colored multi-cultured children, members of Team Earth.

I dream that the wisdom of indigenous people, the wisdom of St. Francis and St. Clare and the Buddha and Jesus, the wisdom of climate scientists and ecologists and spiritual visionaries from all faiths could be welcomed into every heart. Then, we would look across this planet and see not economic resources, but our sacred relations . . . brother dolphin and sister humpback whale, swimming in our majestic indigo oceans, with sister gull and brother frigate bird soaring above them beneath the blue sky. We would see all land as holy land, and walk reverently in the presence of sister meadow and brother forest, feeling our kinship with brother bald eagle and sister box turtle, sister song sparrow and brother swallowtail butterfly, all our relations.

In my dream, the reverence we feel when we enter the most beautiful cathedral we would feel equally among mountains in autumn, beside marshes in spring, surrounded by snow-covered prairies in winter, and along meandering streams in summer. In my dream, even in our cities, we would look up in wonder at the sky, and a marriage between science and spirit would allow us to marvel at the sacredness of sunlight, the wonder of wind, the refreshment of rain, the rhythm of seasons. At each meal, we would feel deep connection to the fields and orchards and rivers and farms where our food was grown, and we would feel deep connection to the farmers and farmworkers whose hands tended soil so we could eat this day with gratitude and joy.

In my dream, our life-giving connection to each other and to the living Earth would be fundamental, central, and sacred . . . and everything else, from economies to governments to schools to religions . . . would be renegotiated to flow from that fundamental connection. In my dream, we would know God not as separate from creation, but as the living light and holy energy we encounter in and through creation: embodied, incarnated, in the current and flow of past, present, and future, known most intimately in the energy of love.

Many will not understand this dream. Some will find reasons to mock it or oppose it. But for those of us who could live this dream in a time of doom, this would be an abundant life, a meaningful life, abounding with beauty, whatever scenarios unfold, whatever the future may hold.

The dance goes on, my loves, without us or with us. Why not join the dance while we have life? Why not find our light and shine bright, together, while we have this one holy moment to do so, even now?

Dear Reader,

When I began this writing project, I thought that the last few chapters would offer some kind of call to action, some clarity about *the plan.* (More about that in the next and final chapter.) I didn't expect it would include a mystical celebration of energy, detachment, and the cosmic dance!

Whether in your journal, or with friends, I invite you to reflect upon how this final chapter sits with you, beginning with my energy epiphany. Even if it feels elusive to you, does it feel enticing?

In the paragraph that begins with "First, you start waking up," I offer a short review of the whole book that continues through five paragraphs. See if those paragraphs can help you review our journey together so far.

At the end of the previous chapter, I shared the story of how Mahalia Jackson told Dr. King to "tell them about the dream, Martin." At the end of this chapter, I imagined that I was standing in front of you, my readers, and Mahalia spoke the same encouragement to me. I didn't plan what I would write: I tried to improvise, and what you read is what flowed out. How does my articulation of my dream land with you? Maybe you could write your own articulation of your dream in under five hundred words (which was the length of Dr. King's improvised ending).

A wise friend once shared an insight that has guided my life, first as a pastor and preacher, then as a writer: "Learning is not the consequence of teaching; learning is the consequence of thinking." What are you thinking about as you finish this chapter and prepare to read this book's final chapter?

21

We Make the Way by Walking

We have multiple uncertainties *and* there is a lot we can do.
—Climate-aware psychotherapist
Caroline Hickman[1]

I exhort everyone to see . . . the Earth is an environment to be safe-guarded, a garden to be cultivated. The relationship of humanity with nature must not be conducted with greed, manipulation, and exploitation, but it must conserve the divine harmony that exists between creatures and Creation within the logic of respect and care. . . .
—Pope Francis

Expect the end of the world. Laugh.
Laughter is immeasurable. Be joyful
though you have considered all the facts. . . .
Practice resurrection.
—Farmer/poet Wendell Berry,
"Manifesto: The Mad Farmer Liberation Front"

When I began learning about ecological overshoot and civilizational crisis and collapse, more than anything, I wanted someone to tell me what to do. I wanted to be a good person in a world falling apart . . . more part of the solution and less part of the problem. To do that, I needed to know The Plan.

Over the years, I've found myself in meetings and conversations with many of the top leaders in movements for environmental healing, spiritual renewal, and social justice. I can't tell you how many times I

---

1 Caroline Hickman is a psychotherapist specializing in climate-related trauma. She is featured in "Are Climate Doomers Right?" Available here: https://youtu.be /JB6smZzFgVY/.

cornered someone in a hallway or bribed them with lunch just to ask them, "Who has the plan? Who will tell us all exactly what to do?"

Here's what I found out:

Nobody had The Plan.[2]

That's because our current situation is not simply a *problem that can be solved* with a brilliant strategic plan, especially a plan designed by people whose imaginations have been shaped by the values and assumptions of our current suicidal economy and anti-ecological way of life! Even if we all bought into someone's version of The Plan tomorrow, that plan would almost certainly be a response to our crisis created within the assumptions of our crisis and would therefore perpetuate our crisis. That's not to say that planning is futile: it's just to say we should see our current situation as a super-complex *predicament that must be lived through* in an evolutionary process.

Evolution doesn't follow a single master plan from A to Z. It branches out like the tendrils of a vine, the branches of a tree, the dendrites of a nervous system. Experiments that don't work fail, like branches that die on a vine. New branches sprout and reach for light. Proven strategies are retained and continue to evolve. If that's the case, rather than one plan designed by one powerful billionaire or government committee, we should expect a thousand plans that must be adjusted ten thousand times as we change in a million ways and as our context changes in a million ways year by year. Millions of agile organizations and initiatives are being launched and led by millions of people at this moment, each one an experiment to address various facets of our current situation. So many good people are doing so much already, and more of us are joining them every day.

Perhaps these millions of plans will eventually coalesce into *the* plan at some point, like some massive chaos theory experiment in which unforeseen order emerges. Be that as it may, you might, at this point, be eager to develop or improve upon *your* plan. In appendix 4, I offer a simple format to help you to do so. One of the most important things

---

2 Actually, a number of authors have offered a number of proposed plans, but none have been accepted as The Plan. See, for example, Bill Gates, *How to Avoid a Climate Disaster* (Knopf, 2021); Paul Hawken, *Drawdown* (Penguin, 2017) and *Regeneration* (Penguin, 2021); and John Doerr, *Speed & Scale* (Portfolio, 2021).

to remember is that your plan must be dynamic, experimental, evolutionary. It will change over time because our situation is complex and our future is uncertain. As Maya Angelou says, "Do the best you can until you know better. Then do better."

For example, you might focus first on a plan to support one condition that will make scenario 1, Collapse Avoidance, more possible. After a few years, you might lose hope in scenario 1, so you shift your focus to help make scenario 2, Collapse/Rebirth, more possible. After a while, you may continue working on scenario 2 while simultaneously doing what you can so scenario 3, Collapse/Survival, will be less horrific than it might otherwise be, if all plans for scenario 2 falter. Someday, you may find yourself focused on scenario 4, Collapse/Extinction, trying to assure that at least some birds and mammals, reptiles and amphibians, insects and fish, trees and ferns and moss survive if we humans do not. But conditions might change, and you might find yourself focused on scenario 2 again. Along the way, you'll realize that all our plans, as important as they are, are less important than an attitude of agile engagement, a commitment to never give up on this f*cked-up world, to keep shining and dancing, whatever scenario unfolds.

Whatever you do, it matters. The same is true for what other people do. It's super tempting, when you're pouring your heart into your own plan, to get mad at everyone else for not joining you. But attacking your allies is counterproductive; who wants to join a team of mean people? And truth be told, what's yours to do may not be what's theirs to do. This is a lesson I learned from one of my heroes, St. Francis of Assisi. Early in his life, he wrote, "No one showed me what I ought to do." In other words, nobody imposed The Plan on him. He felt his way until he found his way. Late in his life, he wrote, "I have done what is mine to do. May Christ teach you what is yours!"

Let me say it like this: *The things you as an individual are doing now really matter, and the many things we come together to do matter even more.*

Like anyone awake to our current situation, I have several front lines of care and involvement. You may have noticed that I write as an expression of my love for this beautiful world and all its creatures in hopes of mobilizing people for constructive action. More specifically, I love birds and turtles and trout and the forests and wetlands and rivers where they live, so I come together with others and volunteer with organizations engaged in wildlife and habitat preservation.[3] I'm also deeply committed to safety, equality, and solidarity across racial, gender, orientation, and religious diversity. That means that I come together with others for political action, even though politics drives me crazy sometimes.[4]

I'm also passionately committed to spiritual and religious reform and revolution, which is why I do public speaking and cohost a conference called Southern Lights.[5] I believe we need a deep change in story, a shift in consciousness, an inner energy conversion, which explains why I invest a lot of my time with the Center for Action and Contemplation.[6] I believe that children and college students deserve special attention in these dangerous times, so I have come together with others to help form a resource network for parents and churches called Raising Kids for Good[7] and a campus network called Zoe.[8]

These commitments (plus writing!) are about all I can handle these days. Meanwhile, you . . . you might be equally passionate about preschool education in your county, about protecting one stream where you live, about the Israel-Palestine situation, about countering voter suppression. You might be wondering why I seldom show up at the school board meeting, and I might be wondering why you seldom show up for sea-turtle nest monitoring. But then I remember: *the small part I am doing now matters, and the combined impact of what we are all doing matters even more.* I recall Michael Franti's wisdom: we need "a billion different people doing a billion different things to make a billion places better today." It all matters. And it matters in surprising ways.

For example, I just heard about some people who have devoted

---

3 See https://rookerybay.org/.
4 See https://www.votecommongood.com/.
5 See https://southernlightsconference.com/.
6 See https://cac.org/.
7 See https://rkfg.org/.
8 See https://www.zoeoncampus.com/.

their lives to restoring sea otter populations because they love sea otters. Guess what they found out? When they restored sea otter populations, the sea otters ate more sea urchins. When sea urchin populations were under control, the kelp forests (which sea urchins eat) got healthier and stronger. And guess what? Kelp forests are excellent collectors of carbon. So by saving sea otters, they were addressing one facet of climate change![9] We all know that harm tends to cascade . . . one liar tempts others to become liars, for example: we must remember that healing can cascade too.

So it's not just that I *can't* offer you The Plan, it's that one single top-down master plan is neither possible nor desirable at this moment. A complex predicament like ours requires us to come together in a complex polyphonic response. I just heard a beautiful song that captures this insight: "You don't have to know the way. The way knows the way."[10]

I want to offer you something that might prove more valuable than The Plan: the assurance that *everything matters, and some things matter more than others.* So here are a batch of ways to focus on what matters and what matters more. I'm making an expanded version of this chapter available online at BrianMcLaren.net, so you can share it with others if you'd like. Even better, add to the list as you share it, because along the way, you'll learn more about what and how the way teaches.

1. *Voicing your concern matters, and voicing your commitment matters even more.* Katharine Hayhoe says it well: the single most important thing you and I can do about our current

---

9 For more on sea otters, see https://www.fws.gov/story/2022-09/sea-otters-are-unlikely-helpers-our-fight-against-climate-change/. It's also important to note that this otter-urchin-kelp story, like so many things, is complicated. For example, warming seas kill kelp and multiply sea urchins. So whether ocean warming will reduce kelp before kelp can reduce carbon which in turn can reduce ocean warming . . . that remains to be seen. See https://regenerationinternational.org/2020/07/03/what-kelp-forests-can-do-for-the-climate/.

10 The song is by community songleader Lyndsey Scott. You can listen and read the lyrics here: https://thebirdsings.com/thewayknows/. Don't miss this beautiful performance and video here: https://youtu.be/Effy3Hyiohg/.

situation is talk about it.[11] So someone says, "How are you doing?" You reply, "I'm healthy, I'm motivated . . . and I wake up every day wondering how we can change our relationship to the Earth and to one another." Someone asks, "How was your weekend?" You reply, "I was reading a book that really has me thinking about ecological overshoot. Have you ever heard of that?" Someone asks, "What's new?" You reply, "I just joined a group that is trying to elect candidates who take climate change and environmental overshoot seriously. I'm really excited about a couple of candidates who are running this year. Can I tell you about them?" Someone complains about political corruption or gridlock, and you reply, "It breaks my heart to see how little is being done. But the worse some people respond to the mess we're in, the more committed I am to setting a positive, creative, alternative example." So as you speak from your heart in your own way, you share the commitment that flows from your dream for the future. Your example of commitment will invite them to involvement, without counterproductive guilt trips or pressure.

2. *Your anxiety matters and your citizenship matters even more.* It will take rapid and radical political and structural change to keep us out of the most lethal scenarios. For that reason, if you're anxious, you're way ahead of those who are oblivious. And if you're anxious but inactive, now is a good time to renew your commitment to be a responsible citizen. Politicians and political parties may try to get you off track with "weapons of mass distraction." But you know what matters, and even if it's a matter of voting for the lesser of two evils, vote. If you can't find enough candidates who get our current situation, maybe you should become a candidate. (In many places, the bar is really low, so you need not feel intimidated!) If not running for office,

---

11 See Eliza Griswold's *New Yorker* article (September 16, 2021) on Katharine Hayhoe (with whom I share a Plymouth Brethren heritage, by the way) available here: https://www.newyorker.com/news/on-religion/how-to-talk-about-climate-change -across-the-political-divide/.

choose a level: local, state, or national . . . and get involved as you are able.[12] Political solutions will almost always disappoint, and in the end, they may fail entirely, but if your efforts reduce harm that your inaction would have intensified, your political work is still good and beautiful.

3. *What you've already learned matters, and remaining curious matters even more.* You've already learned a lot about our current global situation from this book and other resources like it. Congratulations! Hopefully, your curiosity is stimulated rather than satisfied by what you've learned, so you'll keep learning for the rest of your life. As our global situation changes, your curiosity will keep you up to date. Not only that, your curiosity about our global situation can lead you to explore your local situation, your local ecosystem. You'll learn about your watershed, the endangered species there, the main polluters there, the groups working on environmental and social justice there, the groups seeking to strengthen community among neighbors and connection with the land.[13] Cultivate the indigenous spirit we considered in chapters 8 and 9 by digging deep in the writings, music, art, and activism of indigenous leaders. Enjoy and savor the beauty that abounds in your ecological neighborhood. Mourn the harm being done and respond. Belong to the land where you live locally, just as you belong to the Earth as a whole.

4. *What you've already contributed matters, and your ongoing contributions will matter even more.* Celebrate what you've already done . . . in reading this book, in using your voice, in voting conscientiously, and in growing deeper in spirit through all

---

12 For a great resource, see David Pepper's *Saving Democracy* (St. Helena Press, 2023).

13 The rain that falls from your roof drains into a stream somewhere. That's the beginning of your watershed. It then flows into a river that flows into an ocean. You are connected by your watershed to everyone upstream and downstream from you, and ultimately, your watershed connects you with everyone and everything on Earth. For more, see the work of Ched Myers here, https://watersheddiscipleship.org/, and see also https://www.epa.gov/waterdata/hows-my-waterway.

you learn. Then, realize that all of us have room to grow in modeling a new way of life that makes sense in light of our current situation. You'll be curious about how you might improve your diet this year . . . both for your health and the Earth's health.[14] You'll learn about how your home is being heated and cooled, and how you can make improvements in your energy efficiency each year going forward. You'll raise other questions as well. How about transportation? How can you make your transportation choices less harmful and more healing? How can you use and waste less water, or buy and throw out less stuff, especially stuff that can't be recycled or reused? If you have extra space, how might it be shared with those who need a place to live? Don't worry if people call you a hypocrite because you haven't made progress in all areas of your life: of course you are a hypocrite! None of us have arrived at perfect consistency with our values and ideals, so we're all hypocrites to a degree. Far better to be a hypocrite who is growing than a critic or cynic who is doing nothing but criticizing good people who are doing their imperfect best to change and grow!

5. *The salary and benefits of your job matter, but the benefits your work provides to others and to the Earth matter even more.* In a dangerous time like ours, why keep doing a job that harms the environment or produces useless junk when you could find a work that you believe in, work (paid or unpaid) that makes positive difference? If you can't realistically change jobs right now, maybe you can change your job . . . by bringing about needed change in your company or profession.

6. *The return on your investments matters but the impact of your purchases, investments, and donations matters even more.* Why not do business with companies that take good care of the Earth, their employees, and their customers instead of

---

14 Climate Healers, founded by Sailesh Rao, is one of the best organizations to help us all move toward a diet that helps heal the Earth. Their motto is "HELP: Heal the planet. Eat plants. Live simply. Plant trees." More here: https://climatehealers.org/.

companies obsessed with profit only? If you have savings invested in interest-bearing bank accounts, mutual funds, stocks, and the like, why not consult someone to help you move your investments out of harmful companies and into more helpful ones? If you're not a generous giver, why not begin investing in nonprofits and social benefit ventures that contribute to the common good?[15]

7. *Whether or not you have children matters and how much you care for everyone's children matters even more.* Some people feel they shouldn't have children in this dangerous time. Others feel that they should. Whatever you decide, don't let having your own children—or not—keep you from caring about all children, everywhere. It was carelessness about our neighbors and about future generations that got us in this mess. To get out of it, we need a change of heart to exercise "a preferential option for the young," and to think about the well-being of seven and more generations to come.

8. *Your individual actions matter and the institutions and social movements in which you play a part matter even more.* Whether as an employee or volunteer or donor, look for institutions and social movements that are doing good in the world and support them. None of them are perfect, and neither are you; the best you in your imperfections can do is to support the best of the imperfect organizations you can find. Better to be a dishwasher in a good (though imperfect) hospital than a CEO in a company that ruins people's health. Better to become a donor to a good (though imperfect) podcaster than be the well-paid chief of staff for a corrupt president or selfish CEO.

9. *Your mistakes or failures matter way less than what you learn from them.* Don't be surprised if the first steps you take lead to some embarrassing failures or dead ends. Just turn around, learn from your failure, and keep looking for wiser and better ways to get involved. I could tell you some cringeworthy stories of

---

15 For more on this subject, see https://divestinvest.org/.

things I've done, thinking it was so enlightened and helpful . . .
only to find I needed to change course. That's how we often find
our way—by eliminating dead ends.

10. *Your organized religion matters and your spiritual organizing
matters even more.* As I've written elsewhere, I believe that organized religion is already playing some important roles in building a better future, and it can play an even bigger and better role
if it migrates toward being "religion organizing for the common
good."[16] Whether inside, outside, or on the inside edge of religious institutions, we can work together to build a more loving,
just, and generous world within each faith, and in collaboration
with people of all faiths, including secular faith.[17]

11. *What you think matters and how you love matters more.* There
are a lot of mean people out there who *know* they're right about
our current situation and are very impressed with how right
they are. These sincere but misguided people often do more
harm than uninformed people who do little or nothing. We must
bring wise thinking to this work, and even more, we must bring
love to this work . . . love for ourselves, for our colleagues, even
for our opponents. That's another reason coming together in
a love-energized spiritual community is so important (whether
inside or outside of organized religion): it will help you remain
rooted and grounded in love.

12. *Your anger matters and your sadness and joy matter even
more.* Anger is important. Just as pain motivates us to protect
our bodies from harm, anger motivates us to make changes
to reduce harm to what we love. But anger that is not well-
managed can become addictive, degenerating into a kind of
all-pervasive self-righteous hostility. My friend Richard Rohr
has been warning people about this for years: often our anger
is poorly processed sadness, he says. If we can rediscover our
sadness, it will soften us and help us work from a heart of

---

16 See my book *The Great Spiritual Migration* (Convergent, 2016).
17 For more on secular faith, see Martin Hägglund's *This Life: Secular Faith and
Spiritual Freedom* (Anchor, 2020).

love. In fact, hearts broken by sadness are often those most broken open to pour out love.[18] But like anger, sadness too can be overwhelming. That's why joy matters . . . joy in the beauty that abounds, joy in the billion beautiful people doing a billion beautiful things in a billion beautiful places every day, joy in the beautiful dream that glows brighter as the times grow more grim.

13. *Your arguments matter and your agreements matter even more.* Those of us who are working for a more just, generous, loving, and ecologically regenerative world can have major arguments about strategy, timing, tactics, and the like. But we should never forget how fortunate we are to agree about the importance of understanding and addressing our current situation. By the way, I apply this logic to myself: it is my desire to keep appreciating you if you disagree with something (or many things) I've written in these pages. I hope you'll do the same.

14. *Your family matters, and your community of resilience matters even more.* In turbulent times, I expect we'll meet more and more "doomers/preppers" who respond to our deteriorating situation with contraction, pulling their nuclear family into a bunker somewhere. Far better to come together now to build expanding circles of trust and overlapping communities of resilience—so they're alive and well when we and others need them most. Our nuclear and extended families are a good place to start, but not a great place to stop. Churches and other faith communities, neighborhood groups, town and city governments can live out the African adage that if you want to go fast, you go alone, but if you want to go far, you go together.

15. *What I'm telling you on this page matters way less than what you tell yourself when you turn the page.* To paraphrase St. Francis, "I've done what is mine to do in pouring my heart into this

---

18 See Parker Palmer's beautiful article on this subject, available here: https://couragerenewal.org/library/the-broken-open-heart-living-with-faith-and-hope-in-the-tragic-gap/. See also Adam Bucko's *Let Your Heartbreak Be Your Guide* (Orbis, 2022).

book. Now you find what is yours to do, and pour your heart into that." Don't worry: you can't lose, because whatever beautiful thing you do, it matters, whatever scenario unfolds.

Whatever happens to civilization as we know it, you and I—in our own wick, wax, and flame—can find and do what is ours to do right now and shine as magnificently as we can right now, each year that we're given, each day we're awake, each breath that we take. We don't need to know The Plan in advance; we just need to walk our path. In the walking, step by step, the way will unfold like tendrils reaching out from a billion branches, seeking light. The ultimate destination? That is beyond both our control and our capacity to know. So here we are: savoring this gift of this day, in this life, in these times, waking up in the unfolding mystery, and that is gift enough, here and now.

Afterword

I was talking recently to fellow writer on our current situation, Professor Debra Rienstra. She said, "The problem with writing books like ours is that by the time a book is published, it is already out of date." [1]

I cannot imagine what will transpire between this moment as I write this book's final words and the moment you read them.

It is possible that the sense of doom that set the stage for this book will appear overblown by the time you read it. The problems that loom so large right now will have receded and you'll wonder why so many of us were so worried back in the mid-2020s. That's hard for me to imagine, but it's possible.

It is also possible that by the time you read it, the public that now is so divided and distracted will be united and aligned, and a significant portion of Earth's 8 billion human inhabitants will have come together, exercising their nonviolent power to stop the few thousand oligarchs who currently hold the rest of us hostage in the destructive economic, political, and media system they run for their advantage. Again, I don't think that's likely, but I'd be unspeakably happy to be wrong.

It is also possible that the Earth itself, speaking the language of flood, drought, heat wave, fire, famine, and rising seas, will have been

---

1 See her book *Refugia Faith* (Fortress, 2022).

speaking so loudly that everyone (or almost everyone) will be up to their necks in a sense of doom.

I do not and cannot pretend to know the situation you will be in as you read. All I can do is trust that the raw materials I offer here, imperfect as they are, will be sufficient for you to make something life-giving of them.

My friend and colleague Jim Finley often tells a parable in which the worst thing one can imagine becomes a portal to awakening. With his gracious permission, I share a slightly adapted form of it here as a final meditation on life after doom. Jim calls this story "The Awakening":

Imagine you're on a large boat with a lot of people crossing a vast expanse of ocean, and there's a big party going on. Music is playing, people are dancing, and in a moment of carelessness, you fall off the back of the boat and nobody notices you have fallen.

You're waving your arms and yelling, but the music is so loud that no one hears you. You watch the boat disappear in the distance.

You realize you can't tread water for very long, but you can float for a long, long time. So your strategy is to float until they recognize you're missing and come back to look for you.

Now in order for you to float, you have to relax, because if you tighten up, you sink. So you're out on the vast ocean there, lying flat on your back, the big swells of water rising and falling, rising and falling, and you're there relaxing. How would you be relaxing? You'd be relaxing *very seriously,* because your life depends on it. It's a life-saving relaxation!

Hours pass. Darkness falls. You're floating on the water, face-up to a sky full of stars that are brighter than you have ever seen before. Hour after hour, rising and falling in the swells, you wait for morning to come.

Unexpectedly in the darkness, a feeling comes over you, seemingly out of nowhere. You look up at the night sky, stars sparkling like diamonds. The swell of the waves feels like the rhythmic breathing of the Earth and suddenly, unexpectedly, you feel part of it all. Floating on the depths of the ocean, beneath the depths of the sky, you feel an unimagined depth open within you, and in that depth, you feel a poignant awareness that whatever happens, you are alive right now, in this moment. You feel yourself embraced in an infinite generosity that will uphold you whether you live or die. Birth and death, beginning and ending, all are taken up into one unfathomable gift of being alive and grateful and awake in this moment, now. You are so overwhelmed by this mysterious feeling of awakening that words fail you and you begin to cry.

Soon, dawn breaks, and out of the corner of your eye you see the boat coming back to look for you.

When your fellow passengers pull you aboard, you are hugging them, saying thank you, thank you, thank you. You begin to laugh. You are so glad they found you.

That night, you have a nice meal. You take a long hot shower and you're lying in your bunk in a room on the boat, in the dark. You're so grateful they saved your life. But you know, on some deep level, that your life was really saved out there on the sea, amid the rise and the fall of the waves, under the stars, in the darkness, just before dawn.

ACKNOWLEDGMENTS

First, thanks to all the researchers, scientists, authors, artists, journalists, podcasters, activists, organizers, and others directly referenced in this book. Thanks as well to those whose works are not directly referenced, but whose work contributed to this book nonetheless. I thank Kate Rae Davis, director of the Center for Transforming Engagement (https://transformingengagement.org/), and Dr. Jeffrey Olrick, clinical psychologist and author (https://www.growingconnected.com/), who offered insightful feedback on the manuscript.

Sincere thanks to my fellow clergy and other spiritual leaders who teach people that love for God, neighbor, and self are inextricably linked with love for the Earth and for justice, chief among them, Rev. Jim Antal, Katharine Hayhoe, Patrick Carolan, John Cobb, Philip Clayton, and, of course, Pope Francis. Special thanks to the Rev. Michael Dowd who, since I met him many years ago, has always been several steps ahead of me in grappling with the issues in this book. (In the last stages of editing this book, I learned that Michael, a bit younger than me, passed away suddenly of a heart attack. I trust that this book will honor his courage and leadership.)

Deep thanks to Bill McKibben, a hero of mine who started sounding the alarm early and who has given his all for decades to keep from happening what is happening. Thanks to all in Third Act who are joining in the struggle (https://thirdact.org/), and to all activists working for a just, generous, and regenerative world, especially young activists who are being inspired by the brave and brilliant example of Greta Thunberg.

Enthusiastic thanks to my editor, Elisabeth Dyssegaard, and all her colleagues at St. Martin's Press. I happened to send my first draft of this book to Elisabeth in July 2023, the month temperatures were hotter than they had been in over a hundred thousand years. She asked me if I would be willing to move the publication date up by six or seven months because she felt "people need this book now." That request entailed a lot of intense work for a lot of us, and it suggests the sense of partnership that can exist between an author and editorial team, a partnership that is focused on providing readers with what they need, when they need it. That is the same partnership I feel with my literary agent, Roger Freet, who once described himself to me as "a reader's advocate."

Profound thanks also to my colleagues at the Center for Action and Contemplation, and to all who understand that just as we cannot survive by bread alone, so we cannot survive by technology alone, or by politics alone, or by economics, activism, or any other single discipline alone. Personal thanks to Dr. Jim Finley for allowing me to include his beautiful parable in the afterword.

Finally, I thank you, dear reader, for spending this time in my head and heart with me, and for allowing me the honor of spending this time in your head and heart with you. After so many years writing and so many pages written, it still feels like a miracle, really, that this connection can happen and this energy can flow.

APPENDIX 1

Best Resources on Our Predicament

Long before beginning this book, I had for many years been immersed in the literature and online resources related to ecology, economic inequality, and conflict based on race, class, gender, religion, ideology, culture, age, and nation. In writing this book, I worked vigorously to update, broaden, and deepen my research.

As a result, it feels nearly impossible to create a short list of recommended resources when there are so many excellent ones, with new ones appearing hourly. Apologies to all the tremendous content creators who I had to pass over because I've forced myself to limit each category to five. The five I've chosen do not all agree with each other, but their diversity of analysis takes available evidence seriously and will provide you with a broad sense of our current situation.

BOOKS

1. *Overshoot* by William Catton, Jr. (University of Illinois, 1982) is the essential, classic text that puts climate change in a broader, deeper ecological context.
2. *All that We Can Save*, edited by Ayana Elizabeth Johnson and Katharine K. Wilkinson (One World, 2020), is an anthology that brings together women writers with diverse backgrounds and perspectives. It speaks to both head and heart.

3. *We Survived the End of the World* by Steven Charleston (Broadleaf, 2023) brings indigenous wisdom to bear on our current situation.

4. *Climate Church, Climate World* by Rev. Jim Antal (Rowman and Littlefield, 2018, with a new revised and updated edition coming soon) speaks especially to people of faith and leaders of faith communities.

5. *Deep Adaptation*, edited by Jem Bendell and Rupert Read (Polity, 2021), is not an easy read, but brings together a wide array of contributors who take seriously the threat of collapse.

VIDEO/AUDIO

1. Michael Dowd's YouTube channel, TheGreatStory.org, hosts the series Post-Doom Conversations. Michael describes his editorial position as "post-doom/no gloom." The channel's assumption is that collapse is inevitable and near-term human extinction is a real possibility. Michael unflinchingly faces the most disturbing evidence and curates intelligent conversations with all the luminaries here: https://www.youtube.com/@thegreatstory/.

2. Sid Smith's How to Enjoy the End of the World series combines a grim prognosis with a compassionate tone of presentation: https://www.youtube.com/@bsidneysmith/.

3. The Post Carbon Institute's video/podcast series, *What Could Possibly Go Right?*, takes a less dire approach while still taking very seriously the interrelated economic, energy, environmental, and equity crises that we face in this century: https://www.youtube.com/@postcarboninstitute/videos.

4. If you'd like to go straight to the scientists, you can listen in on their conversations on climate-related threats at the World Climate Research Program's channel, here: https://www.youtube.com/@WCRP1980/videos.

5. David Borlace's popular Just Have a Think channel addresses twenty-first-century crises and focuses on possible responses. He does his homework and synthesizes information well: https://www.youtube.com/@JustHaveaThink.

PODCASTS

1. *Breaking Down: Collapse* is an accessible podcast that introduces readers gently but firmly to the many facets of civilizational collapse. It is available here: https://collapsepod.buzzsprout.com/. The hosts recently launched a follow-up podcast, *Building Up: Resilience*, available on a variety of platforms.

2. *How to Save a Planet* offers a large archive of interviews and conversations related to a wide array of climate-change topics: https://gimletmedia.com/shows/howtosaveaplanet/episodes/.

3. *The Climate Pod* presents conversations with leading experts on the politics, economics, activism, culture, science, and social justice issues at the heart of the climate crisis: https://podcasts.apple.com/us/podcast/the-climate-pod/id1469270123.

4. *The EcoCiv Podcast* hosts conversations about the kinds of transformations required to create a more sustainable, peaceful, and just society: https://ecociv.org/the-ecociv-podcast/.

5. *Outrage and Optimism*: As its title suggests, this podcast seeks to integrate an honest look at disturbing realities with an optimistic outlook: https://www.outrageandoptimism.org/.

APPENDIX 2

Using This Book for Small Groups, Classes, Sermon Series, and Retreats

The Dear Reader questions and prompts at the end of each chapter can easily serve as conversation prompts for a small group or class (in person or online). A simple way to proceed would be for the leader or convener to invite each person to respond to each question prompt, or to ask each member to choose a favorite question or prompt to respond to. Of course, make it easy for people to pass if they are not ready to speak.

Another option, instead of or in addition to using the questions and prompts, is to encourage people to underline or copy sentences or paragraphs that are especially interesting or meaningful to them. Then in the group, a participant can share a selected passage and why they found it interesting or meaningful, followed by discussion. You may find it useful to use a talking stick or other object, so all feel the importance of honoring and listening to each speaker. After a speaker shares, they can pass the talking stick to a person they choose or who volunteers.

An ideal time frame for reading the book closely would be thirteen weeks (or an academic quarter), as follows:

Week 1: Introduction, Chapter 1
Week 2: Chapters 2–3

Week 3: Chapters 4–5

Week 4: Chapters 6–7

Week 5: Chapters 8–9

Week 6: Chapters 10–11

Week 7: Chapters 12–13

Week 8: Chapter 14–15

Week 9: Chapters 16–17

Week 10: Chapter 18–19

Week 11: Chapters 20–21

Week 12: Afterword, Appendices, and Review

Week 13: Party or Campfire

For faster readers, or for a retreat setting, the book could be read and processed together in five sessions, reviewing parts 1 through 4 of the book in four sessions, and then doing a review and closing ritual for the final session. Here are two suggestions for a closing ritual, but you may come up with a much more appropriate closing ritual for your group and setting.

1. Each willing member of the group shares his or her experience of reading the book and participating in the group. Each speaker might begin or close by lighting a candle or adding a stone to a cairn or writing a word on a piece of poster paper or giving or receiving a gift of some sort. Each speaker might conclude by saying, "I have spoken," and others would respond by saying, "We hear you."

2. Each participant completes (in advance, or at the gathering) three to five elements of Appendix 4: Your Plan, and shares their plans with the group. The speaker might finish by saying, "This is my plan," and the others would respond by saying, "We support you."

Whatever the format, I recommend that the group establishes some guidelines or ground rules at the first session and reviews or mentions them at each subsequent session. Here are five ground rules that I have found helpful for groups I've been part of:

1. Come prepared. If you aren't prepared, still come, but please tell your group at the beginning that you aren't prepared so you don't feel pressured to pretend.

2. Assign a timekeeper. Decide, for example, to give each person three or five or seven minutes to speak without interruption in response to each question. Allow people to pass if they would rather not participate, and welcome silence as an important part of the conversation. End on time.

3. Participate but don't dominate. In general, don't speak twice until everyone has been invited to speak once. If you're normally quiet, take some extra effort to open up.

4. Be curious, but don't engage in cross talk. Feel free to ask sincere questions after a person speaks, and whenever possible, begin with the words, "I'd be curious to know." (Thanks to Jim Henderson of 3Practices.com for this practice.) But don't correct, disagree, fix, diagnose, teach, and so on.

5. Be grateful and respect confidentiality. Thank your fellow members for honesty, courage, and vulnerability, and respect their privacy by sharing information only with explicit permission.

I highly recommend the four Way of Council guidelines, readily available online: 1. Listen from the heart, 2. Share from the heart, 3. Be lean of speech, and 4. Be spontaneous.

If you are a minister, priest, or rabbi, and you would like to develop some sermons or lectures on the book, I would recommend selecting three to five of the chapters or themes that resonated most deeply with you. Feel free to reference the book, but I would encourage you to center your own thoughts, feelings, and stories: your congregation is far more interested in what comes from your heart than from someone they've never met.

APPENDIX 3

Three Conversation Starters for
Courageous Conversations

In chapter 21, we noted the importance of speaking up about our current situation whenever we can, and in chapter 16, we emphasized developing "the courage to differ graciously" whenever necessary. Here are three simple scripts to help you use your "right to not remain silent."

1. When someone says something you consider harmful, untrue, or inaccurate, say, "Wow, I see that differently." This statement has power because it is an act of self-reporting rather than argument and it is non-directive, non-accusatory, and non-shaming. Often this response will prompt your conversation partner to ask why. Sometimes it may be appropriate to answer, especially if you are in private. If you're in public, disagreeing may put the person in a defensive mode, which seldom leads anywhere productive. So I recommend responding, "I don't need to go into it now. I just want you to know that I see it differently. If you're curious, give me a call sometime and I'll be glad to share with you privately." In so doing, you show that your relationship doesn't depend on agreement, and you invite your conversation partner into a place of curiosity rather than argument.

2. When people ask how you are or what's new, often, they are just making small talk. But if it feels appropriate and they actually seem

to care, you can answer with honesty. I recommend you choose a word that describes your emotion: "Thanks for asking. I've been feeling . . . troubled, excited, brokenhearted, motivated . . . lately." Then you can explain why.

3. Sometimes, the best way to have a needed and meaningful conversation is to ask permission: "Could I ask you a personal question?" If they say yes, continue: "I'm feeling really concerned about (name your issue—climate change, political division or corruption, racism and white supremacy, economic inequality, etc.). I wonder if you feel the same way."

You may find many other good ways to start needed and meaningful conversations, but I've found these three to be simple, honest, direct, non-manipulative, and effective. For more information on this subject, check out Ecoamerica's "Five Steps to Effective Climate Communication," available here: https://ecoamerica.org/climate-action-sheet/5 -steps-to-effective-climate-communication/.

APPENDIX 4

Your Plan

In chapter 21, I wrote, "When I began learning about ecological overshoot and civilizational crisis and collapse, more than anything, I wanted someone to tell me what to do. . . . I needed to know The Plan." Then I suggested that nobody has The Plan, at least not for all of us, and not at this moment. That means that many of us will want to design our own plan.

Below I offer a framework to help us begin to do that in three steps. First, this is not a to-do list! Please do *not* try to respond to all twenty prompts right now (unless you feel super-motivated): that would be overwhelming. Instead, I recommend you (and maybe your family or friend circle) *choose a few* that appeal to you most right now. Second, *do your research and write your plan* for these prompts and *place it in a prominent place* . . . on a bathroom mirror, or on your desk, or have it come up for review on your calendar once a week or month. Third, when you've incorporated your first plan elements into your daily life and you're ready for a new challenge, *choose a few more*. You can repeat that process and keep improving and updating your plan as long as you feel motivated to do so.

Again, please remember that this is not a to-do list. You don't need another set of obligations to feel pressured or guilty about. This is simply a way for you to be intentional about making changes that you sincerely want to make when you are sincerely ready to make them.

1. Your plan to reflect on what you've learned in this book. (Forming a group using guidelines from appendix 2 might be a good place to start.)

2. Your plan to use your voice and exercise your right to not remain silent. (See appendix 3 for ideas.)

3. Your plan to keep learning about overshoot and collapse scenarios, authoritarianism, racism and other inequalities of wealth and power, nonviolence and peacemaking, and related subjects. (See appendix 1 for more ideas.)

4. Your plan to improve your diet for your own health and planetary health.

5. Your plan to improve your home's energy use and production, and if you have a yard or property, your plan to maximize your property for environmental health and the well-being of your neighbors.

6. Your plan to improve your transportation.

7. Your plan to reduce your consumption of fossil fuels, electricity, water, plastics, clothing, etc., in other ways.

8. Your plan to improve or change your job.

9. Your plan to transition your spending and financial investments toward ecological and ethical companies and instruments.

10. Your plan to use your vote, citizenship, political power, and presence (at meetings, protests, etc.).

11. Your plan to increase your concern for children and future generations. (See appendix 5 for ideas.)

12. Your plan to support and improve key institutions.

13. Your plan to support and improve key social movements and organizations.

14. Your plan to re-indigenize and deepen your religious/spiritual life. (See chapters 8 and 9.)

15. Your plan to deepen your roots in love as your prime motivation. (See chapter 6.)

16. Your plan for self-care and managing anger, grief, sadness, fear, and other difficult emotions.

17. Your plan to manage argument and agreement among allies, antagonists, and the unconvinced.

18. Your plan to build multiple communities of resilience. (See chapter 15.)

19. Your plan to nurture joy, gratitude, and celebration of goodness, truth, and beauty. (See chapter 17.)

20. Your plan to revisit, celebrate, and improve this plan.

You'll find a lot of specific ideas to integrate into your plan in Ecoamerica's Climate Action Sheets, available here: https://ecoamerica .org/resources/climate-action-sheets/.

APPENDIX 5

Talking to Children About Our Current Situation

Here is a letter I have written for my grandkids, ages eight to fourteen. I hope it will give you ideas and inspiration for supporting children you love in these turbulent times. You can even copy some or all of it, or add to it or adapt it to make it what you want to say. You'll notice that I:

- Introduce the subject through a story.
- Ask questions to create conversation rather than monologue.
- Create space—but not pressure—to go deeper.
- Make room for difficult emotions.
- Use a metaphor to "tell them about the dream" (Team Earth).
- Avoid adding blame, shame, fear, and guilt to their lives.
- Offer them some things to do now, as kids.
- Give them permission to be kids now, and adults later.
- Focus on our relationship as a place of safety and love.

Dear Grandkids,

Some of you remember my dad, your great-grandpa.

When I was a boy, many nights after dinner, he would tell me I had to sit and watch the news on TV with him. I wanted to go out and play with my friends, but he would make me sit on the couch and watch a half hour of news first. "You need to understand what is going on in the world," he would say.

But I didn't agree. Grown-ups could take care of the great big world, I thought. I was a kid and all I wanted to do was have fun outside.

My dad understood that, but still, he made me sit there in front of the TV. And even though I didn't have a great attitude, most evenings I learned a little bit more about what was going on in the world: wars, politics, poverty, crime, business, scientific discoveries, weather, natural disasters like earthquakes and tornadoes, and other current events.

Now I understand why my dad wanted me to watch the news. He knew that I would be a grown-up myself sooner than I expected. If I started learning as a child about how the world works and what is going on, it would help me be a better grown-up someday. It would help me do my part to make the world, or at least some small part of it, a better place.

Do you see why my dad felt the way he did, and why I felt the way I did?

Kids, the reason I'm writing you this letter is that there is something going on in our world, the world you have been born into. It's often called climate change or global warming.

I know you have heard about it, and sometimes, you might worry about it and want to talk about it.

Or maybe you say, "It's not my problem. I'm just a kid. The grown-ups will take care of it." However you feel, it's OK if you feel that way. But if you want to know a little more about what's going on with climate change, I want to help you figure it out.

Here's my best explanation: Until very recently, most grown-ups didn't understand one of the most important, basic things about how the world works. They didn't understand that the Earth isn't just a planet we live on: it's a team we're part of.

Team Earth is made up of all plants and animals, and it includes air, land, water, ice, and sunlight, too. For millions of years, Team Earth has been working to maintain a balance so that things don't get too hot or too cold, too wet or too dry. Trees and grass play their part. Ice and oceans play their part.

Honeybees and bison play their part. Oceans and winds play their part.

But a long, long time ago, many humans forgot that they were members of Team Earth. They did what they wanted to the Earth and they didn't care much how it hurt other animals, plants, the air, the land, the water, and the ice. Sometimes, they didn't care if other people got hurt either. They formed their own little teams and they hurt Team Earth in many ways. They didn't realize that if Team Earth loses, all humans lose too.

So, we were born into a bad situation. For a long time, without even realizing it, our civilization has been hurting the balance that we depend on to have a good life. Things people do every day, without meaning any harm, are heating up the air and the oceans. Things people do every day are hurting plants and animals and the land, water, and air they depend on. Lots of people are getting hurt too. What we're doing isn't smart. It isn't good. And it isn't fair.

More and more grown-ups and kids are trying to figure out what we can do to change things and to make things better and to be part of Team Earth again. I imagine you feel the same way.

Of course, some grown-ups want to keep doing exactly what they've been doing because it is what they're used to and it makes them a lot of money. They won't even think about the harm being done to Team Earth. They only care about their little team. That's sad, but can you understand why they would feel this way? Maybe someday, they'll join Team Earth too.

When I was a boy watching the news with my dad, every night the reporters talked about a war that our country was fighting far away. It scared me. I wondered if I would have to go to war when I got older. And I imagine that sometimes you feel scared too when you hear about global warming. You might not know who to talk to about it.

I want you to know you can talk to me about this or any subject anytime. And of course, you can talk to your parents too. If you asked me what you can do right now as a kid to be a good member of Team Earth, here are five top ideas I would offer you.

First, give yourself a pat on the back for being interested in what is going on in the world. Then give yourself a bigger pat on the back for caring and wanting to be a good person, part of Team Earth. That's amazing! Welcome to the team!

Second, do everything you can to learn more about the Earth itself . . . about sunlight, the atmosphere and climate, land and soil, oceans and ice, snow and rain, streams and rivers . . . and how all the parts work together. Since we're part of Team Earth, it makes sense to understand it better, right?

Third, do everything you can to learn more about plants and animals and how they work together as part of one web of life on Team Earth. Lots of kids are so busy with video games, social media, and sports teams that they hardly ever think about Team Earth. That's understandable, but I think life is way better when you understand how much we depend on the animals and plants who are also part of Team Earth.

Fourth, whenever you feel afraid or confused, find someone you trust to talk about it . . . your parents, older family members, your teachers, or maybe a pastor or counselor. And always remember that I am here for you!

And fifth, maybe you can be a good example for your friends. You can share with them what you're learning and doing. If they feel worried or afraid about climate change and grown-ups arguing about what to do about it, you can be a person they can talk to.

As you get older, you'll learn a lot of things you can do as a good adult member of Team Earth. Someday, you might even help your children and grandchildren understand what is going on in the world so they can join Team Earth too.

Most of all, always remember how much I love you, and how glad I am to be part of Team Earth with each of you.

Sending you a big bear hug,
Pop-pop

APPENDIX 6

A Short List of Biases

Why do people so often delay facing reality until it's too late?

Anything that we humans perceive as a threat will elicit a strong reaction in our bodies, whether it's a threat to our own survival, to our family and friends' survival, or even to our prosperity and comfort. Hormones like cortisol and adrenaline are released to prepare us to fight, flee, freeze, flock, or fawn. A fight response might energize us to mock or hate someone who brings disturbing news, or to dismiss them with a disparaging label (liberal, alarmist, heretic, extremist, or kook, for example). A flight response might tempt us to change the TV channel when disturbing news comes on, or to put down a book when it threatens to unsettle us. A freeze response might give us that "deer in the headlights" feeling, shutting us down and leaving us feeling paralyzed. A flock response might motivate us to find people who do not believe in the threat or issue that has disturbed us, so we can feel safe in their company. A fawn response might motivate us to call in to a radio talk show or attend a political rally or religious gathering where we can show our submission to a bold and confident leader who will assure us that we're good, we're right, and we're going to be OK.

As flight, fight, freeze, flock, and fawn impulses course through our bodies, the three primary committees of our brains (as we described them in chapter 3) will start constructing coping strategies to deal with the unwanted information. Sometimes, the lightning-fast negotiations result in a willingness to address reality, sometimes to deny it, sometimes to color or distort it to make it more palatable.

Over recent years, I've been curating a growing list of our most common distortions, defenses, or biases. Here's my latest version, with a brief explanation of how each bias distorts our understanding of our current situation.

1. *Confirmation Bias:* Our brain committees screen new ideas based on the ease with which they fit in with and confirm the only standards we have: old ideas, old information, and trusted authorities. Doing so simply saves time and energy, so we aren't constantly having to rethink everything we know when new data presents itself. As a result, our preexisting framing story, belief system, or paradigm prefers to exclude whatever doesn't fit. Most of our framing stories embed inevitable progress and happy endings as normative, so any story with an unhappy or uncertain ending is already suspect. In addition, those of us who are older have spent our whole lives, or at least our whole childhood, not taking ecological overshoot into account. When the idea of overshoot comes along and changes the rules of the game as we understand it, our brains will resist it before we even have a chance to think about it. For example, if we have always been told that economic growth is a good and necessary thing, and then someone tells us that economic growth hastens environmental collapse, we find that notion impossible to even fathom.

2. *Complexity Bias:* The human brain often prefers a simple lie to a complex truth. When we hear large amounts of complex information about a quickly destabilizing geosphere and biosphere, both the content and complexity of that information repels us. When a politician, scientist, or religious leader comes along and says, "I alone can fix this," or "We have the technology to fix this," or "God won't let this happen," our brains often find that one simple reassurance more acceptable and believable than a mountain of complex data.

3. *Community Bias:* Your brain finds it very hard for you to see something your community or in-group doesn't want you to see. Also known as social confirmation bias, this bias puts tribe over truth.

If you grew up in a capitalist economy where capitalism was good and any alternative was evil, any critique on capitalism will feel like an attack on your tribe, and you will feel defensive. If you grew up as a white person in a predominantly white culture, any critique of white history or white privilege will feel like an attack on your tribe, and you will feel defensive. If you are convinced that your government should stop fossil-fuel subsidies, but your family, church, party, and business are all in favor of continuing those subsidies, you will feel afraid to speak your mind for fear of rejection by your community, and may even decide to change your mind to be in line with what your community thinks.

4. *Complementarity Bias:* If people are nice to you, you'll be open to what they see and have to say. If they aren't nice to you, you won't. So if you feel that people judge you because you drive a gas-guzzling car or eat a lot of meat or make a lot of transatlantic flights, you will be less likely to agree with them on the urgency of ecological overshoot because you don't want to be aligned with people who you feel are unsympathetic toward you.

5. *Contact Bias:* If you lack contact with someone, you won't see what they see. That means that if all your friends are in climate denial or climate despair, or if all your friends believe nuclear energy or geo-engineering will solve all our problems, or if all your friends think that because you recycle, there's nothing to worry about, and if you have no personal relationships with people who see differently, it will be easy to ignore what people outside your in-group say and only listen to what people inside your in-group say.

6. *Conservative/Liberal Bias:* Because of community bias and contact bias, our brains like to see as our party sees. Political parties aggregate people who see alike. Social psychologists have noticed that liberal parties aggregate people who see through a "nurturing parent" window, and conservative parties aggregate people who see through a "strict father" window. Liberals primarily value moral arguments based on justice and compassion; conservatives also place a high value on arguments based on purity, loyalty, authority, and tradition.

When conservatives begin to understand the gravity of global climate disruption, they realize that government may have to grow stronger in order to stop the environmental harm done by big business. But because big government is the enemy to conservatives and big business is the friend, conservatives will find it hard to keep thinking about the reality of global climate disruption. Or when liberals begin to understand that government in its current form is largely controlled by fossil fuel and other interests that keep politicians from taking the bold action necessary to address global climate disruption, they may feel paralyzed, because government is the primary driver of progress among their tribe, and without government leadership, they feel helpless.

7. *Consciousness Bias:* Our brains see from a location. A person's level of consciousness—from dualistic to pragmatic to critical to integral—makes it possible to see some things and impossible to see others.

   If we're at a dualistic stage, we assume that we're the good guys and we will win, and if we use fossil fuels, that's OK, since we're the good guys and we're doing it. If we're at a pragmatic stage, we think of every problem as fixable or solvable; we just need the right technology or strategy, working within our existing structures and assumptions, and we will "win the war against climate change." If we're at the critical stage, we develop the ability to see that our existing structures or assumptions may be the problem, so all strategies or technologies used within our structures are subject to scrutiny. In this stage, we may feel that ecological overshoot is overwhelming, leading us to despair, paralysis, or acquiescence. If we're at the integral stage, we begin to be able to integrate dualism, pragmatism, and critical thinking—with all their strengths and weaknesses—to face reality creatively.

8. *Competency Bias:* Our brains prefer to think of ourselves as above average. As a result, we are incompetent at knowing how incompetent or competent we are, so we may in fact be less or more informed and competent than we think. When we have been raised, trained, and rewarded by a civilization that is out of sync with the planet, we don't realize that our ways of thinking have been limited by that system. Our competence in playing by the rules of our

civilization may translate into incompetence in fitting in successfully with the rules and limits of our environment, but we have no
standard by which to identify our incompetence.

9. *Confidence Bias:* Our brains prefer a confident lie to a hesitant truth.
   We mistake confidence for competence, which renders us vulnerable
   to the lies of confident people (many of whom are con artists, which
   means artists at manipulating others by their confidence). When scientists are modest in their claims, or when con men and demagogues
   are bold in their claims, we are highly susceptible to being misled.

10. *Conspiracy Bias:* When we feel shame, we are vulnerable to stories
    that cast us as the victims of an evil conspiracy by some enemy
    "other." Our brains like stories in which we're either the hero or the
    victim . . . never the villain. The story of human civilization in eco-
    logical overshoot doesn't easily cast us as heroes, so our next best
    option is to be the victim. If we create an external villain and cast
    ourselves as helpless victims, we disempower ourselves.

11. *Comfort/Convenience/Complacency Bias:* For a majority of us, our
    brains welcome optimistic information that allows us to relax and
    be happy, and our brains reject pessimistic information that might
    require us to adjust, work, or inconvenience ourselves. Whatever
    the future holds, it will likely be less comfortable and convenient
    than most of us wish, which means that many of us will be tempted
    to retreat into a bubble of denial to preserve our complacency and
    avoid facing reality as long as possible.

12. *Catastrophe/Negativity Bias:* Our brain's primary job is to keep us
    alive, which means being vigilant about the approach of immediate
    and catastrophic danger. As a result, when under stress, we are wired
    to notice and remember bad news and bad experiences, and to mini-
    mize good news and good experiences. That can lead us to becoming
    magnets for bad news that sucks us into a vortex of crippling despair
    and an inability to recognize positive options when they present them-
    selves. (Catastrophe Bias and Comfort Bias work in dynamic tension.)

13. *Constancy/Normalcy/Baseline Bias:* Our brains are wired to set a
    baseline of normalcy and assume what feels normal has always been
    and will always remain constant. Whatever happens repeatedly

becomes normalized for us. This bias makes it easy for us to get used to the latest reports about record-high temperatures or collapsing glaciers or a species going extinct. When disturbing news becomes normalized for us, it becomes virtually invisible and ceases to count. It is normal and therefore negligible. As a result, we become blind to tipping points until it's too late, because we assume that environmental deterioration and decay are constant and normal. We become like the person who gets so used to receiving past-due notices from his creditors in the mail that he is shocked when they repossess his car and evict him from his house.

14. *Cash Bias*: Our brains are wired to see within the framework of our economy, so whatever helps us make money, we consider good. It is very hard to see anything that interferes with our way of making a living. One of the great challenges of overshoot is that we are facing collapse not because we failed at building a profitable economy, but rather, because we succeeded. We can't imagine how the rules of the economy that made us rich, safe, and comfortable in the short term set us up for such loss, danger, and suffering in the long term.

15. *Certainty/Closure Bias*: Our brains find it difficult to rest with uncertainty, so we would rather close in on an unwarranted certainty than live in uncertainty. Whether it's the optimistic certainty of techno-optimism or the pessimistic certainty of extinction, certainty has an undeniable appeal to our brains. The ability to hold unknowing requires real practice.

16. *Cleverness/Deception Bias*: Our brains know that deception comes in many forms, from a venomous snake camouflaged in fallen leaves to an internet scammer trying to get our bank information by posing as a friend in need. To protect ourselves, we must become more clever than those who deceive us, which requires constant vigilance. When we become bias aware, our challenge intensifies: we must become not only more clever than others, but also more clever than our own biases! As a result, we may become so habitually skeptical that we become cynical: we become biased against anyone who brings good or hopeful news. In our desire to avoid deception, we unintentionally reject hope and encouragement.

As you can imagine, in writing this book, I have tried my best to be on alert for bias in the experts and texts I encountered in my research. And I have also been on alert to discern my own biases. I have often thought of Jesus' words about taking the board from our own eyes before trying to extract the splinters from the eyes of others. In other words, before calling out the bias of others, it makes sense to face bias in oneself or one's in-group. Bias awareness becomes an exercise in self-examination and humility.

For more on this subject in relation to climate change and ecological overshoot, see "Are We Wired to Deny Climate Change?" (*The Agenda*, November 8, 2022, available here: https://www.tvo.org/video/are-we -wired-to-deny-climate-change) and see George Marshall's *Don't Even Think About It: Why Our Brains Are Wired to Ignore Climate Change* (Bloomsbury, 2014).